DATE DUE

Dec 11 ??			
Aug ?8 ?4			
GAYLORD			PRINTED IN U.S A

THE SOCIAL HISTORY
OF BOURBON

*An Unhurried Account of
Our Star-Spangled American Drink*

Bourbon, pronounced "ber-bun" in Kentucky where they ought to know, is the distinctive spirit of the Western world, the *fine champagne cognac* of the United States. Its place in American culture has long waited for objective treatment. The saga is a lively one, intimately associated with valor and splendor and the graces of life; with villainy, too, and folly and man's inhumanity to man. And it has dramatic events such as the Whisky Rebellion, the scandals of the Whiskey Ring, the notorious "whiskey forts" of the fur trade, the fate of the American Indian and the toil of civilizing a continent.

Combining happily patient research with an urbane and witty style, Gerald Carson presents in sweeping narrative and apt anecdote the first comprehensive account ever written of drinks and drinking in America from the early settlements to the present day.

Not a recipe book or barman's guide, but a fascinating contribution to Americana, this lusty book reflects an aspect of the American experience that has long been suppressed or disregarded. A few chapter headings suggest the panorama of the contents:

Also by Gerald Carson

THE OLD COUNTRY STORE

CORNFLAKE CRUSADE

THE ROGUISH WORLD OF DOCTOR BRINKLEY

ONE FOR A MAN, TWO FOR A HORSE

THE SOCIAL HISTORY
OF BOURBON

An Unhurried Account of
Our Star-Spangled American Drink

BY GERALD CARSON

Illustrated

". . . Why should not our countrymen have
a national beverage?"

HARRISON HALL, *The Distiller*
Philadelphia: 1813

Dodd, Mead & Company
New York

Printed in the United States of America
by Vail-Ballou Press, Inc., Binghamton, N.Y.

The author and publishers wish to thank the following for permission to reproduce selections in this book: University of Oklahoma Press, for permission to use a passage from *We Pointed Them North* by Edward C. Abbott. Harcourt, Brace & World, Inc., for permission to use a passage from *The Politicos* by Matthew Josephson. Carl Fischer, Inc., for permission to use three lines from the song, *Kentucky Moonshiner*, in a setting by Elie Siegmeister. The Bobbs Merrill Company, for permission to use a passage from *The Life of Billy Yank* by Bell Irvin Wiley. Copyright © 1951, 1952 by The Bobbs Merrill Company, Inc.

In slightly different form some of the chapters of this book appeared as articles in *American Heritage* and *The Virginia Quarterly Review*.

For Lettie

ACKNOWLEDGMENTS

Picture credits will be found on the pages with the illustrations.

While it is not possible to mention here all who wrote a letter, sent a book, explained an obscure point or otherwise responded generously to the needs of the author, I must mention as prominently as I can my obligation to those who read the typescript either in whole or in part, and made available to me their criticisms, suggestions and comments: Mr. Gordon Bass, Professor Thomas D. Clark, Messrs. Paul E. Lockwood, Tom Maloney, L. R. Rodenberg and Dr. J. W. Spanyer, Jr. None of these good counselors bear any responsibility, of course, for the final manuscript.

Other individuals who helped to bring this book into being are: Miss Lucy L. Addams, Lee Adler, Samuel Aker, Professor John Q. Anderson; Dwight E. Avis, Director, Alcohol and Tobacco Tax Division, Internal Revenue Service, U.S. Treasury.

Also Nelson Bengston, Professor Walter Blair, Jacob Blanck, Herman Blum, Ben Botkin, Mr. and Mrs. John D. Briscoe, Robert Tate Caldwell, Jr., Pat. B. Cleary, Clifford Dowdey, Grant Dugdale, Mr. and Mrs. Charles Farnsley, Professor J. DeLancey Ferguson, Mrs. Bessie B. Martin Fightmaster, Mrs. David W. Forden, Lee E. Grove, Tom Haines, Alvin F. Harlow, Dan Hecht, Professor Atcheson L. Hench, Alexander Izsak, U.S. Senator Jacob K. Javits, Sydney M. Kaye, Mark Kiley, Wathen R. Knebelkamp and Bill Koch.

For courtesies extended, assistance rendered, facilities opened up, I thank Perry Luntz, Philip Lukin, William F. Mac Queen, Bob McIlwaine, C. Kenneth Meeker, Miss Katherine Megibben, Don Mitchell, Robert B. Patterson, Professor Norman Holmes Pearson, Tom Ramage, John F.

Reed, John W. Ripley, Lawrence B. Romaine, Mrs. Marc A. Rose who deserves a *cum laude*. I remember gratefully, too, Sam Simpson, Julian P. Van Winkle, Sr., Al Wathen, D. K. Wilgus and my old friend, Professor James Harvey Young, who introduced me to the frightening world of government documents.

I wish to thank for various forms of assistance the following libraries and librarians, historical societies, universities, state agencies and business firms: Oliver Field, Director, Bureau of Investigation, American Medical Association, Admiral William J. Marshall, President, The Bourbon Institute, and Miss Lorraine Roach. At Brown-Forman Distillers Corporation I received valuable assistance from Robert D. Henry, Manager of External Communications, Joseph B. Scholnick, Director of Public Relations and Dr. Spanyer, already mentioned; also from Allan R. Ottley, California Section Librarian, The California State Library; Miss Dorothy English, Librarian, Pennsylvania Division, Carnegie Library of Pittsburgh; Miss Margaret Scriven, Librarian, and Grant Talbot Dean, Cataloger, Chicago Historical Society; Harry Rigby, Jr., City Historian, City of Kingston, New York; Miss Sara T. Tenney, Sterling and Francine Clark Art Institute, Williamstown, Massachusetts. Miss Jean K. Taylor, Head, Business and Technical Department, Cleveland Public Library pursued a point for me with great ingenuity and inexhaustible patience.

I am indebted also to Francis M. Taylor, Communications Counseling Services; The Council of the Southern Mountains, Berea, Kentucky, and Ralph J. Shoemaker, Librarian, *The Courier-Journal,* Louisville, Kentucky. James M. Babcock, Chief, The Burton Historical Collection, Detroit Public Library, answered repeated inquiries, as did also William E. Staiger, Division of Research & Statistics, Distilled Spirits Institute; Miss Elizabeth C. Littsinger, Head, Maryland Department, Enoch Pratt Free Library and Mrs. Dorothy Thomas Cullen, Curator and Librarian, The Filson Club.

Thanks are due also to Jack E. Hodge, Fort Worth Public Library; Misses Mary B. Nesmith and Ella A. Jones, *Fortune;* and at the Glass Container Manufacturers' Institute, Bush Barnum, Director of Advertising and Public Information and Miss Frances Meade Perry, Librarian. I am under obligation to Harvard University Library; Mrs. C. E. Berry, Librarian, and Mrs. Frank Mercer, Edsel Ford Memorial Library, Hotchkiss School; Miss Margaret A. Flint, Assistant State Historian, Illinois State Historical Library; Nyle H. Miller, Secretary, and Joe Snell of Kansas State Historical Society.

At the Library of Congress I received valuable assistance from Miss Virginia Daiker, Reference Librarian, and Milton Kaplan, in the Print and Photograph Division. John S. Dydo, Assistant Director, Research Division,

Licensed Beverage Industries, and Mrs. Ora C. Glasgall, Librarian, were unfailingly helpful; also Mrs. Norman L. Johnson, Head, Reference Department, Louisville Free Public Library; Mrs. Polly G. Anderson, James P. Brock, Leon Karpel, Director, Mid-Hudson Libraries; Mrs. Malcolm Hunter, Millerton Free Library, and the Montana State Historical Society.

Executives at National Distillers Products Company who provided information, suggestions and facilities are Thomas F. Brown, Gerald Kirschbaum, Lester Rodenberg and L. R. Rodenberg, previously mentioned. I thank also the National Library of Medicine; Newberry Library; Malcolm E. Scheer, Assistant Librarian, New School for Social Research; Miss Gertrude L. Annan, Librarian, New York Academy of Medicine Library; and at The New-York Historical Society, Miss Geraldine Beard, Chief of the Reading Room, Arthur B. Carlson, Curator of Maps and Prints, Miss Rachel Minnick, Bibliographer, Carolyn Scoon, Assistant Curator—indeed, the whole staff.

I am indebted to many divisions and specialized collections in The New York Public Library, especially to Mr. Robert W. Hill, Keeper of Manuscripts; also the New York State Library—Miss Ida M. Cohen, Senior Reference Librarian and H. Lansing Mace, Assistant Reference Librarian. Others are: S. K. Stevens, Executive Director, Pennsylvania Historical and Museum Commission; Mrs. Alice Wallace, The State Historical Society of Colorado; Mrs. Gertrude Morton Parsley, Reference Librarian, Tennessee State Library, Miss Dorothy Fey, Executive Director, The United States Trademark Association.

At the University of Kentucky Libraries I am under deep obligation to Dr. Jacqueline P. Bull, Archivist, Miss Norma B. Cass, Reference Librarian, Dr. Lawrence S. Thompson, Director and Mrs. Elizabeth Underwood. I thank William S. Powell, Librarian, North Carolina Collection, University of North Carolina Library; the University of Pittsburgh Library; E. L. Inabinett, Director, The South Caroliniana Library, University of South Carolina; Miss Llerena Friend, Librarian, Barker Texas History Library, The University of Texas Library; Alderman Library, University of Virginia; Vassar College Library; Mrs. Laura P. Abbott, Assistant to the Librarian and Museum Director, Vermont Historical Society; Milton C. Russell, Head, Reference and Circulation Section, Virginia State Library; Mrs. Ruth J. Bradley, Chief, Historical Division, Wyoming State Archives and Historical Department; and Miss Dorothy W. Bridgwater, Assistant Head, Reference Department, Yale University Library.

Both author and book have benefited in countless ways because Raymond T. Bond and his associates at Dodd, Mead & Company regard publishing as a profession. Willis Kingsley Wing has been patient, helpful, a good counselor and friend. I salute affectionately my wife, Lettie Gay Carson, who remembers this little book in its first state, second state and so on and has ever urged a valuable point of view on how to write a book. It may be expressed succinctly in the words of St. Luke: "Give, and it shall be given unto you."

G.C.

FOREWORD

"If you want to find out about something of which you know nothing," Professor Morris Bishop of Cornell University has suggested, "write a book about it."

I have adopted Dr. Bishop's excellent maxim and applied it to bourbon whiskey, a noble and exhilarating subject whose place in American cultural history has long waited for objective treatment. Distilled from our own native maize, given character by limestone water and yeasts from the salubrious air of the bourbon belt, cradled during a long slumber in barrels of charred white oak, bourbon whiskey is the distinctive spirit of the United States. With its fruity bouquet, its rich color suggesting the golds and russets of our autumn foliage, a well-finished bourbon worthily holds place among the classic spirituous beverages of the world.

Spirits distilled from rye came among us first. But rye is an Old World grain. Only bourbon can be called with propriety our all-American drink which, Colonel Edmund H. Taylor, Jr., creator of the beneficent Old Taylor, declared in a deposition, was originated in the year of the Declaration of Independence and will endure as long as the liberties set forth in the Declaration itself.

The story of bourbon is recorded in many lively pages of our history. American whiskey is intimately associated with valor and splendor and the graces of life; with villainy and folly; with dramatic events such as the Whisky Rebellion, the scandals of the Whiskey Ring and later with the Whiskey Trust; with the "whiskey forts" of the fur trade, the fate of the American Indian and the toil of civilizing a continent. Whiskey and government, finally, are yoked together in an uneasy relationship derived from the power of Congress to levy taxes.

The liquor industry as it was constituted up to 1920 turned in a shabby performance so far as social responsibility was concerned. Generally it behaved in a manner which might be characterized by the words the hero of the Sut Lovingood stories applied to himself; it acted like a "Nat'ral-Born Durned Fool." Any critical remarks which may appear in the pages which follow should be viewed against the historical setting. They are not intended to describe the modern industry which has since Repeal avoided the old arrogance and fully assumed its obligations toward the public, setting up agencies of its own for safeguarding the general welfare, such as the Distilled Spirits Institute, Licensed Beverage Industries, Inc., and Kentucky Distillers' Association. The point of view taken here was expressed as long ago as Roman times, *abusus non tollit usum;* abuse is no argument against proper use.

Because they are large topics in themselves, I have omitted the temperance movement except for incidental mention; also the long and complicated subject of compulsory Prohibition. There are necessarily, however, scattered references to the social climate which made it prudent for a prominent citizen, when angling toward the hotel bar, to try to look as though he was going to the washroom to get his shoes shined.

Bourbon, referring not to the royal family of France but to the whiskey, is pronounced by Kentuckians, who are entitled to priority in this matter since Kentucky is where bourbon whiskey came from, "Ber-bun," not "Boor-bon." Bourbon rhymes with urban. But *whiskey* may be spelled with or without the *e* before the *y.* The best modern practice distinguishes between *ey* for the American whiskey and *y* for Scotch or Canadian whiskies. Some writers have spelled the word both ways within the bounds of a single paragraph. When quoting, I have followed the usage of the document.

Helpful criticisms and suggestions have been received from various sources (see Acknowledgments). Mistakes of fact or interpretation remain the lonely responsibility of the author. Some of my friends, a jolly lot, have visualized the leading distillers as dropping off cases of choice bourbons at my study to keep the wheels turning. To this pleasant conceit, the answer must be—no; no free sipping for the author, no subsidy of the text. The only purpose here is to bring pleasure and information to the intelligent but nonspecialized reader.

"In the Early days of Kentucky," wrote an old papermaker, Ebenezer Hiram Stedman, in appreciation of his state's red elixir, "one Small drink would Stimulate the whole Sistom. . . . It Brot out Kind feelings of the Heart, Made men sociable, And in them days Evry Boddy invited Evry Boddy That Come to their house to partake of this hosesome Beverage."

Stranger, will you join me in a horn of old bourbon at the bar of history? Then step right this way. . . .

G. C.

Carson Road
Millerton, New York

CONTENTS

ACKNOWLEDGMENTS vii

FOREWORD xi

1. DRINKS AND DRINKING IN EARLY AMERICA 1

2. WATERMELON ARMIES AND WHISKEY BOYS 11

3. BOURBON'S COUNTRY COUSIN 24

4. THE FIRST TRUE BOURBON 33

5. A NAME WITH A MELODY ALL ITS OWN—KENTUCKY 50

6. THE DARK AGE OF AMERICAN DRINKING 62

7. WHISKEY IN THE CIVIL WAR 71

8. GOLDEN YEARS OF THE BOURBON ARISTOCRACY 81

9. DRINKING DOWN THE NATIONAL DEBT 94

10. MOONSHINE AND HONEYSUCKLE 102

11. THE GREAT WHISKEY STEAL 114

12. THE HIGHWINE TRUST 128

13. WESTWARD THE JUG OF EMPIRE TOOK ITS WAY 137

14. A SOFA WITH EVERY CASE 149

15. BUT—WHAT *IS* WHISKEY? 163

16. WHISKEY FUN AND FOLKLORE 174

17. THE SWINGING DOOR 187

CONTENTS

18. THE ZENITH OF MAN'S PLEASURE   207

19. BOURBON: FROM 1920 TO THE DAY BEFORE YESTERDAY   218

    CHRONOLOGY   231

    GLOSSARY   235

    CHAPTER NOTES   239

    INDEX   271

ILLUSTRATIONS

	Facing page
A tavern bill	12
General Washington	13
Things that made Kentucky	44
General Taylor flask	45
I. W. Harper bourbon in a special bottle	45
Design for Star Whiskey	45
The Edgewater Distillery	76
John G. Carlyle and others at Churchill Downs	77
A pot still	108
General Orville E. Babcock	109
A dance house in Leadville, Colorado	140
Two specimens of liquor advertising	141
Colonel Edmund H. Taylor, Jr.	172
Making Home Comfortable For Him	173
Lincoln liquor bond	204
Hoffman House bar, New York City	205
Taft's Holdup Saloon, Red Lodge, Montana	220
Barrels aging in warehouse	221

THE SOCIAL HISTORY
OF BOURBON

An Unhurried Account of
Our Star-Spangled American Drink

Chapter I

DRINKS AND DRINKING
IN EARLY AMERICA

LONG before recorded history, primitive man discovered that the molecular readjustment of the carbon, hydrogen and oxygen atoms in a watery solution of fruit pulp which had been alllowed to stand, produced a beverage which made the world seem a wonderful place. Fermentation was regarded, literally, as a gift from the gods, and seems to have been arrived at by widely separated peoples who used whatever was at hand that would take on the new and magical charm not present in the fresh juice. Dates and honey were tried with satisfactory results, the palms of the tropics, mare's milk and, in Mexico, the sap of the maguey.

Alcohol is a snap to make. It will even make itself. Julian P. (Pappy) Van Winkle, Sr., at present writing the nation's oldest active distillery executive, tells the story of a Kentucky fabricator of mountain dew who was apprehended by a revenue officer. The moonshiner insisted that his jug contained nothing but spring water. The federal agent took a swig, choked and insisted that the mountaineer sample the contents.

"What do you know!" the old man sputtered. "The good Lord's gone and done it again!"

There is some debate as to whether the North American Indians may not have been one of the few peoples of the earth who

1

did not know how to obtain alcohol. In any event, they made up for lost time once they became acquainted with the Frenchman's brandy and the cheap, fiery rum of the *Bostonnais*.

Fermented drinks and social development advanced together. Alcohol may have stimulated the beginning of agriculture and a settled way of life. Alcohol entered into religious observances at a very early date, for it seemed to possess a spirit, or perhaps it was itself a spirit. The flowing bowl introduced a touch of civilizing ceremony, the graces of politeness. And sometimes ancient man found himself to be very, very drunk. Thus the risks became known as well as the benefits conferred by vinous liquor. Christianity and viticulture spread in western Europe together. One of the miracles ascribed by monkish chronicles to St. Remi in the sixth century is commemorated by a bas-relief on the north doorway of Rheims Cathedral where the saint is shown making the sign of the cross over an empty barrel, which reputedly and miraculously became filled with wine.

Although a concentration of up to fifteen per cent alcohol can be obtained by fermentation, the possibility of beverages of greater strength had to wait upon the invention of the still. The process whereby alcohol is first developed in a fruit pomace or a mash of cracked grain, then vaporized by heat, caught again in a cool coil, redistilled and fashioned into a beverage of potency, finesse and solace, constitutes an old and respected art, described intelligently by Albertus Magnus in the eleventh century. But long before Albertus put it down in good, strong black and white, some ingenious, or lucky, man had discovered that alcohol and water have different boiling points. Despite their strong affinity for each other, they can be separated. So an alembic or crude still was devised. Out of it came a raw, searing, formidable but drinkable distillate, direct ancestor of our western rivermen's "Tiger Spit."

Thus, in some such way as has been briefly sketched, wines and malt liquors and spirits began their long and tempestuous career as curse and boon. There is nothing in alcohol itself which is poisonous or injurious to man's health, despite a large propagandistic literature to the contrary. Indeed, the blood stream of the average healthy human normally contains a small amount of it. William Jennnings Bryan, the advocate of unfermented grape juice, John B. Gough, the great anti-whiskey orator, when he was sober, even hatchet-wielding Carry Nation—she, too, had .003 per cent of alcohol frisking through her arteries. There is quick energy, but no vitamins and minerals in alcohol. The pink elephants and other terrifying hallucinations associated with excessive indulgence in alcohol are brought on by a deficiency of vitamin B_1. Millions have enjoyed alcohol. Millions have abused it. Millions have come to hate it. The peoples of the world have reached no final decision about it yet. They probably never will. But the reasons for drinking are not likely to disappear, since they include such disparate motivations as revolt, despair, anodyne, compliance with social custom, casual pleasure and a lifting of the veil in which drink "maketh glad the heart of man."

The first settlements on the eastern shores of the present United States were marked by the transit of the social customs of England and Europe to the New World, which included the conception that beer, ale, wine and spirits were pleasant, beneficial and necessary in the prevention of malaria. The Pilgrims were comforted by liquor on the *Mayflower*. The *Arabella*, which carried Governor John Winthrop, first governor of Massachusetts Bay Colony, also transported forty-two tuns of beer. Nor did the ship's company lack something stronger, for Winthrop observed of his fellow-passengers, "they gave themselves to drink *hot waters* very immoderately."

By 1639 brewing had been started in Massachusetts on a small scale. The ingenuity of the colonists was equal to the challenge. Fermented drinks were made from pumpkins, parsnips, grapes, currants and elderberries. They distilled ardent spirits from plums, cherries, the pawpaw, blackberries, whortleberries, persimmons, potatoes both white and sweet, turnips, carrots and the small grains. "Old peach" came from peaches. "Perry" was a liquor made from pears. From honey and honeycomb our grandsirs distilled "old metheglin," a deep, dark brown liquor said to have packed a tremendous kick. According to Vermont tradition, if one put down a glass of it he could hear the bees buzz.

Apple trees were "prospering abundantly" in Massachusetts by 1671, John Josselyn wrote in his *Voyages*. Soon every New

England homestead had an apple orchard for making hard cider. It was a necessity at all barn-raisings, weddings and town meetings. When attending funerals was a major recreation in New England, comparable to going to meeting and spying on the neighbors, a table with liquor was always provided by the family of the deceased. The mourner entered, took off his hat with his left hand, smoothed down his hair with the other. Walking to the coffin, he gazed at the corpse with an expression suited to the occasion and the degree of his grief, and passed on to the table loaded with pitchers and decanters. Later, the men gathered in front of the house to talk politics or swap heifers. The Quakers of Pennsylvania followed the same custom. So enthusiastic did they become over the sugar cakes and hot liquors provided, on one occasion, at "Burralls" that Chester Meeting admonished "ye friends" to take care not to push the liquor but let every one partake as they chose, but "not more than will doe them Good."

This still left the mourners a good deal of latitude.

In New England, reflecting the temperament of the people, drinking was usually associated with some useful activity, such as shearing sheep. Hard cider and applejohn, the saying goes, built the stone walls of the region, a gallon per rod of wall. The customs of Virginia were equally significant of the culture developed there. The Virginians took pleasure for its own sake. The planter class, up to the Revolution, rode to hounds and hit the bottle liberally in the pattern of the English gentlemen back "home." They dined with the help of such amenities as claret, Fayal, Madeira and Rhenish wines. Imported and native brandy flowed when the appraisers fixed the value of an estate, or the commissioners met to accept a new bridge. Gout was endemic. The yeoman farmers drank their beer and ale, while the frontiersmen danced their reels and square dances with homemade whiskey generously present in an open tub, the gourd dipper beside it. Before whiskey became the leading beverage, a brandy made of peaches was a favorite all through the South under the name "Virginia drams."

The first settler to plant a peach orchard on the Broad River was one Micajah McGehee, who set up a small country distillery and consumed most of his own product. But so hard was his head that it took him all day to get capsized. In a moment of religious excitement he joined the Methodists; so, of course, he was spoken to about his drinking. McGehee replied that his peach brandy was necessary to the preservation of health. But as a gesture of good faith he agreed to limit himself to a quart a day. The allowance proved to be too small, for Micajah lost his battle with the angel of death at the age of eighty.

New Jersey took a commanding lead at a very early date in distilling apple whiskey whose potency is suggested in the name Jersey Lightning, so called because it struck suddenly and produced an affliction known as "apple palsy." Firm information on the applejack distilling industry of the state is fragmentary and difficult to come by, since local history was usually compiled by emeritus pastors to whom the moral stance on total abstinence was more compelling than the moral imperative to write objective history. Thus the distillers of apple hardly got a fair shake. At any rate, we do know that apple whiskey helped along the infant glass industry in Salem County with its demand for containers and occupies a prominent place in the drinking folklore of the United States because of its supposed capabilities for trapping the unwary into an indiscretion.

In cold fact, the horsepower of "jack" or of any other distilled spirit depends on the kind of beverage drunk, the speed of drinking, the proof, the quantity, the amount of dilution and individual constitutional and psychological factors. According to granny medicine, applejack was rated as "good for a weakly constitution" and taken liberally as a tonic. The pineys of south Jersey developed a kind of immunity or at least a remarkable ability to cope with their native Calvados. As Exhibit A one may present Owley Lemon who lived in a small cabin in Southampton township at Ewansville and was known as King of the Pinehawkers. Owley drank a quart a day without inconvenience. Once, to oblige a friend, Owley put down a pint in one draw, smacked his lips, drew his hand across his mouth, and remarked that it was a fine day.

But New Jersey had no patent on the fermented and distilled juice of the American apple. In Tennessee applejack was plentiful at twelve and a half cents a quart. And those who had experience with double-distilled Kentucky apple held that if a piece of fatback was thrown into the liquor the pork would simply disappear. They knew this powerful drink in Maryland, too, as early as the mid-eighteenth century, for a young tobacco factor described life there around 1740 to an English friend in these terms:

> Our fires are wood, Our Houses as good;
>   Our diet is Hawg & Hominie
> Drink juice of the Apple, Tobacco's our staple,
>   Gloria tibi Domine.

Early distilling in North America was an agricultural activity, no different from tapping the sugar maples or retting and scutching flax to obtain linen fiber. Various forms of malt and spirituous liquors were available not only in the home but at retail by the drink or "by the smalls," according to a contemporary phrase, at the tavern or public house. The barroom operated under the eye of a circumspect Ganymede who had been carefully chosen for his post by the justices of the county court or, in New England, by the board of selectmen, "as a Person of sober life and Conversation" and therefore fit "to keep a House of Entertainment."

On cold winter evenings the loggerheads were kept cherry-red in the great fireplaces, ready to be plunged into the mugs of flip, a mixture of rum and beer, sweetened and then heated with the hot metal ball at the end of the loggerhead handle. This same appurtenance of the colonial fireplace also came into play for making the "Yard of Flannel" whose recipe called for cider, rum, cream, beaten eggs and spices. And sometimes, when the talk turned to politics or a point of church doctrine, the loggerhead became an offensive weapon. The colonial "ordinary" operated under a system of control that was strict and even paternalistic. Hours, prices, such matters as cockfighting and gambling and loud singing, were all the subject of legislation. Details were spelled out minutely. The objective was public order. But the system of licensing and supervision was quite innocent of any abstract theory of social control.

Before the evangelical churches and "comfortable drinks" came to a sharp parting of the ways, the deacons and vestry carried on the business of the church in front of the wooden wicket of the public house bar. There the justices held court. On the day of the militia trainings, the newly elected officer was expected "to wet his commission bountifully." All convocations of a public nature gathered as a matter of course at the barroom where deals were consummated, elections settled. Many tavern names come to mind because of their associations with the main stream of American history. Paul Revere and Sam Adams knew well the Green Dragon in Boston. Patrick Henry had tended bar in his father-in-law's establishment at Hanover Courthouse. The Sons of Liberty held rendezvous at the Burns Coffee House just north of Trinity Church in New York. The connections between General Washington and Fraunces Tavern are still cherished and celebrated. The place in history of John Buckman's house of hospitality at Lexington, Massachusetts, will not be forgotten; where in the chilly darkness of April 19, 1775, the Minutemen put down their ale or hot toddy and stepped out on the Green to face destiny.

Around the middle of the seventeenth century a flourishing trade developed between New England and the islands of the Caribbean, first in West India rum, later in molasses. A distilling industry centered on Salem, Newport, Medford and Boston turned the molasses into rum—originally "rumbullion"—which penetrated deeply into the social and economic life of Americans for the next one hundred and fifty years. A relative newcomer among the world's spirituous drinks, and not a native one to the continental United States, rum nevertheless became the most profitable manufactured article produced in New England. In 1807 Boston had no fewer than forty rum distilleries, Rhode Island about the same number, and it used to be said that for every missionary sent out to Christianize Africa, ten thousand gallons of rum went along for more secular purposes.

The arduous occupations of lumbering, coopering, shipbuilding, grubbing out the farms, fishing on the Grand Banks all called for strong drink to wash down the Indian corn and salt provisions. So did the rigors of the American climate. Rum, and later whiskey, offered an attractive form of central heating. The status of ardent spirits was clearly conveyed by the Spanish commander at St. Louis when he remarked in a report to the

governor-general at New Orleans in 1779: "There have arrived at this post . . . five boats, all loaded with rum, sugar,
and coffee, which for these people are the world, the flesh, and
the devil."

The West Indies needed slaves to grow the sugar cane and
make the molasses. New England needed the molasses to make
its rum. The African chiefs of the Gold Coast needed the stimulus of rum to keep their slave pens filled. Thus arose the famous
or infamous "triangular trade" in which rum functioned as the
currency of the slavers. The New Englanders dominated the
carrying trade, moving the molasses to the ports of Massachusetts and Rhode Island and the rum to Africa. Then the
sloops, brigantines and snows of Newport and Boston became
blackbirders, returning from the Guinea coast crammed with
slaves lying like cordwood in handcuffs and leg-irons. The
Yankees had tried various kinds of trade goods in connection
with this business. But the best lure was liquor. These entre-
preneurs did not prefer wet goods to dry. Rum just worked
better. So they sailed with hogsheads and tierces to trade for
the "black ivory" which, after the long journey from Sierra
Leone to the West Indies, and back to the home port with more
molasses, would often net more in one voyage than the ship was
worth.

Under British economic theory, the colonies were regarded as
a source of raw materials which were carried home in British
ships to be exchanged for British manufactures. New England
had little in the way of raw materials to send to England. But
the rum trade did provide exchange for settling British balances.
In pursuit of the objectives of empire, Parliament in 1733 passed
what was called the Molasses Act, levying prohibitive duties on
molasses of non-British origin, with the purpose of compelling
the importation of the British product. Since the American
colonies imported the greater part of their molasses from the
French and Spanish islands, the Act might have brought ruin
upon the distilling industry, except for the fact that they wisely
paid no attention to it. The law, like the later Sugar Act, contributed much to the spirit of '76, but little to the British treasury. Since the French and Spanish molasses was better in quality, cheaper in price, and there wasn't enough British molasses

anyway, smuggling became universal. Politically as well as economically a mistake, the measure engendered disrespect for all law, gave smuggling the cachet of social approval, laid the basis for the subsequent and more famous defiance of the Stamp Act.

Rum gave a great impetus to drinking in America, assisted by its reputation as a medicine. When an old chap had acquired the family cough, he turned to rum in some combination with tansy. Rum was esteemed for its power to open the pores of the skin. The treatment for gallstones was liverwort and rum; a small quantity of liverwort, plenty of rum. Rum and milk was a "restorative." Even the fishermen rated rum above cod-liver oil.

The wars of the eighteenth century also advanced the social esteem of rum. In the old "French war" of '55 the troops were furnished a ration of rum. Rum-sellers followed the soldiers and provided such abundant supplementary supplies that General Amherst ordered that every man taken up for intoxication should be lashed twenty times a day until, the Reverend Dr. Daniel Dorchester noted approvingly in his book, *The Liquor Problem in All Ages* (1884)—"until he disclosed the name of the person from whom he procured the liquor." It should be observed that the Reverend Doctor was here giving the nod to torture, provided that it was employed in a cause he approved of.

Congress, in Revolutionary times, voted supplies of rum or whiskey for the American army as a necessity for those who were facing hardships and danger. So once more, in Dr. Dorchester's super-heated prose, "the diseased appetite was . . . fostered." Toward the end of the century rum slipped in popularity but left behind a legacy of quaint and slangy names for the various stages of intoxication; among them, as enumerated with relish by the Reverend Mason Locke Weems, "boozy, groggy, blue, damp, tipsy, fuddled, haily gaily, how came you so, half shaved, swipy, has got a drop in his eye, cut, has got his wet sheet aboard, cut in the craw." A special Georgiaism was "high up to picking cotton."

The production of whiskey before the Revolution was insignificant. It is not known certainly what grain was first used in the primitive mash tubs. As the settlers moved west they found rye made a bumper crop in western Maryland and Pennsylvania; and in Kentucky the corn grew green and tall. It was probably rye whiskey which began to supplant rum in popular favor. Two heavy blows fell upon the rum trade in quick succession. First, in 1807 the Embargo Act interdicted land and sea commerce with foreign nations and cut off the supply of molasses. Then in the next year Congress abolished the slave trade. There was smuggling of both molasses and slaves. But these two events, plus the increasing cost of freighting rum from the seaboard over the Appalachian mountains, hastened the decline of rum.

There were other factors. The Scotch-Irish were pouring down the Shenandoah Valley, over the Pennsylvania ridges and through the Cumberland Gap. These men were old hands with the pot still. And they were *grain* distillers. As one Pennsylvania distiller cannily observed, when men found that they could make three gallons of whiskey from one bushel of grain, the business became "sufficiently respectable." By the time the nineteenth century rolled around, when the men of the new West toasted Independence Day, they did it in a tumbler of what we would be able to recognize as American-style whiskey, distilled by a people known at the time as the Irish. The "Irish" were actually Scotch who had been colonized in north Ireland during the reign of James I. They came to America in large numbers, passed west through the Pennsylvania Germans to whom they were unfavorably known as *die dummer Irisher,* filled up the Cumberland valley, advanced along the old Indian trading path, settled the Juniata country, pushed on into southwest Pennsylvania. They brought with them the strongly held opinion that whiskey, not bread, was the staff of life, the equipment for distilling and an expert knowledge of the distiller's art. By the 1790's western Pennsylvania was occupied by a bustling race of farmers and whiskey-makers, millers, traders, peddlers, frontiersmen, recruits for the coming Indian campaigns, all of whom liked their whiskey and most of whom depended upon their country distilleries for a commodity to take to market. When the new federal government taxed their Monongahela, the western counties exploded with oratory and the squirrel hunters began to oil their guns.

Chapter 2

WATERMELON ARMIES
AND WHISKEY BOYS

WHEN one recalls that the President of the United States, the Secretary of War, the Secretary of the Treasury and the governors of four states once mobilized against the farmers of western Pennsylvania almost as large an army as ever took the field in the Revolutionary War, the event appears at first glance as one of the more improbable episodes in the annals of this country. Thirteen thousand grenadiers, dragoons, foot soldiers and pioneers, a train of artillery with six-pounders, mortars and several "grasshoppers," equipped with mountains of ammunition, forage, baggage and a bountiful stock of tax-paid whiskey, paraded over the mountains to Pittsburgh against a gaggle of homespun rebels who had already dispersed.

Yet the march had a rationale. President George Washington and his Secretary of the Treasury, Alexander Hamilton, moved to counter civil commotion with overwhelming force because they well understood that the viability of the United States Constitution was involved. Soon after he assumed his post at the Treasury, Hamilton had proposed, to the astonishment of the country, that the United States should meet fully and promptly its financial obligations, including the assumption of the debts contracted by the states in the struggle for independence. The

money was partly to be raised by laying an excise tax upon distilled spirits. The tax, which was universally detested in the
West—"odious" was the word most commonly used to describe
it—became law on March 3, 1791.

The news of the passage of the measure was greeted with
a roar of indignation in the back country settlements. The duty
was laid uniformly upon all the states, as the Constitution provided. If the West had to pay more, Secretary Hamilton explained, it was only because it used more whiskey. The East
could, if it so desired, forgo beverage spirits and fall back on
cider and beer. The South could not. It had neither orchards
nor breweries. To Virginia and Maryland the excise tax appeared
to be as unjust and oppressive as the well-remembered Molasses
Act and the tea duties of George III. "The time will come,"
predicted fiery James Jackson of Georgia in the House of Representatives, "when a shirt shall not be washed without an excise."

Kentucky, then thinly settled, but already producing its characteristic hand-made, whole-souled liquor from planished copper stills, was of the opinion that the law was unconstitutional.
Deputy revenue collectors throughout the Bluegrass region were
assaulted, their papers stolen, their horses' ears cropped and
their saddles cut to pieces. On one wild night the people of
Lexington dragged a stuffed dummy through the streets and
hanged in effigy Colonel Thomas Marshall, the chief collector
for the district.

Yet in no other place did popular fury rise so high, spread so
rapidly, involve a whole population so completely, express so
many assorted grievances, as in the Pennsylvania frontier counties of Fayette, Allegheny, Westmoreland and Washington. In
these counties, around 1791, a light plume of wood smoke rose
from the chimneys of no less than five thousand log stillhouses.
The rates went into effect on July first. The whiskey maker
could choose whether he would pay a yearly levy on his still
capacity or a gallonage tax ranging from nine to eleven cents
on his actual production.

Before the month was out, "committees of correspondence,"
in the old Revolutionary phrase, were speeding horsemen over
the ridges and through the valleys to arouse the people to arm
and assemble. The majority, but not all, of the men who made

A TAVERN-BILL,

Rated at the GENERAL QUARTER-SESSIONS, held at ~~Salem~~ *Bridgetown* for the County of ~~Salem~~ *Cumberland,* the *twenty fifth* Day of *February* Anno Domini 17*9*0   *June 1792*

THE beft Dinner or Supper, with a Pint of good Beer or Cyder,		-	0 .. 1 .. 6	1/10 1/2
Second beft or Family ditto, with ditto,	-	-	1 .. 2	1/3
Beft Breakfaft of Tea, Coffee or Chocolate, with Loaf Sugar,	-	-	1 .. 0	1/3
Ditto of cold Meat, with a Pint of good Beer or Cyder,	-	-	" 10	—
Good Madeira Wine,	per Pint,	- 3 ..	6	3/9
Other good Foreign ditto,	per ditto,	— 1 ..	6	—2/
Fruit Punch of good Spirits and Loaf Sugar,	per Quart Bowl,	— 1 ..	6	1/6 1/2
Mim of good Rum and Loaf Sugar,	per Quart,	— 1 ..	0	1/3
Mull'd Cyder,	per ditto,	..	9	1/10 1/2
Egg or other Sling, with a Gill of Weft-India Rum in it and Loaf Sugar,	-	—	9	1/1 1/2
Weft-India Rum,	per Half Pint,	—	10	1/1 1/2
Ditto,	per Gill,	—	5	1/6 2
Cherry ditto,	per ditto,	—	5	1/6 2
Gin or Brandy,	per ditto,	—	6	1/8 2
Cyder-Royal,	per Pint,	—	6	1/8
Metheglin,	per ditto,	—	9	1/11
Good double Beer,	per Quart,	—	6	1/9 2
Good Cyder,	per ditto,	—	6	1/6 2
A good clean Bed, with clean Sheets, for a fingle Perfon,	per Night,	—	6	1/6 3
Ditto with two Perfons in a Bed, each Perfon,	per ditto,	—	4	1/4 3
~~Oats or Corn,~~ *Corn*	per Quart,	—	2 3/8	1/3
Good Pafture for a fingle Horse, *per* Night, or 24 Hours,	-	—	8	
Good Stabling for ditto, Clover Hay, *per* ditto, *or Timothy*	—	1 .. 6		1/6 3
~~Baiting with Clover Hay for an Hour, before Oats or Corn,~~		1/6 3		
~~Ditto in good Pafture, in the like cafe,~~	—			

By order of Court.

Giles, Clk:

Courtesy of The New-York Historical Society

The county courts in most colonies regulated the business of keeping an inn, including the fixing of prices. Above: a schedule established by Cumberland County, at Bridgeton, New Jersey.

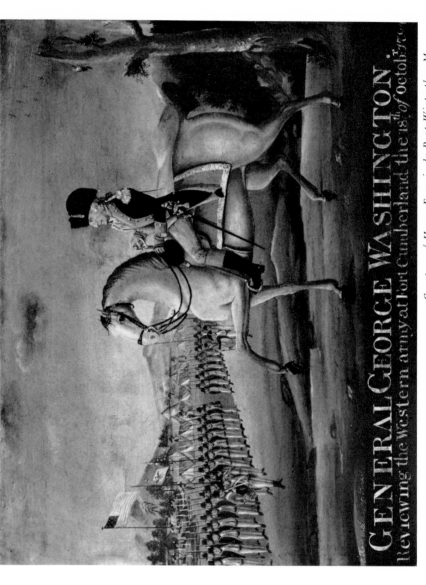

GENERAL GEORGE WASHINGTON.
Reviewing the Western army at Fort Cumberland the 18.th of Octob.r 1794.

Courtesy of Henry Francis du Pont Winterthur Museum

An incident of the Whiskey Rebellion. Oil painting by Frederick Kemmelmeyer, an artist active
in Baltimore from *circa* 1788 to 1803,

the whiskey decided to "forbear" from paying the tax. The revenue officers were thoroughly worked over. Robert Johnson, for example, collector for Washington and Allegheny counties, was waylaid near Pigeon Creek by a mob disguised in women's clothing. They cut off his hair, gave him a coat of tar and feathers and stole his horse.

The Pennsylvania troubles were rooted in the economic importance and impregnable social position of mellow old Monongahela rye whiskey. In 1825, for instance, when the Philadelphia Society for Promoting Agriculture offered a gold medal to the person in Pennsylvania who carried on large-scale farming operations without providing ardent spirits for his farm workers, the medal could not be awarded. There were no entries for the uncoveted honor.

The frontier people had been reared from childhood on the family jug of farmer whiskey. They found the taste pleasant, the effect agreeable. Whiskey was usually involved when there was kissing or fighting. It beatified the rituals of birth and death. The doctor kept a bottle in his office for his own use under the deceptive label "Arsenic—Deadly poison." The lawyer produced the bottle when the papers were signed. Whiskey was available in the prothonotary's office when the trial-list was made up. Jurors got their dram, and the constable drew his ration for his services on election day. The hospitable barrel and the tin cup were the mark of the successful political candidate. The United States Army issued a gill to a man every day. Ministers of the gospel were paid in rye whiskey, for they were shepherds of a devout flock, Scotch Presbyterians mostly, who took their Bible straight, especially where it said: "Give strong drink unto him that is ready to perish, and wine unto those that be of heavy hearts."

With grain the most abundant commodity west of the mountains, the farmers could eat it or drink it, but they couldn't sell it in distant markets unless it was reduced in bulk and enhanced in value. A Pennsylvania farmer's "best holt," then, was whiskey. A pack-horse could move only four bushels of grain. But it could carry twenty-four bushels if it was condensed into two kegs of whiskey slung across its back, while the price of the goods would double when they reached the eastern markets. So whiskey became the remittance of the fringe settlements for salt, sugar, nails, bar iron, pewter plates, powder and shot. Along the western rivers where men saw few shilling pieces, a gallon of good, sound rye whiskey was a stable measure of value.

The bitter resistance of the western men to the whiskey tax involved both practical considerations and principles. First, the excise payment was due and must be paid in hard money as soon as the water-white distillate flowed from the condensing coil. The principle concerned the whole repulsive idea of an internal revenue levy. The settlers of western Pennsylvania were a bold, hardy, emigrant race who brought with them bitter memories of oppression under the excise laws in Scotland and Ireland, involving invasion of their homes, confiscation of their property and a system of paid informers. Revenue collectors were social outcasts in a society which warmly seconded Doctor Samuel Johnson's definition of excise: "a hateful tax levied upon commodities, and adjudged not by the common judges of property, but wretches hired by those to whom excise is paid."

The whiskey boys of Pennsylvania saw it as simply a matter of sound Whig doctrine to resist the exciseman as he made his rounds with Dicas' hydrometer to measure the proof of the whiskey and his marking iron to brand the casks with his findings. Earlier, Pennsylvania had taxed spirits. But whiskey produced for purely private use was exempt. William Findley of Westmoreland County, a member of Congress at the time and a sympathetic interpreter of the western point of view, looked into this angle. To his astonishment, he learned that all of the whiskey distilled in the west was for purely personal use. So far as the state's excise tax was concerned, or any other tax, for that matter, the sturdy Celtic peoples of the Monongahela region had cheerfully returned to nature: they just didn't pay. About every sixth man made whiskey. But all were involved in the problem, since the other five took their grain to the stillhouse where the master distiller turned it into liquid form.

The state had been lenient. But now matters had taken a more serious turn. The new federal government in Philadelphia was dividing the whole country up into "districts" for the purpose of collecting the money. And the districts were subdivided into smaller "surveys." The transmontane Pennsylvanians found themselves in the grip of something known as the fourth survey, with General John Neville, hitherto a popular citizen and leader, getting ready to enforce the law, with a reward paid to informers and a percentage to the collectors, who appeared to be a rapacious set.

The first meeting of public protest against the 1791 federal tax was held at Redstone Old Fort, now Brownsville. The proceedings were moderate on that occasion, and scarcely went beyond the right of petition. Another meeting in August, more characteristic of others which were to follow, was radical in tone, disorderly, threatening. It passed resolves to the effect that any person taking office under the revenue law was an enemy of society.

When warrants were issued in the affair of Robert Johnson, the process server was robbed, beaten, tarred and feathered and left tied to a tree in the forest. As the inspectors' offices were established, they were systematically raided. Liberty poles reappeared as whiskey poles. The stills of operators who paid the tax were riddled with bullets in attacks sardonically known as "mending" the still. This led to a popular description of the Whiskey Boys as "Tom the Tinker's Men," an ironical reference to the familiar, itinerant repairer of pots and kettles. Notices proposing measures for thwarting the law, or aimed at coercing the distillers, were posted on trees or published in the *Pittsburgh Gazette* over the signature, "Tom the Tinker," nom de plume of the insurgent John Holcroft and other anti-tax agitators. Findley, who tried to build a bridge of understanding between the backwoodsmen and the central government, described the outbreak as not the result of any concerted plan, but rather as a flame, "an infatuation almost incredible."

An additional grievance grew out of the circumstance that offenders were required to appear in the federal court at Philadelphia, three hundred miles away. The whiskey-makers saw this distant government as being no less oppressive than one seated in London, and often drew the parallel. The Scotch-Irish of western Pennsylvania were, in sum, anti-federalist, anti-tax, and it may be added, anti-Indian. West of Pittsburgh lay Indian country. The men of the west held to a simple concept of how to solve the Indian problem: extermination. The Indians had the same program, in reverse, and were getting better results. The bungling campaigns, which generals Hamar and St. Clair had conducted in the early 1790's made the people of the fringe settlements despair of the ability of the Union to protect them.

Congress amended the excise tax law in 1792 and again in 1794 to lighten the burden on country distillers. A further conciliatory step was taken. To ease the hardships of the judicial process, Congress gave to the state courts jurisdiction in excise offenses so that accused persons might be tried in their own vicinity. But some fifty or sixty writs already issued and returnable at Philadelphia resulted in men being carried away from their fields during harvest time. This convinced the insurgents that the federalist East was seeking a pretext to discipline the democratic West.

One day in July, while the papers were being served, William Miller, a delinquent farmer-distiller, and political supporter of General Neville, saw the General riding up his lane accompanied by a stranger who turned out to be a United States marshal from Philadelphia. The marshal unlimbered an official paper and began to read a summons. It ordered said Miller peremptorily to "set aside all manner of business and excuses" and appear in his "proper person" before a Philadelphia judge. Miller had been planning to sell his property and remove to Kentucky. The cost of the trip to Philadelphia and the fine for which he was liable would eat up the value of his land and betterments. The farm was as good as gone.

"I felt my blood boil at seeing General Neville along to pilot the sheriff to my very door," Miller said afterward. "I felt myself mad with passion."

As Neville and the marshal rode away, a party from the county militia which was mustered at Mingo Creek fired upon them, but there were no casualties. When the General reached Bower Hill, his country home above the Chartiers Valley, another party under the command of John Holcroft awaited him there and demanded his commission and official papers. The demand was refused and both sides began to shoot. As the rebels closed in on the main house, a flanking fire came from the Negro cabins on the plantation. The Whiskey Boys were driven off with one killed and four wounded.

The next day, Major James McFarlane, a veteran of the Revolution, led an attack in force upon Neville's painted and wallpapered mansion, furnished with such marvels as carpets, mirrors, pictures and prints and an eight-day clock. The house was now defended by a dozen soldiers from Fort Fayette at Pittsburgh. A fire-fight followed during which a soldier was shot and McFarlane was killed—by treachery, the rebels said, when a white flag was displayed. The soldiers surrendered and were either released or allowed to escape. Neville was not found, but his cabins, barns, outbuildings and finally the residence were all burned to the ground. Stocks of grain were destroyed, all fences leveled, as the victors broke up the furniture, liberated the mirrors and clock, and distributed Neville's supply of liquor to the mob.

The funeral of McFarlane caused great excitement. Among those present were Hugh Henry Brackenridge, author, lawyer and one of the western moderates, and David Bradford, prosecuting attorney for Washington County. The former wished to find ways to reduce the tension; the latter to increase it. Bradford was a rash, impetuous Marylander, ambitious for power and position. Some thought him a second-rate lawyer. Others disagreed. They said he was third-rate. But he had a gift for rough mob eloquence. Bradford had already robbed the United States mails to find out what information was being sent east against the conspirators. He had already called for the people to make a choice of "submission or opposition . . . with *head, heart, hand* and *voice."*

At Major McFarlane's funeral service Bradford worked powerfully upon the feelings of his sympathizers as he described "the murder of McFarlane." Brackenridge also spoke, using wit and drollery to let down the pressure and to make palatable his warning to the insurgents that they were flirting with the possibility of being hanged. But the temper of the throng was for Bradford, clearly revealed in the epitaph which was set over McFarlane's grave. It said "He fell . . . by the hands of an unprincipled villain in the support of what he supposed to be the rights of his country."

The high-water mark of the insurrection was the occupation of Pittsburgh. After the fight and the funeral, Bradford called out the militia regiments of the four disaffected counties. They were commanded to rendezvous at Braddock's Field, near Pittsburgh, with arms, full equipment and four days' rations. At the field there was a great beating of drums, much marching and counter-marching, almost a holiday spirit. Men in hunting shirts practiced shooting at the mark until a dense pall of smoke hung over the plain, as there had been thirty-nine years before at the time of General Braddock's disaster. There were between five and seven thousand men on the field, many meditating in an ugly mood upon their enemies holed up in the town, talking of storming Fort Fayette and burning Pittsburgh as "a second Sodom."

Bradford's dream was the establishment of an independent state with himself cast as a sort of Washington of the West. Elected by acclaim as Major General, he dashed about the field on a superb horse in a fancy uniform, his sword flashing, plumes floating out from his hat. As he harangued the multitude, Bradford received applications for commissions in the service of—what? No one quite knew.

Marching in good order, strung out over two and a half miles of road, the rebels advanced on August first toward Pittsburgh in what was hopefully interpreted as a "visit," though the temper of the whiskey soldiers was perhaps nearer to that of one man who twirled his hat on the muzzle of his rifle and shouted, "I have a bad hat now, but I expect to have a better one soon." While the panic-stricken burghers buried the silver and locked up the girls, the mob marched in on what is now Fourth Avenue to the vicinity of the present Baltimore and Ohio Railroad station. A reception committee extended nervous hospitality in the form of hams, poultry, dried venison, bear meat, water and whiskey. They agreed to banish certain citizens obnoxious to the insurrectionists. One building on a suburban farm was burned. Another attempt at arson failed to come off. The day cost Brackenridge four barrels of prime Monongahela. It was better, he reflected, "to be employed in extinguishing the fire of their thirst than of my house." Pittsburgh was fortunate in getting the main body in and then out again without a battle or a burning.

All through the month of August armed bands continued to patrol the roads as a "scrub Congress," in the phrase of one scoffer, met at Parkinson's Ferry, now Monongahela, to debate, pass resolutions and move somewhat uncertainly toward separation from the United States. Wild and ignorant rumors won belief. It was said that Congress was extending the excise levy to plows at a dollar each, that every wagon entering Philadelphia would be forced to pay a dollar, that a tax was soon to be established at Pittsburgh of fifteen shillings for the birth of every boy baby, and ten for each girl.

With the terrorizing of Pittsburgh, it was evident that the crisis had arrived. The President requisitioned 15,000 militia from Pennsylvania, New Jersey, Virginia and Maryland, of whom about 13,000 actually marched. Would the citizens of one state invade another to compel obedience to federal law? Here one gets a glimpse of the larger importance of the affair. Both the national government and the state of Pennsylvania sent commissioners to the West with offers of pardon upon satisfactory assurances that the people would obey the laws. Albert Gallatin, William Findley, Brackenridge and others made a desperate effort to win the people to compliance, though their motives were often questioned by both the rebels and the federal authorities. The response to the offer of amnesty was judged not to be sufficiently positive. Pressed by Hamilton to have federal power show its teeth, Washington announced that the troops would march.

The army was aroused. In particular, the New Jersey militia were ready for lynch law because they had been derided in a western newspaper as a "Water-mellon Army" and an uncomplimentary estimate was made of their military capabilities. The piece was written as a take-off on the kind of negotiations which preceded an Indian treaty. Possibly the idea was suggested by the fact that the Whiskey Boys were often called "White Indians." At any rate, in the satire the Indians admonished the great council in Philadelphia: ". . . Brothers, we have that powerful monarch, Capt. Whiskey, to command us. By the power of his influence, and a love to *his person* we are compelled to every great and heroic act. . . . We, the Six United Nations of White Indians . . . have all imbibed his principles and passions —that is a love of whiskey . . . . Brothers, you must not think to frighten us with . . . infantry, cavalry and artillery, composed of your water-mellon armies from the Jersey shores; they would cut a much better figure in warring with the crabs and oysters about the Capes of Delaware."

Captain Whiskey was answered hotly by "A Jersey Blue." He pointed out that "the water-melon army of New Jersey" was going to march westward shortly with "ten-inch howitzers for throwing a species of mellon very useful for curing a *gravel occasioned by whiskey!*" The expedition was tagged thereafter as the "Watermelon Army."

The troops moved in two columns under the command of General Henry (Light Horse Harry) Lee, Governor of Virginia. Old Dan Morgan was there and young Meriwether Lewis, five nephews of President Washington, the governors of Pennsylvania and New Jersey, too, and many a veteran blooded in Revolutionary fighting, including the extraordinary German, Captain John Fries of the Bucks County militia and his remarkable dog to which the Captain gave the name of a beverage he occasionally enjoyed—Whiskey.

The left wing marched west during October, 1794, over General Braddock's old route from Virginia and Maryland to Cumberland on the Potomac, then northwest into Pennsylvania, to join forces with the right wing at Union Town. The Pennsylvania and New Jersey corps proceeded via Norristown and Reading to Harrisburg and Carlisle. There, on October 4th, President Washington arrived, accompanied by Colonel Hamilton. The representatives of the disaffected counties told the President at Carlisle that the army was not needed but Hamilton convinced him that it was. Washington proceeded with the troops as far as Bedford, then returned to Philadelphia for the meeting of Congress. Hamilton ordered a roundup of many of the rebels and personally interrogated the most important ones. Brackenridge, incidentally, came off well in his encounter with Hamilton, who declared that he was satisfied with Brackenridge's conduct.

By the time the expedition had crossed the mountains, the uprising was already coming apart at the seams. David Bradford, who had been excluded from the offer of amnesty, fled to Spanish Louisiana. About two thousand of the best riflemen in the West also left the country, including many a distiller, who loaded his pot still on a pack horse or a keel boat and sought asylum in Kentucky where, hopefully, a man could make "the creature" without giving the public debt a lift.

The punitive army moved forward in glorious autumn weather, raiding chicken coops, consuming prodigious quantities of the commodity which lay at the heart of the controversy. Richard Howell, governor of New Jersey and commander of the right wing, revived the spirits of the Jersey troops by composing a marching song, "Dash to the Mountains, Jersey Blue":

> To arms once more, our hero cries,
> Sedition lives and order dies;
> To peace and ease then did adieu
> And dash to the mountains, Jersey Blue.

Faded diaries, old letters and orderly books preserve something of the gala atmosphere of the expedition. At Trenton a Miss Forman and a Miss Milnor were most amiable. Newtown, Pennsylvania, was ticketed as a poor place for hay. At Potts Grove a captain of the cavalry troop got kicked in the shin by his horse. Among the Virginians, Meriwether Lewis enjoyed the martial excitement, wrote to his mother in high spirits of the "mountains of beef and oceans of Whiskey"; sent regards "to all the girls" and announced that he would bring "an Insergiant Girl to se them next fall bearing the title of Mrs. Lewis." If there was such a girl, he soon forgot her.

Yet where there is an army in being there are bound to be unpleasant occurrences. Men were lashed. Quartermasters stole government property. A soldier was ordered to put a Scotch-Irish rebel under guard. In execution of the order, he ran said insurgent through with his bayonet, of which the prisoner died. At Carlisle a dragoon's pistol went off and hit a countryman in the groin; he too died. On November 13, long remembered in many a cabin and stump-clearing as "the dismal night," the Jersey horse captured various citizens whom they described grimly as "the whiskey pole gentry," dragging them out of bed, tying them back to back. The troopers held their prisoners in a damp cellar for twenty-four hours without food or water, before marching them off at gun point to a collection center at Washington, Pennsylvania.

In late November, finding no one to fight, the army turned east again, leaving a volunteer force under General Morgan to conciliate and consolidate the position during the winter. Twenty "Yahoos" were carried back to Philadelphia and were paraded by the Philadelphia Horse through the streets of the city with placards marked "Insurrection" attached to their hats, in an odd federalist version of a Roman triumph. The cavalry was composed, as an admirer said, of "young men of the first property of the city," with beautiful mounts, uniforms of the finest blue broadcloth. They held their swords elevated in the right hand while the light flashed from their silver stirrups, martingales and jingling bridles. Stretched over half a mile they came, first two troopers abreast, then a pair of Yahoos, walking; then two more mounted men, and so on.

The army, meditating upon their fatigues and hardships, called for a substantial number of hangings. Samuel Hodgson, Commissary-general of the army, wrote to a Pittsburgh confidant, "We all lament that so few of the insurgents fell—such disorders can only be cured by copious bleedings. . . ." Philip Freneau, friend and literary colleague of Brackenridge, suggested in retrospect—ironically, of course—the benefits which would have accrued to the country "If Washington had drawn and quartered thirty or forty of the whiskey boys. . . ." Most of the captives escaped any punishment other than that of being held in jail without a trial for ten or twelve months. One died. Two were finally tried and sentenced to death. Eventually both were let off.

Gradually the bitterness receded. In August, 1794, General Anthony Wayne had crushed the Indians at the Battle of Fallen Timbers. A treaty was concluded with Spain in October, 1795, clearing the Mississippi for western trade. The movement of the army into the Pennsylvania hinterland, meanwhile, brought with it a flood of cash which furnished the distillers with currency for paying their taxes. These events served to produce a better feeling toward the Union.

If the rising was a failure, so was the liquor tax. The military adventure alone, without ordinary costs of collection, ran up a bill of $1,500,000, or about one third of all the money that was realized during the life of the revenue act. The excise was quietly repealed during Jefferson's administration. Yet the watermelon armies and the Whiskey Boys made a not inconsiderable contribution to our constitutional history. Through them, the year 1794 completed what 1787 had begun; for it established the reality of a federal union whose law was not a suggestion but a command.

Chapter 3

BOURBON'S
COUNTRY COUSIN

DOWN-RIVER from Redstone Old Fort the pioneer settlers from Pennsylvania and the upper valley of Virginia, Catholics from Maryland who knew the art of distilling Maryland rye whiskey, floated to Kentucky with their burr-mills and copper stills. They were raising their cabins, cultivating a corn patch, setting up furnaces and stills when American Independence was barely won and when that sound in the velvety Kentucky night might be either the hoot of an owl or an exchange of signals among skulking Indians. Other movers gathered at the Blockhouse in the Holston section of North Carolina to "settle out" in the wilderness. Men came with names like Harrod, McAfee, Calloway, Beam, Bond, Boone, Bryan, Dant, Logan, Floyd and Wathen; men named Thompson, Todd, Breckenridge, McDowell, Innes—some of them men who had read law and knew Quintilian's *Institutes of Oratory;* also gentlemen of mystery, like one called "Ready-Money Jack" who didn't mention what his name was back East.

The names of the places where they settled tell a vivid story of their own—Doe Run, Pigeon Roost, Stamping Ground and Stillhouse Branch. This was a name which was soon to be appropriate to almost any stream in central Kentucky. The first

counties which were laid out filled up rapidly after the collapse
of the Whiskey Rebellion. But even before that, the whiskey of
the West was making a name for itself. As early as 1789, the
year the Constitution was adopted, George Thatcher, Harvard
1776, eminent jurist and representative from Massachusetts in
the first six Congresses, in praising the merits of New England
rum, took an ungracious dig at what he termed "some new-
fangled distillates produced in other states. . . ." By 1791 dis-
stilling was a major adjunct to farming in the Bluegrass counties
and the events of 1791–1794 in Pennsylvania were followed with
the liveliest anxiety and indignation.

After the use of force against the distillers of the Monongahela country, the feeling in Kentucky was "We are next." Governor Isaac Shelby declared he believed "the Executive of the
United States was disposed, upon slight pretext, to send an army
into the State . . . to quell a disorderly spirit which had been
represented to exist. . . ." The distillers formed a loose sort of
confederation. There was a lot of talk. Indignant meetings were
held and the collector of the excise for Kentucky wrote of "the
distillers' infernal temper." Some of the deputy collectors were
roughed up and, says a modern Kentuckian cautiously, ". . .
there sprang up . . . a rather general opinion . . . that it was
not altogether disgraceful to oppose the payment of the new
federal whiskey taxes." The Kentucky whiskey-makers did not
go as far or react as violently as the Pennsylvanians; but they
kept at it longer. Some complied with the law, more or less.
Others quit the business, as did Major Peyton Short, who advertised in the *Kentucky Gazette* in the spring of 1792, "several
valuable stills of different capacities, mashing tubs and other
appendages to a distillery."

As in Pennsylvania, it was a particular grievance that the tax
was required to be paid in hard money. Kentucky had land and
grain and cool, pure water which flowed from limestone ledges.
The air was full of yeasts. But there was no cash. The government proceeded, however, with patience and moderation. For
years the federal court calendar was choked with "whiskey
cases." Finally, in the autumn of 1798 in Judge Harry Innes'
United States district court in the Old State House in Frankfort,
one hundred and seventy-seven of the pioneer 'stillers pleaded to

their tax liabilities, including Thomas Tunstall, the clerk of the court, who had to get up the considerable sum of $76.32.

The first settlers found that wheat was difficult to produce among the stumps of their clearings, and they lacked the mills to grind it. But corn, the American maize, thrived among the girdled trees. It could be planted in early May with the most sketchy preparation. Even a tomahawk could scarify the rich soil sufficiently. By July they had roastin' ears, or could harvest matured corn in October with an assured yield of three to four times that of wheat. Corn provided "hog and hominy," a husk bed to sleep on, cobs for fires and the liquid refreshment celebrated in the old song, "Just Hand Me Down My Jug of Corn."

Perhaps the first account of corn growing in what is now Kentucky appears in the series of reports on America known by the short title of *Jesuit Relations*. The author, presumably the Jesuit Hierosme Lalemant, had no personal knowledge of Kentucky. He wrote down what the Indians told him. But their stories must have made him think of the biblical Promised Land "for," this old chronicler wrote in the seventeenth century, "to mention the Indian corn only, it puts forth a stalk of such extraordinary thickness and height that one would take it for a tree, while it bears ears two feet long with grains that resemble in size our large Muscatel grapes." This is tall talk, but it scarcely exceeds the enthusiasm of later generations of Kentuckians, grateful for the largesse of *Zea mays*. A pamphlet published in connection with the World's Columbian Exposition in Chicago, entitled *Kentucky's Distilling Interests,* and issued in 1893 from Lexington, says of corn, "The blood of brave men nourished its branching roots and the hands of noble matrons gathered its golden ears. The pollen of its nodding tassels sifted down upon the heads of playing children and the graves of buried sires." Homesick Kentuckians would dream of their native maize in the shadow of the Pyramids, this unnamed Psalmist of the Kentucky Distillers' Bureau Co. continued, and the Kentucky scholar at Heidelberg University would look down upon the old university town and the enchanting valley of the winding Neckar only to sigh for just one morsel of Kentucky cornbread.

The first "improvers," poor amid their abundance, found in whiskey the means of moving their grain to market. The pattern came from Maryland and Pennsylvania where the farmers had done the same thing with their rye crops; not because rye was better, but because it was there. The seaboard states, being the home of rye, then mainly an eastern grain, became accustomed to rye whiskey, while the frontiersmen of the new West settled down happily with their crock of ambrosia condensed from the corn-spirit. Thus local tastes and habits developed which persisted long after the reasons for their existence had disappeared.

The date and location of the first distillery of corn squeezings in Kentucky is a matter long in dispute and the researches of modern historians have not settled the argument. This much may be said in summary: Corn was growing in Kentucky during the Revolution. Men who understood the art of the master distiller were arriving. Stills were being set up here and there and the local distillate, sometimes referred to as "paleface," was present in copious quantities. In 1775 Nicholas Cresswell, an English traveler, recorded in his diary that he had had a drink of whiskey at Leestown. In 1781 Captain John Bailey, stationed at Vincennes in the Illinois country, wrote to Colonel George Slaughter, commander of the fort at the Falls of the Ohio—Louisville— stating that his troops had been on half-rations for fifteen days, that he could not get provisions on credit, and would the officer at Louisville please send food, or whiskey, "which will answer as good an end." For whiskey would restore the credit of the government of the United States and with it he could obtain food. There are other scattered evidences of the presence of whiskey in very early times. George Rogers Clark in 1780 impressed a keg at Louisville from Eli Cleveland for his soldiers. The sale of whiskey at retail, by the drink, was being regulated in Kentucky taverns in 1781. Whiskey stills were offered for sale in 1787; and where there are stills, surely there is whiskey.

The late Augustus Owsley Stanley, former Governor and Senator from Kentucky, told Alvin W. Harlow, the author of *Weep No More, My Lady* (1942), that the first Kentucky whiskey was made from rye; "naturally," he said, "as the distillers had been in the habit of making it in the East." Then one spring, Stanley continued, the rye crop was nearly a failure. The Kentucky distillers mixed corn meal with their rye mash as a desperate expedient, and so discovered the proportions of what became famous later as bourbon. This statement, like so many of the legends about conditions on the old frontier of "Kentucke" is reasonable, but unsupported. This much is true. Rye whiskey was made in Kentucky along with a corn-base distillate. Richard Monarch, scion of a Maryland family gifted in the distilling line, turned out what has been described as "the most superb rye whiskey on earth" in the neighborhood of Owensboro, as well as his light-bodied, fruity Glenmore bourbon.

For a long time, and just how long no one knows, whiskey was just whiskey in Kentucky. Peddlers with pack animals toured the rural counties to barter eastern manufactured goods for newly distilled farm whiskey of variable strength, quality and purity. Packaged in uncharred barrels and with no identification as to source, the liquor was colorless, with a sharp odor and biting taste. But it commanded attention. In 1812 "Kentucky whiskey" and "western whiskey" were established commercial terms in the eastern markets, for Harrison Hall refers to them under those names in his manual, *The Distiller,* published the following year in Philadelphia. Hall gives a high mark to the Kentucky goods.

Western whiskey moved north and south, too. Among the borderers of Illinois, two-thirds of whom in the state's territorial days were of southern stock, whiskey was the universal solvent. They took it right from the bottle, known affectionately as "Black Betsy." Tafia, a kind of rum, and claret were used too, but for the "iron-throated Illinoisans" Kentucky corn whiskey and Monongahela were favored for serious drinking and keeping off chiggers.

Collected at Louisville or Cincinnati, much of the fruitage of Kentucky corn floated down the Ohio and Mississippi rivers on the barges or arks called broadhorns. John James Audubon, the naturalist, once a merchant at Henderson, Kentucky, his capital being three hundred barrels of sound whiskey, loaded his merchandise on a boat at Henderson, its value then twenty-five cents a gallon. Audubon sold the cargo at Ste. Genevieve, Missouri, for two dollars a gallon.

Large quantities of whiskey from the upper South went all the way down to New Orleans. Hall, in the manual already referred to, wrote that the mellowing effects of age upon American whiskey were discovered because the Kentucky product had to wait for the spring rise of the rivers before it could be moved to market. Thus it acquired some age out of necessity. The rocking motion of the boat and the time required for the slow journey produced a further improvement. By the time the packages reached the lower Mississippi their contents were merchantable as "old" whiskey. Starting out as "bald face," said to be a reference to bald face hornets—they're hot, too—the raw distillate picked up a pale amber color, lost some of its rough edges and, it has been conjectured, these evidences of enhanced value suggested the desirability of adding still more age and breeding.

There have been similar modern instances. During the years of Prohibition, Kansans drank corn liquor which had benefited from time and motion. The best of it came from southeast Kansas, the virile Third District sometimes called the Balkans, and was known as Deep Shaft because the moonshiners, all recessive types, conducted their business in the shafts of abandoned coal mines. Says John W. Ripley, long-time accurate and sympathetic observer of the manners and tribal customs of the Sunflower State, "I know for a fact that commercial travellers working out of Topeka would regularly pick up one or two ten gallon charred oak kegs of Deep Shaft on their visits to Pittsburg, which served admirably as ballast. Word had gone around that two months of travel in the trunk of a Dodge roadster was the equivalent of a trip around the world in the hold of a slow freighter, for aging."

Mr. Ripley points out that the standard container for less than keg lots was the one-quart Mason jar, and adds, thoughtfully: "Today indentations on the bridge work of many a man in the Social Security set are reminders of the past."

Down to the period of the Civil War, most whiskey was sold "white," although sometimes it was colored with caramel to imitate the amber tint of brandy which had the prestige of upperclass acceptance and foreign origin. Much native whiskey was passed off as brandy; but it was whiskey, all right. The formulas were designed to produce whiskey with a heavy body and maximum flavor, since most of it would be mixed later with grain spirits. A distillate was wanted which would "cover" a large amount of alcohol.

Kentucky did not originate the idea of distilling liquor from

Indian corn. More than a century and a half before the Bluegrass region had been visited by white men, Captain George Thorpe, a gentleman pensioner and a scholar of Cambridge University, known for his "godliness and learning," fired up a still on the banks of the James River and produced authentic corn liquor. No whiskey company, so far as the present writer knows, has ever honored Captain Thorpe with the compliment of an "Old George Thorpe" brand name. They should have, if only because of this happy bit of whiskey promotion which the Captain sent off to his friends in London:

"I have found a way to make so good a drink of Indian corn as I protest I have divers times refused to drink good strong English beer and chosen to drink that." This intelligence, which was received in England no doubt with unbelief, was important in the annals of American drinking. A Spanish visitor noted that the Virginians were a sickly lot and put his finger on the reason: ". . . they have . . . nothing to drink but water . . . which is contrary to the nature of the English." This was said, of course, before Thorpe's successful experiment. The Captain was also interested in making Christians out of the local Indians. In that venture he was less fortunate, for early in the morning of Good Friday, March 27, 1622, they ungratefully clubbed and stabbed him to death, bringing to an untimely end the life of a great humanitarian. When a Louisville newspaper editor, Mr. John Ed Pearce, heard for the first time of Captain Thorpe's corn whiskey he was so shocked he could only mutter "it is a sure thing that this stuff was not bourbon."

No, it wasn't bourbon. It was "corn"—bourbon's country cousin. But Virginia kept right on turning corn into a potent juice, substantial amounts of which, during the Great Drought of our own century, traveled a far piece to places like New York and Philadelphia. It found its way across the Potomac to Washington hotels where the porter, smelling of cloves, would poke around in the baggage room and produce a trunk full of old fruit jars with screw tops. They contained a fluid which, Gene Fowler has recorded, "tasted as though it had been keeping company with old 'tater sacks.' "

Other states, too, have their tales and memories of corn whiskey. An old gentleman sitting on a coil of rope in a country store in Texas recalled in the '80's the privations of his youth in rural Georgia—no shoes until he was twelve, wooden plates, wooden noggins to drink out of; "but Lor' bless your soul! we never wanted for somethin' to put in them . . . whiskey! I should say so! Most everybody made their own: but, if you wa'n't fixed to make it yourself, you had only to carry a bushel of corn to a neighbor's still, and come back with a demijohn of pure juice. When we had a corn-shuckin', a log-rollin', a house-raisin', or any such frolic, the whiskey just sloshed around like water. We only got coffee on Sundays; but we had whiskey all the time, and it was whiskey as was whiskey, not the adulterated pizen they call by that name now. You could hev got fullernagoose on it, and it wouldn't hurt you."

The old-timer sighed and shook his head regretfully as he thought of the good old days when whiskey just "sloshed around." An editor who was riding a Mexican mustang in the general direction of the Rio Grande and happened to be present, set it down in his notes that upon invitation the old gentleman consented graciously to sample "some of the juice of these degenerate days. He . . . apologized for the size of the drink he took by saying that the soil was dry. . . ." Georgia corn has continued to be drunk when the dew was falling or the sun was rising. New York sports writers who were guests of Wilbert Robinson when he was manager of the old Brooklyn Dodgers during the Georgia game bird season appreciated "Uncle Wilbert's" pleasant custom of sending up hot toddies well laced with Georgia corn whiskey at daybreak each morning.

"This will start the blood," Uncle Wilbert was wont to say.

The corncrackers of Kentucky had their jug whiskey to go along with the shinbone soup. "Every Boddy took it," wrote Ebenezer Hiram Stedman, the papermaker, whose reminiscences reflect the life not of the high sock people but the artisans, mechanics, tradesmen and river folk. "It ondly Cost Twenty Five Cents pr. Gallon. Evry Boddy," he continued, "was not Drinkhards . . . a Man might Get Drunk on this whiskey Evry Day in the year for a Life time & never have the Delerium Tremens nor Sick Stomack or nerverous Head Achake."

Long after Stedman composed his memoirs in which whiskey is so affectionately remembered, science confirmed the old man's observations. Chemically, ethyl alcohol is the same, regardless of source. Theoretically, then, the individual drinker should get the same reaction to a given quantity of alcohol from any source. Yet it doesn't work out this way. Brunton and Tunnicliffe found that different beverages have different effects upon the same drinkers. In plain words, when a man starts to drink, and after he stops—then he finds out the quality of the liquor he has downed. The alcohol is unchanging, but the effects of the other constituents present can produce quite disparate results.

When the belles of what Professor Thomas D. Clark has called "the rampaging frontier" danced in their short-waisted dresses of linsey-woolsey with coonskin aprons, they expected a toddy as refreshment, while the young bucks passed the 'jorum for a long pull, or added brown sugar to a tumblerful, stirred with the forefinger. At the minister's cabin the corn whiskey was set out on Sunday morning. As Lincoln's kinsman, Dennis Hanks, said, everybody took a sip, "preachers and Christians included." And as one imagines the buckskinned publican in a backwoods tavern serving the last cruet, snuffing the candles and sending his patrons home, one can perhaps hear faintly down the corridors of time the blithe spirts of an early and earthy America—in Kentucky, Indiana, Illinois, or wherever the settlement line was —proceeding on their dark but happy way, singing loudly of

> The turbaned Turk that scorns the world
> And struts about with his whiskers curled,
> For no other man but himself to see.

It was not bourbon whiskey as we know it today that they drank. But it prepared the way for bourbon. To what family and what county—for in Kentucky life county ranks close to family as an important social fact—shall we pay tribute for originating a beverage as urbane and "breedy" as bourbon whiskey? We turn to this subject in the pages which follow.

Chapter 4

THE FIRST TRUE BOURBON

SOME time around 1776 Elijah Pepper settled at what came to be known as the "Old Pepper Spring" near Lexington, Kentucky, on the Frankfort Pike. There he built a log cabin distillery about 1780. Elijah was followed by a son, Oscar, and then a grandson, James E. Pepper, who became a great name in distilling annals. The family continued in the business until 1900, maintaining the trademark "Old 1776" and flaunting the advertising slogan, "Born with the Republic." Outside observers have viewed the historicity of this claim with reserve, and have said that Elijah's first run of corn juice was not made until years later.

But the Peppers and their successors stuck to their story. When Jack Johnson, after giving Jim Jeffries a severe drubbing at Reno, Nevada, collected his share of the $121,000 purse on the evening of July 4, 1910, at the Hotel Golden, headquarters of the promoters, he did it under a banner stretched across the street in front of the hotel saluting James E. Pepper Whiskey which continued to be "Born with the Republic." Later still, at the time of World War I, the first evidence that one was approaching Lexington by train from the West was a sign in box car letters on the wall of the old Pepper Distillery, emphasizing again the 1776 war cry. One disgruntled doughboy, returning from the war to make the world safe for democracy, and finding Pepper whiskey no longer a lawful beverage, suggested the sign be brought up to date to say, "Born with the Republic—Died with Democracy."

Other voices have been raised to name John Ritchie as the patriarch of bourbon distillers. He is said to have set up a still at Linn's Fort, east of Bardstown, in 1777. The Wathen family, who have been connected with whiskey-making in Kentucky for well over a century and a half, cherish a family tradition which says that Henry Hudson Wathen, the first Kentucky ancestor, set up a still near Lebanon in 1788. Descendants of Jacob Beam report that recently uncovered family material indicates that the first Beam may have started distilling in that same year. We get closer to contemporary documentary evidence when we come to Daniel Stewart, who offered for sale in an advertisement published in June, 1789, "a Copper Still of 120 Gallons Capacity, with a Good Copper and Pewter Worm." Stewart may have used the still in the distilling season of 1788–89 and perhaps before that.

Colonel Reuben T. Durrett, long the presiding genius of the distinguished historical society in Louisville known as the Filson Club, wrote that Evan Williams, who erected a small distillery in Louisville in 1783 at the foot of Fifth Street, was the first man to make whiskey in Kentucky. This was not bourbon. Apparently it was not good whiskey, either, but a low order of popskull, because Williams, a city Trustee, was censured by his colleagues, first for introducing liquor into the deliberations of the city fathers, and second, for offering such a poor article. However, Colonel Durrett wrote that the bottle went home empty.

Claims of a similar nature have been advanced for Captain John Hamilton and for Jacob Spears who set up a still in Bourbon County. His stone foundation could be traced as late as 1897, the masonry of the walled-in spring well preserved, the malt house standing and filled then with stock feed.

The arguments for the priority in bourbon manufacture of the different counties in the Bluegrass region are confusing because of shifting county lines. Before 1776 all of Kentucky was part of Fincastle County, Virginia. In that year it became Kentucky County, but was still in Virginia. This vast tract was cut up into Jefferson, Lincoln and Fayette counties in 1780. Bourbon County, which once covered a large area in the north central portion of Kentucky, was taken from the northern part of Fayette in 1785 and became one of nine big counties organized by the Virginia legislature before Kentucky became a state in 1792. The others, in addition to those already named, were Nelson, Mercer, Madison, Mason and Woodford. Later, thirty-three counties were carved from the original Bourbon County. Some of these represent territory where whiskey was distilled before the area had been divided off from Bourbon County.

Place names such as Bourbon, a word complimenting the royal house of France; Paris, the county seat town in Bourbon county, once also called Bourbontown; Versailles and Fayette, the latter referring to the Marquis de La Fayette, all reflect the enthusiasm felt in the West for France because of French aid received in the war for American independence when the lilies of the royal Bourbons whipped in the breeze beside the republican red, white and blue. Many old-time distillers of bourbon whiskey have believed that their distinctive type of whiskey originated in Bourbon County. Kentucky Senator Garrett Davis told the United States Senate in 1862, "The liquor that is termed 'old Bourbon' had its origin in the county in which I reside, and a great deal of the genuine article is distilled there." Since Davis was admitted to the bar in Paris and practiced there, he was in a position, from the point of view of time and place, to be well informed on the origins of bourbon whiskey. But this testimony does not eliminate the possibility that Kentucky whiskey in general was known in commerce as bourbon.

Perhaps we come closer to the mark if we think of bourbon as coming from a *region*. The late H. F. Willkie, Vice President in Charge of Production, Seagram-Distillers Corporation, observed in his *Beverage Spirits in America* (1949), "All the whiskey sent back East was called Kentucky Bourbon by dealers to distinguish it from Pennsylvania rye." This much is certain, the bourbon belt turned out a liquor possessing an individual and delightful depth of flavor with subtle overtones and undertones, a lingering aroma known to appreciative Kentuckians as the "farewell." Old Van Hook, made in Cynthiana in Harrison County, had the essential bourbon character and also Rolling Fork, Chicken Cock and Belle of Nelson and other famous early names which were burned into the end of the barrel before bottled goods were sold. Oddly enough, Bourbon County now produces no bourbon whiskey.

Some say, with a very good show of reason, although no contemporary evidence has survived, that since Pennsylvania called its whiskey by a geographical name, Monongahela, the Pennsylvanians who engaged in distilling after they removed to Kentucky were only following a familiar custom when they gave Kentucky whiskey a place name, "Bourbon." The special characteristics of bourbon whiskey were, first, the mingling of the properties of corn and rye grain; corn for strength and body, the rye for its smoothing effect and mellow flavor. Secondly, there occurred a fortuitous discovery by the bourbon distillers that aging in charred white oak barrels enormously improved the whiskey which slumbered for several summers in the casks.

There are many legends about the origin of charring. But it appears to have been completely a matter of chance. One account attributes the discovery to a primitive distiller who saved money by storing his liquor in barrels previously used for the shipment of salt fish. To get rid of the fish smell, he started scorching the inside of the barrels, and subsequently found that the liquor from the toasted kegs had a smoother flavor, an intriguing ruddy color. Another version tells of an old-time cooper who was heating barrel shooks in order to make them more pliable and carelessly charred a batch. Being a thrifty man, he delivered a keg made of the scorched staves to a distiller without saying anything about it. Months later, when the customer sampled the liquor stored in that barrel, he was so pleased with it that he instructed the cooper to char all of his packages.

Gordon Bass, the well-known collector of old glass, including whiskey flasks, and a close student of whiskeyana, relates that the slow journey by water to New Orleans demonstrated the beneficial effect upon whiskey of resting in wood. So the Kentucky distillers began to age their whiskeys. That called for more barrels than were available. They burned out the inside of used barrels so the whiskey would not pick up off-flavors, and found the taste improved still more.

A widely circulated account of the beginnings of bourbon, and one which is popularly accepted as having an historical basis, has it that the Reverend Elijah Craig created bourbon whiskey.

Craig's great contribution is declared to have been the development of the bourbon formula. Those who would like to make Craig seven feet tall also insist that he discovered that whiskey aged in charred kegs would lose its sharpness and acquire that perfume which made great-grandfather smell wonderful when he entered a room. The fact is, however, so far as aging is concerned, that until the Civil War period, the Kentucky distiller disposed at once of his white whiskey, usually to the whiskey trade in Cincinnati or Louisville. The aging, if any, was carried out by the purchaser.

There is no doubt, though, that Elder Craig was an active distiller in the 1790's. He was one of the reluctant whiskey men who in 1798 composed their differences with the United States government. The Reverend Craig settled up for excise taxes amounting to $140 on September 26th of that year. Something of a promoter and capitalist, Craig owned a thousand acres of land and a valuable water-power site on the Big Spring Branch of the North Elkhorn Creek at Lebanon, later Georgetown, in what shortly became Scott County. The preacher-capitalist-entrepreneur installed a dam, built a paper mill, a grist mill and a mill for "fulling" cloth. "The first Bourbon whiskey," says Richard H. Collins in his *History of Kentucky* (1874), "was made in 1789 at Georgetown, at the fulling mill at the Royal Spring." This location, incidentally, was never in Bourbon County.

Craig was a Virginia Baptist, brother of the even more celebrated, in Baptist annals, Reverend Lewis Craig. Both held "unlawful conventicles" in their home state and were often carried before a magistrate on charges of preaching contrary to law. They thrived on persecution. Elijah, taken from behind his plow in 1771 and lodged in the Culpeper County jail, exhorted the people powerfully through the grates. He was also personally acquainted with the dungeon of the Orange County jail. In 1786 Elijah removed to Kentucky. There he plunged into complicated business affairs, wrote contentious pamphlets on church matters and preached emotional sermons, performing great works of grace as well as officiating, according to a prominent school of thought, at the birth of bourbon whiskey.

Nothing that is said here about Craig as a distiller should be construed as a suggestion that the Reverend was hypocritical. The frontier churches had not yet taken a stand on temperance. Most of the folks in the western settlements regarded those who took care of their need for alcoholic restoratives as public bene-factors and made no distinction between grinding sorghum cane for syrup and corn "chops" for whiskey. In the old minute book of one Kentucky church, an entry of 1795 raises the question of whether it is "consistent with true religion . . . to carry on a distillery of spirits." The record shows, after discussion, that it was voted, "Not Inconsistent."

A modern skeptic and a Virginian, Mr. John A. Schools, has questioned whether it was Kentucky whiskey at all that Craig distilled when he made his first run of singlings. In a spirit of fun, Schools wrote to the Richmond *Times-Dispatch* a few years back expressing feelings of dismay over the upstart claims of Kentucky. For, as he saw it, Craig was first of all a Virginian. "He was forty-four years old when he left Virginia in 1787, and I contend that any man who is going to make whiskey is going to learn how before he gets to be forty-four years old. He must have learned how in Virginia. Our Reverend Craig had been in Kentucky hardly two years, yet they pounce upon him and claim his talents as new and their very own." Schools could have made his argument even stronger if he had pointed out that when Craig made his fermentation, if he did it before 1792, Kentucky was still a part of Virginia.

But—*did* the Reverend turn out the first true bourbon? It has been said that he did countless times in magazine articles and books, which quote each other and refer to previous writers as "the authorities." All of this commotion reminds one of the definition of history as "fiction agreed upon." The case for Craig traces back only to 1874 when Richard H. Collins, editor, law-yer and antiquarian, published his 1600-page *History,* a work so highly thought of at the time that the Kentucky state legisla-ture gave it a kind of official status by ordering five thousand copies for use in the schools, while James Lane Allen, the novel-ist, saluted him as "Collins, the Kentucky Froissart."

It is Collins who constitutes the earliest authority for bourbon being made at Georgetown in 1789. Collins was a tireless col-lector of Kentucky historical data, and although much of it was not prime source material, he did preserve a wealth of early incident. It is also pertinent that his father, Judge Lewis Collins, wrote on the early times of Kentucky in his *Historical Sketches of Kentucky,* published in 1847. This was considered to be the standard work on the state until superseded in 1874 when his son revised and enlarged it. Lewis Collins mentions Craig's paper mill, but is silent on the subject of whiskey. Born near Lexington in 1797, this Collins could have known people who had first-hand knowledge about Craig as a whiskey-maker. But then Lewis Collins does not mention *any* distiller.

The position of modern investigators is, regretfully, that no one knows for certain who made the first bourbon whiskey. "Craig was making some kind of corn whiskey in Scott County in 1789," Lawrence S. Thompson concludes in his *Kentucky Tradition* (1956), "but there is no evidence that he called it bourbon."

As a counterpoise to Elder Craig and the claims advanced for Scott County as the birthplace of bourbon, the case for Bourbon County is strengthened through some knowledge we have of James Garrard. Also a Baptist preacher, Garrard was indicted in 1787 by the first Grand Jury impaneled in Bourbon County. The charge was retailing liquor without a license. In the same year he helped to organize the Cooper's Run Baptist Church. Later the church ejected him, not for keeping a saloon or violating the liquor laws, but because he held unconventional views upon the doctrine of the Trinity. Garrard later rose to high position in public life, helped to shape Kentucky's state constitution and governed the state for two terms.

Two other tavern keepers, not otherwise known to history, were presented along with Garrard for non-payment of their liquor license. Willard Rouse Jillson, a careful modern investigator of Kentucky distilling records, considers the circumstance that three individuals were retailing whiskey at this early date in or near Paris as firm evidence that the liquor was of local origin. He concludes that "it was in Bourbon, as the name implies, rather than Scott County that the first sour mash whiskey was made in Central Kentucky." Mr. Jillson's hypothesis, if confirmed, would set aside the priority so frequently claimed for Craig. But perhaps there has been altogether too much emphasis upon who was the first man to make old-fashioned small-tub whiskey of the bourbon type, and in what county he did it. Distilling was common work incidental to western pioneer life, as prosaic as building a fodder stack. Let us look back upon the accomplishments of our sturdy grandsirs and agree that there is glory enough for all. Some distiller experimented. Or some imaginative observer had a flash of intuition, and bourbon was born. Perhaps fortune, as Pasteur once said, favored the prepared mind.

Most of the historians of the Bluegrass counties have displayed a bias against the distilling interests. One annalist of Scott County, for example, B. O. Gaines, after repeating the declaration that the first bourbon whiskey was made at Craig's mill, and that Scott was subsequently famous for maturing whiskeys which were the best in the world, added the comment, "if the word 'good' may be, without violence, applied to the greatest known evil in existence."

The manufacture of whiskey expanded rapidly after the 1790's. By 1810 in the vicinity of Lexington, Lawrenceburg, Harrodsburg, Frankfort, Louisville and Bardstown, there were from one to ten plants. In Fayette County alone, in 1811, one hundred and thirty-nine were counted and it was estimated that there were 2,000 in the state. Economically, a distillery was of great value to a community. It provided a market for local grain and for cordwood to fire the stills. Barrel staves and headers and hooppoles were needed for the cooperage shops. Perhaps hooppoles need explaining. A hooppole was a straight sapling of hickory or white oak suitable for splitting to make a withe or hoop for holding together a cask. Finally, teamsters were required to haul the whiskey to market. Yet all of this activity scarcely constituted an industry. It was more in the category of a special kind of farming.

A distinctive feature which sets bourbon off from other whiskeys of the world is the use of new, charred barrels. Scotch whisky casks are re-used and not charred. Canadian whisky packages are charred but not new. The modern consumer in most instances knows nothing of the chemistry of whiskey maturation. But by an ancient and agreeable organoleptic examination—by taste and smell—he can make his own observations on properties which cannot be found by chemical analysis. When spirit is on wood there is a change. The liquor becomes aromatic, smoother and sweeter. It rests but it is not loafing.

New whiskey contains volatile secondary products or impurities which are modified or eliminated when a whiskey spends four years or more in charred barrels. Known in modern terminology as "congeners," they are members of the large alcohol family; but they belong to the amyl or black sheep branch. These congeners, a term borrowed from the vocabularies of zoology and botany, consist of fusel oil, acids, esters, aldehydes, furfural and other complicated substances. Congeners are potentially toxic. Yet they give whiskey its character. They can be removed up to a point by leaching through charcoal. They can be removed completely by distillation. But if they are, the end product isn't whiskey but neutral grain spirits. The congenerics are tamed through cycling; that is, the expansion and contraction of the whiskey into and out of the "red layer" behind the char in the barrel. When the temperature rises, the whiskey expands into the char. When it falls, the whiskey contracts. A ripening occurs. The liquid is gentled. An oily feeling and a strong "bead," visible around the edge of a glass, develop.

Both water and alcohol can pass through the oak staves of a whiskey barrel. Water vapors escape faster than the alcohols. Therefore the strength or proof of barrel whiskey rises with age. During aging, when the whiskey is being modified by the tannin and other extractives from the wood, there is a loss of about two and a half gallons of the liquor per annum. This "outage" is never recovered. After four years about twenty-two per cent of the whiskey is gone. After eight years the loss by leakage and evaporation is thirty-six per cent. Contrary to popular belief, whiskey does not continue to improve indefinitely. If kept too long, it becomes woody.

Distilling practice up to the end of the 1860's involved relatively simple procedures of heating, vaporization and condensation. The corn was first cleaned, coarsely ground either by water power or a horse treadmill. The distiller or a helper mashed the chopped kernels in a small wooden tub, working about a bushel at a time. "Mashing" meant mixing the corn grits with limestone water and a proportion of rye meal, and scalding the mixture with fresh, hot "slop" from a previous distillation. This brought the mass to the consistency of a thick mush or pudding. The mash was allowed to cool until the following day —the souring period—when it was stirred or broken up. Then barley malt was added. This hastened the conversion of the starch in the grain to soluble sugar.

After a cycle of heating and cooling, the mash was broken up with a paddle or "mashing oar" and poured into an open-topped wooden fermenting tank. Yeast, which has been termed a "prolific micro-organism with a voracious appetite for sweets" was then introduced. It fed on the sugar and caused a violent agitation, producing alcohol and carbon dioxide gas which rose to the surface of the mass as it "worked." The liquid was called "distiller's beer." This is not the familiar beverage produced in a brewery, although men have been known to drink it. The alcoholic concentration rose to about seven per cent. The beer remained in the fermenter for from seventy-two to ninety-six hours, depending upon the process used, standing at a temperature of seventy-five degrees, as tested by the distiller's hand. Heat control was important. But the method was crude. From first to last, the quality of the run depended upon the intuition of the master distiller, and chance. Wide variations were inevitable.

Ignorant of chemistry or sanitation, the early distillers got results on an empirical basis. Each had his own formula, techniques and discoveries about which he was less than garrulous. One early whiskey-maker, Jonathan Taylor, who kept a diary between 1794 and 1796, left some comments on the art of "making." "In the first place," he wrote, "the Distiller must be an Industrious man, a Cleanly Sober, Watchful man." Some distillers examined the tip of each ear of corn. They would shell off by hand any kernels that were rotten or mildewed, before tossing the ear to a helper to be put through a hand-cranked sheller. Other master distillers insisted upon using a particularly flinty type of corn, which not only yielded more liquor to the bushel, but also was believed to provide more and better congeners for governing taste and aroma.

The still consisted of two principal parts. The still itself was made of copper, shaped somewhat like a tea kettle with a broad, rounded bottom and topped by a head or globe with a long, tapered neck connected with the second part, the condenser. This was a spiral of copper tubing called a "worm" and was immersed in a tub through which cold water circulated. Such an apparatus was known as a pot still. The still was set into a low masonry furnace and heated over open flames. The fermented beer was thrown into the chamber of the beer still. The vapor rose and passed into the chilled worm which received water by gravity flow. There were no pumps when whiskey distilling was a domestic handicraft in the United States. The circulating water liquefied the alcoholic steam in the worm and it was drawn off from a cock. A distiller could make whiskey with one still. But since it required two distillations to produce whiskey, the pot stills were often arranged in pairs or "sets," each bricked up over its own furnace, a larger one for the first distillation and a smaller, called the doubler, with its own worm, for the second run. The country distiller had to buy the pots and the worms and the jug for his yeast. The rest of his equipment, such items as tubs, barrels and tackle for handling them, piggins, mash sticks, dippers and funnels of copper, a "thief" for drying samples, could be made at home.

The stillhouse was often no more than a low-roofed shack, with a mud floor and one face open to the weather. The location was usually in a hollow under a hill where clear, cold, limestone water flowed to the worm in a wooden trough. Why *limestone* water? In distilling, water loaded with calcium, the kind that makes the bluegrass blue, the horses frisky, and perhaps its virtues may even be stretched to explain the beauty of Kentucky women—limestone water teams up perfectly with yeast. "It keeps bourbon on the alkaline side," explains Jim O'Rear, Schenley executive and bourbon authority. "Limestone in bourbon lets you wake up next morning feeling like a gentleman."

A distillery might be located on a creek or branch. A flowing spring was even better because it was necessary to have the water as cold as possible to condense the steam. If the water was warmer than in the range of fifty-six to sixty degrees, the distiller had to suspend operations or move to another location.

Since water boils at 212 degrees and ethyl alcohol at 173, it would seem that when the "wash" was heated to a temperature just above 173, only the alcohol would become vapor. But it is not so. The boiling point of the mixture lies in between because alcohol and water cling together. Also, ethyl alcohol, the grand object of the whole procedure, is only one of many alcohols present, all of which have different boiling points. The fire had to be gentle, not hurried along. The 'stiller's Negro kept the wash in motion with a bar to prevent burning. At the moment when the still began to work, the head was "luted" on—closed, that is—by a composition of clay. "It is no easy matter to hit the exact time . . ." remarked an early writer on the art.

The first rush of vapor, called the "foreshot," carried considerable amounts of solid matter, and the various complicated varieties of alcohol and some water. Later increasing amounts of water came over. The percentages were always shifting. The distillate, known as "singlings" or "low wines," yielded the largest amount of potable alcohol in the middle part of the run. The object was to draw off as much alcohol and as little water as possible at the discharging cock of the worm. There were hazards. Sometimes the stillhouse caught fire and burned to the ground. Sometimes the pot "ran foul"; i.e., boiled over and blew its top. Sometimes, since the fire was directly under the copper, the whiskey had a scorched flavor. Some consumers liked the empyreumatic taste. As late as 1900 whiskey merchants would get orders for some of "that bourbon with the burned flavor."

A considerable portion of the first running of the charge, the foreshots or heads, and of the last part of the run, the tails or feints, was discarded because of the very high concentration of impurities. These discards contained most of the substances which render raw whiskey harsh. Often colloidal particles were entrained in the vapor stream as it left the beer still and gave the low wines a cloudy appearance. When the singlings were boiled again in the doubler the second distillation eliminated this cloud. What the worm spigot discharged was a powerful, clear spirit known as "high wines," flowing from the still at from 140 to 160 proof. The double-distilled spirit had buried in it the traditional properties of whiskey although not yet entitled to be called bourbon until the civilizing effects of time and the oak char taught it good manners.

Things that made
Kentucky
its Reputation

"SHE WAS BRED IN KENTUCKY"

COPYRIGHT, 1907, BY M. H. PHILLIPS

Horses and whiskey, beauty and gunsmoke provide the Bluegrass region with romance, recreation, humor and tourists.

(*Left*) General Taylor flask. Decorative flasks, now choice collectors' items, were treasured possessions to be filled and refilled, until distillers found a way to identify their products clear through to the ultimate buyer. (*Right*) I. W. Harper bourbon in a special bottle, made for the veterans of the Union armies when they held their first reunion on Southern soil.

This design was lithographed on paper and placed on the end of the barrel of bulk whiskey.

A hundred years ago it was a big day's work to make around ten gallons of high wines. A week's production, drawn to the nearest shire town by oxen, would be about two barrels. This was the style in which Coon Hollow, Cumberland, Cedar Brook, Old Jordan and many another early bourbon was made, involving hand work and small batches. Some of the primitive stills were constructed of wood. A poplar log was halved, hollowed out, withed together and bottomed. The beer entered at the top and a copper pipe introduced steam to heat up the 'stiller's beer and vaporize the alcohol. There was no fire, of course, under a wooden still. The low wines were carried to the conventional copper pot still for doubling. The backwoodsmen spoke of this method as "making it on a log" or "running it on a log," and the product as "log and copper" whiskey.

The spent stillage was valuable as stock feed. A distillery usually maintained pens for raising hogs so that the distiller was, in a sense, making pork from the same equipment that produced his whiskey. Often to the delight of the old corncrackers who hung around stillhouses, the pigs would get the staggers on, and squeal with such delight as to arouse the envy of the loafers. Lacking the ready for buying whiskey, even at stillhouse rates, they would revive their flagging spirits by leaning over the side of the fermenter vat, filling their nasal passages with the heady fumes. If the distiller didn't have the skill or the will to make a clean distillate, to "get the pig tracks out of it," in an old, homely phrase, he wasn't making a first-class article, what the trade called "family whiskey," but ordinary redeye.

"Proof," the technical term indicating alcoholic strength, referred originally to "gunpowder proof." Primitive distillers determined the potable strength of their product in this way: an equal amount of spirit and gunpowder were mixed and a flame applied. If the powder failed to burn, the liquor was too weak. If it burned brightly, it was too strong. If it burned evenly, slowly, with a blue flame, it was said to be "100 per cent perfect" or "proved." This did not mean 100 per cent alcohol. It represented the drinkable mean, which was approximately fifty per cent alcohol by volume. The rest is water. The human system can tolerate a spirit which is a bit above 100 proof in strength, but not very much higher. So experience suggested that the half-and-half mark was about right. It became the standard for gauging spirits, a subject in which the United States government is even more interested than most consumers of spirituous beverages; for the tax which Uncle Sam collects is based upon the quantity of alcohol present.

One major variant in the manufacture of bourbon is expressed in the terms "sweet mash" and "sour mash." Both refer to ways of producing fermentation. Sweet mash is made with fresh yeast and all fresh yeast for each batch. Maryland rye, for instance, is a sweet mash fermentation. Bourbon can be made either way. The sour mash method prevails today. It involves scalding the meal with the thin, spent beer left over in the still from a run. The procedure is called, somewhat inelegantly, "sloppin' back." The stillage has a slightly acid taste; hence the term sour mash. But the whiskey which results is not sour or tart. All bourbon, as a matter of fact, is sweet in taste. Advocates of sour mash bourbon claim for it a more pronounced character and greater uniformity.

Many bourbons made by the sour mash method today do not say so on the bottle, probably because some public relations expert has declared that the consumer will think the whiskey is sour. But many of today's famous bourbons, among them Old Fitzgerald and Beam's Choice, proudly place the term on their labels. It does not seem to have scared off such informed appreciators of good bourbon as John Nance Garner, the venerable former Vice President of the United States, or the late William Faulkner or Lucius Beebe, the *arbiter elegantiae* of good living in our time. Irvin S. Cobb, the writing son of Paducah, who was not unacquainted with the qualities of a well-finished sour mash distillate, has his Colonel Attila Bird say in the novel, *Red Likker,* that by "distilling back" the master distillers get "exciting properties for the next batch, so that the very soul of the grain goes on perpetuating itself, reincarnating itself, world without end."

The mystery of the days when the whiskey was good and the days when it was "off" was gradually replaced by a clearer understanding of whiskey production after Dr. James C. Crow, a Scottish physician and chemist, appeared in Kentucky in 1823.

Crow had a significant effect upon distilling practice. It has been handed down for a hundred years that Crow introduced the sour mash process, the use of instruments such as the saccharometer and the thermometer as well as strict standards of cleanliness. Stressing quality instead of quantity, Crow made only two and a quarter to two and a half gallons of whiskey to the bushel at a time when others were striving for the highest possible return from each bushel of grain.

After Dr. Crow died in 1856, the firm of Gaines, Berry and Company, later W. A. Gaines & Co., decided to keep the name alive and to make bourbon by old man Crow's method. The last decanter of Jim Crow's whiskey known to exist on this earth was used by Joseph C. S. Blackburn of Versailles, Kentucky, in the hot political campaign for Representative he made against Ed Marshall in 1875. Marshall was a brilliant campaigner, but Joe Blackburn had one advantage: a ten gallon cask of Old Crow in his cellar. With his political career at stake, Blackburn decanted the precious fluid into small cruets. He would take a stubborn Marshall supporter aside and tell him all about Crow and his wonderful whiskey and then, as an old account puts it, he "poured the liquor into his soul."

"As you drink that, sir," Blackburn would say, "I want you to remember that you are helping to destroy the most precious heirloom of my family. It is the last bit of genuine Crow whiskey in the world. Observe, sir, that you do not need to gulp down a tumbler of water after swallowing the liquor to keep it from burning your gullet. On the contrary, you know instinctively that to drink water with it would be a crime. All I ask of you is to remember that you are getting something in this liquor that all the money of an Indian prince cannot buy. Drink it, sir, and give your soul up to the Lord. Then if you can vote for Ed Marshall I cannot complain, because it will be the Lord's act!"

Blackburn beat Marshall handsomely.

Many major figures of our political past, Henry Clay, Andrew Jackson, Calhoun, General Grant and William Henry Harrison have been recorded as samplers of Crow whiskey who came back for more. A reporter said of Crow whiskey, "Webster's breath was flavored with it when he replied to Hayne."

More often than not, bourbon whiskey was called by some

other name in James Crow's days. Common usage described it as Kentucky or domestic whiskey, table or family whiskey. Or they just called it whiskey. And the term whiskey covered a multitude of drinks—grain spirits, "rectified" or blended liquor, the raw white distillate of the stillhouse, or ripe bourbon, frequently referred to simply as "sour mash" or "fire copper" whiskey. Here is a parallel. The English and Scotch did not say Scotch whisky before the middle of the nineteenth century. They simply said whiskey; but they meant Scotch.

Early references to bourbon often include a suggestion of age; they said "Old Bourbon." W. F. Bond, a distiller whose personal memory reached back to the business as it was conducted before 1840, testified in court that ordinarily "whisky was used up just as it was manufactured in the early days." Old bourbon, then, was acknowledged to be something special, in which age had balanced out the flavor, fused and mellowed it into a smooth maturity. Stedman, the Kentucky diarist quoted before, says that in the 1830's there was fine fishing in the old main Elkhorn, and bank presidents and other wealthy men came for a week of sport, equipped with the best of provisions, "and alwais The Best of old Bourbon. . . . The president of the bank alwais Kept his Black Bottle in the Spring and the mint grew Rank and Completely Hid the Bottle." Here is an indication that the term "bourbon" was common in the 1830's. But we cannot be sure; the diary was written in 1878 and may reflect a later usage.

James B. Beck, Representative in Congress for Bourbon County and later U.S. Senator from Kentucky, received from political admirers in 1868 a precious bottle of bourbon made in 1837, thirty-one years before! One more probing of the antiquity of the bourbon name as applied to whiskey leads back to Henry ("Marse Henry") Watterson, Kentucky statesman, sage, editor and social philosopher. Watterson gave a friend whom he addresses as "Colonel" a phial of Nelson County whiskey made in 1845 "whose pedigree and antecedents are undoubtedly Bourbon." His letter makes it impossible to resist further quotation. Watterson wrote to his friend of the gift:

"It was re-barreled in 1860 by James Ford.

"It never paid no taxes.

"It was hid in the bushes . . . in spite of its disloyal practises and Ku Klux associations, it is soft and mild, and can say as Champ Ferguson [Confederate guerilla in the Civil War] said when he cut Billy Still's ears off, 'Why, I wouldn't hurt a fly.' "

A recent search of original sources before 1850—lists of "prices current," early local histories and city directories—produced no instance of the use of the word bourbon as applied to whiskey. The earliest printed mention of bourbon which the present writer knows of appears in 1846. Scattered examples have been collected for 1850, 1851, 1855, and several occur in the 1860's. The term becomes common after the Civil War.

Called by whatever name, however, the world well knew of the existence of a delicately proportioned distillation of corn, rye and barley malt, mixed with sparkling limestone water, singled and doubled in copper over open fires, passed through heavy copper worms into charred oaken barrels. There, youthful fire changed to a genial ruddy glow. And old-time distillers say that each summer when the wind blows the pollen from the tassels of the growing corn, the spirit strives to break its bonds just as the wine in deep cellars frets when grape blooms scent the air.

Wayne Wheeler, the eminent counsel for the Anti-Saloon League, once expressed the opinion that Scotch was to be preferred to bourbon and so there was no reason to manufacture whiskey in the United States. Tell it not in Owensboro, publish it not in Frankfort! Whisper it not in the streets of Louisville! "Kentucky Bourbon," said the Louisville *Herald* in indignant rebuttal, "bears no resemblance to the pale, emaciated, sickly soured stuff the world knows as Scotch."

The graciousness, the special quality of an extraordinary culture, are all reflected in the whiskey which originated in that garden spot of the world, Kentucky. Those who know the Grand Old Commonwealth understand and sympathize with the emotion of the pioneer preacher who, wishing to recommend Heaven to his congregation, described it as "a real Kentuck of a place."

Chapter 5

A NAME WITH A MELODY
ALL ITS OWN–KENTUCKY

THE people who before 1789 came over the trace from points on the Ohio River or walked out to Kentucky from the Yadkin and the Holston rivers had something to escape from—the post-war depression, the weak Confederation, taxes, the political and economic ascendancy of the federalists. They had something to search for—land. These pilgrims sought, too, that earthly paradise, perhaps, which ancient chronicles had variously located and now was reliably reported by wandering hunters and surveyors to be Kentucky, a vale of loveliness. As an Ohio boatman expressed the garden myth to Charles Fenno Hoffman, the poet and novelist, "No, stranger, there's no place on the universal 'arth like old Kaintuck: she whips all 'Out-west' in prettiness; and you might bile down cr'ation and not get such another State out of it."

When one considers the cross-section of early immigrants, Scotch-Irish, plain Irish, gentlemen from Virginia, pineys from North Carolina, French bourgeoisie, thrifty Swiss, German farmers, Shakers, Millerites, gamblers, lawyers, speculators, highwaymen, adventurers and smoothies, the suspicion arises that the new paradise was to be more a state of the flesh than the spirit, that the travelers came, actually, to raise hell in the

Garden. Well—some did and some didn't. An agrarian society with romantic overtones developed in a land dripping with fatness, a way of life involving blooded horses, barbecues, fairs where the women showed their jellies and the men their whiskeys; of court days, Christmas festivities, duels, shootings, open drunkenness. Kentuck became a state of mind—a land of chivalry and social graces, of "tempestuous expression" generally—all life carried on, as it were, to the music of violins. The Kentucky of polite literature became populated with gentlemen entitled to hold a pew in Bruton Parish church and high-born ladies who had danced in the great plantation houses on the James River. The solid fact is that most of the early Kentuckians were honest, plain folks who already lived west of the Fall Line before they made "The Crossing" into Kentucky and were well-schooled in coping with a wild environment.

By the first decade of the nineteenth century Kentuckians were recognized as heroes in a new style, the western screamer or "Salt River Roarer" of American folklore, great on the brag, quick on the draw, who spoke in extravagant language, using what Professor Walter Blair has happily called a "toothsome vernacular." One such shaggy character with the bark still on him, affirmed, "I'm the *ginewine* article. . . . I can out-run, out-jump, out-swim, chaw more tobacco and spit less, and drink more whiskey and keep soberer than any other man in these localities!" "Kaintuck" became a generic term for the frontiersman from the Monongahela to the mouth of the Mississippi.

The Kentuckian was the half-horse, half-alligator man, full of fun and fight, with a gargantuan capacity for punishing his jug without getting ramsquaddled. Here was America's first Superman, realized most perfectly in the character of Davy Crockett, who *grinned* the coon out of his tree, used a bobcat as an outboard motor, lounged in the stern of his broadhorn, the old Free and Easy, regaling himself first with a horn of whiskey, then dipping up a tin of Mississippi River water. Crockett was a folk hero in his own generation, the "Yellow forest flow'r" of an admiring poem, a full colonel of militia, too, and although unacquainted with public affairs or the meaning of a tough word like "judiciary," he was sent to Congress three times. In one of his campaigns, when a political opponent offered to lead the electorate to the cannon's mouth, Crockett countered with a proposal to lead them to the "mouth of a barrel of whiskey." He went to Congress by a majority of three to one.

By the time the Kentucky kingdom of coal, cattle and corn had been established, the pioneer types had been pushed off-stage. The noble child of nature, the son of the soil who could play it by ear, found out who the best man was—the lawyer well-grounded in land claims who turned up with a valid deed to his farm. The Nimrod characters moved on, leaving behind many a warrant for debt docketed "gone to Missouri." Social changes could be enumerated in various ways. "Corn bread and common doings" gave way to variety and decorum at the table. The banjo in the cabin was succeeded by the melodeon in the parlor; the whiskey gourd by the crystal decanter of old bourbon, twinkling in the candlelight on an heirloom sideboard. The gratuitous assault and battery of the flatboat bullies, conceived as sheer sport, was superseded by a more knightly conception of homicide, as instanced in the Kentuckian whose reason for killing his man was "Because, sar, he resembled, sar, a man I do not like, sar."

As the frontier receded into the purple past, the symbolic Kentuckian evolved into a well-set-up gentleman wearing a goatee and broad-brimmed Panama hat, a jimswinger coat and a cane. The cane had a big crook that could be conveniently hooked over the arm, leaving both hands free for dealing with the free lunch in the saloons of the United States. For him, ear-chewing was passé but he liked to fight the "tiger." His hand had not lost its cunning in the decoction of mixed drinks with a bourbon base, and his ear was attuned to the thunder of dainty hoofs on a fast track. Such a man, perhaps, was Judge Ira Julian. The judge was sitting on the portico of the Capital Hotel in Frankfort when Bob Tyler, who had ridden with Duke in the Second Kentucky Cavalry—Basil Wislon Duke came from Scott County. His mother was a Currie. He married Henrietta Hunt Morgan, the sister of General John Hunt Morgan—but where was I? Oh—Tyler. He had been excited by the international yacht race in which Lord Dunvaren had challenged the holders of the America's Cup.

"Judge, Valkyrie wins!" Tyler called out.

Judge Julian thought a moment.

"He did? Whose horse was that?"

Always genial, frequently dashingly handsome, with match-less social gifts, an air *degagé*, unpredictable, individualistic to the point of eccentricity, a philosopher or at least a humorist, the Kentuckian looked like a lord, lived like a lord and some-times acted like one. Lawrence S. Thompson has told the "semi-fabulous story" of Jack Cole of Franklin County who went to Paris, France, not Kentucky, and read of a grand ball being given in honor of the marshals of France. Since he was a marshal of the United States census, Cole decided that he was eligible to at-tend. He produced his credentials and was received with all honors as a Marshal of America.

Tradition and custom and leisurely ways count in Kentucky. It is significant that it was a Kentucky man, courtly Judge George M. Bibb, one of the "War Hawks" in the U.S. Senate in 1811, who was the last man in Washington to be seen wearing eight-eenth-century knee breeches and long silk stockings. In Ken-tucky every man who is an esquire can spell out his genealogy at the drop of a Panama to the last outer circle of consanguinity. Kentucky still preserves the pretty custom of a gentleman ad-dressing a married woman of close acquaintance as "Miss"; as Arthur Krock, for instance, when he was a working newspaper-man in Louisville, would address Mrs. Henry Watterson, wife of the beloved and distinguished "Marse Henry," as "Miss Rebecca." "Old" was the important qualifying word associated with excellence. One said Old Woodford County, Old Virginia Military Institute where one had gone to school, old bourbon whiskey, as already noted, and of course Old Kentucky. "Old Kentucky!" Henry Watterson once exclaimed in a homecoming speech at the Armory in Louisville. "The very name has had a charm, has wrought a spell, has made a melody all its own; has woven on its sylvan loom a glory quite apart from the glory of Virginia, Kentucky's mother, and the glory of Tennessee, Ken-tucky's sister."

Kentuckians who leave the state are still known as "trans-plants." If they prosper in alien climes, they return regularly to see the floral horseshoe hung on the winner of the Derby, drop their howdies to old friends and renew a mystic contact with the earth-rhythms of that beloved soil whence cometh a Kentuckian's strength. The story has been told as typical of a lonely son of the Bluegrass who was a sojourner in a European port city, most probably Hamburg. On a pier he saw a barrel of Kentucky bourbon, the fragrant produce of his home precinct. Impulsively and joyously, he threw his arms around the cask.

"You must be a Kentuckian," a stranger remarked.

All citizens of the northern states are "damn Yankees" in Kentucky, we like to believe, a tradition which Mr. Charles Farnsley of Louisville exploited amusingly a few years ago when he applied to the Copyright Office in the Library of Congress for the registration of a whiskey label. The design which he wished to protect was called Damyankee. The Copyright Office rejected the application and returned it with a notation, in blue pencil, "In bad taste." It is not true, as widely reported, that Farnsley promptly filed again, this time for the name Old Bad Taste. But he admits that the idea did occur to him. Mr. Farnsley, a man who wears many hats as civic leader, former mayor of Louisville, lawyer, scholar in the field of rare Americana, is also the proprietor of a label for Kentucky straight bourbon known as Rebel Yell, and another called Lost Cause, decorated with a mourning border in heavy black. Thus even loyal Kentuckians occasionally have a bit of fun with the Kentucky *mystique*.

Despite the popular notion to the contrary, a certain reserve about Yankees existed south of the Ohio long before the War Between the States. The New England peddler of clocks, razorstrops and notions, with his sweet talk, shoddy merchandise, holier-than-thou attitude, had made Yankee a pejorative word. The feeling dated back as far as the War of 1812 when New England resistance to the war outraged the new West. There was, too, a well-established prejudice in Kentucky which came out in the remark "mighty few Yankees can carry their liquor." This, in turn, led on to a natural question, "Are there any gentlemen, sir, among the Yankees?" The purpose was not to give offense but to elicit information. It was, rather, the kind of innocent and rustic inquiry which Sir Roger de Coverley might have made had he lived in that time and place. The question was, indeed, asked of the New Yorker, Hoffman, at the inn in Manchester in 1833.

Among the Kentucky sovereigns the urge to hold public office is especially strong. This may explain why of all the arts, the one most admired in Kentucky has been oratory, including the art of picturesque invective. Young men read law with the local judge, studied medicine at the Louisville Medical Institute, wrote stilted verses in the neoclassic fashion, read *Gil Blas* and books on surveying, farming and distilling. But the proper study of mankind was—public speaking. When a youth who had learned the knack of projecting himself to an audience rose to claim for Kentucky the best card players, the fastest horses, the prettiest girls, or to praise, in an orotund phrase, the "life and character" of John C. Breckinridge, it was second nature for him to draw flattering analogies between local political lights in the Democratic party and the Nestors of ancient Greece. He learned to throw in the watchword of the Democratic party in Latin, *Fiat justitia ruat coelum,* explaining how that meant "Justice be done even if the Heavens should fall," and sling the language of eloquence, involving such admired phrases as "without a stain upon his bright escutcheon," and five-dollar words like "guerdon" and "never recreant." The borrowings from Greece and Rome were in part conventional ornamentation of the period and in part valued because both republican Rome and the Athens of Pericles presented remote and therefore respectable examples of glorious states which practiced slavery. A bright young attorney, gifted in wind and tongue, who owned a copy of the *Kentucky Statutes,* and had gotten off some good speeches, might legitimately dream of being sent to represent his district at Frankfort, or of someday sitting in the House of Representatives with his own spitbox, and appear before the home folks at picnics as a great man, saying: "Mr. Chairman, Daughters of the Confederacy, Confederate veterans, Ladies and Gentlemen: Standing on this sacred soil, hallowed by your mighty deeds . . ."

In antebellum elections, each candidate provided a free barrel of whiskey with his name lettered on the side. Into the barrel was thrown a bouquet of mint, a few pounds of sugar, with tin cups festooned around the barrel. Sometimes the whiskey bucket near the polling place was productive of fights and gougings.

Indubitably it put some zing into an election. Yet it had its uses, for it must have taken a man well fortified with "Dutch courage," in the days when elections were settled by voice vote, to call out, in 1860, "Lincoln and Hamlin!"

The prevailing method of campaigning was burlesqued by William Littell, the first humorist of Kentucky letters, in a mock petition presented to the people by Gregory Woodcock, the perennial unsuccessful candidate, who "most humbly sheweth . . . that your petitioner hath grown grey and poor, and become an idler and a drunkard, in attempting to serve his country in the capacity of a legislator." Woodcock said that in the course of running repeatedly for the Assembly but never being elected, "your petitioner moreover contracted a disrelish for all ordinary industry, and such a relish for strong drink, that it is utterly impracticable for him to retrieve his circumstances." He asked nothing for lost time, but did apply for reimbursement of out of pocket expenses incurred "in frequenting taverns, tippling houses, gambling tables, dram shops, and every other hole and corner where your majesties were to be met with. . . ."

A statement of account was appended, with such items as "For introducing myself as a candidate, 100 half pints of whiskey" and "Treating those who had voted for me last year, 200 half pints"; and another 100 half pints purchased "merely for the purpose of shewing that I was attached to diets and drinks of domestic growth and manufacture, and was disposed to encourage them."

In New England the stranger at the gates was asked his name, destination and business. In Kentucky the salutation was, "Stranger, sit down. What will you take?" Unforgettable was the gesture of the courtly Kentuckian who uncorked his last bottle of W. L. Weller Straight Kentucky Bourbon, distilled in 1917 and not a day younger than forty-five years, to compliment this undeserving writer who was neither a colonel, a lawyer nor kinfolks, and whose Kentucky forebears struck out for Illanoy a hundred and thirty years ago for reasons not pertinent to this discussion. The whole atmosphere of Kentucky tradition is suffused with the aroma of fine whiskey. A Kentucky historian, J. Stoddard Johnston, once declared that the nations who lead the march of civilization and Christianity, who are patrons of art, science and literature are also alcohol-drinking peoples. On such a scale of values, Kentuckians could claim a high rank for their services to religion and the arts, at least up to the time when a temperance speaker could assert, without fear of contradiction from his audience, "God is a Prohibitionist." Of this incident, *Bonfort's Wine and Spirit Circular* observed editorially as a melancholy sign of the times, "the rapidly increasing number of people who profess to speak with authority concerning the opinions and designs of Inscrutable Providence in matters of political economy, taxation, social science and sumptuary legislation."

As to these matters, Kentucky took a schizophrenic course. Famous for its fine whiskeys, with $160,000,000 in capital invested in distilleries in 1908, the state was in the same year ninety-seven per cent dry and went on from there to pass a universal local option law which made the home of bourbon legally a dry state long before the passage of the Eighteenth Amendment. Not everyone agreed that the millennium was at hand. Henry Watterson, who had had a whiskey named after him and whose editorial offices were within sniffing distance of the fermenting vats of the Old Forester plant, wrote, "I should not like to take the hand of a prohibitionist if I knew him to be a prohibitionist. I should not like it because in the event he be not a fool outright . . . he must be sterile of mind and heart as well as a traitor to the institutions of his country."

Kentuckians have always been good at picturesque verbalization. The swearing of mighty oaths became a branch of oral literature. The butchers of Covington are said to have been top stylists in this field of endeavor. A state capable of devising such place names as Bar, Malt, Rye and Sip, would also give us Temperance. "Viper" prepares us for Governor William Goebel's nickname for a man about whom he was unenthusiastic, "Gonorrhoea John." It is a measure of the distaste which Theodore Hallam felt for Goebel that he said of Goebel's candidacy that he would vote for a yellow dog if duly nominated in the Democratic primary. But, he said, he would not go lower than that. It comes almost as anticlimax to note that one governor, who once had been a mason, was known to the electorate as "Old Stone Hammer," while another answered to the sobriquet of "Hog-Jaw" Taylor; that two William Pierces of Barren County were called, to avoid embarrassing mistakes, Sycamore Bill and Hypocrite Bill; or that Alvin Harlow, the author, who has a Kentucky background, had an Uncle Willie known as Piddlin' Bill.

The eminence of Kentuckians in oratory, in castigation, in marksmanship, in statecraft and just plain craft has been attributed by philosophers with some knowledge of geology to the commonwealth's remarkable understratum, the blue limestone of the Lower Silurian of the Trenton period. It's the lime in the water which gives Kentucky bourbon its special geniality and velvety flavor. It has been credited with making Kentucky soldiers the bravest. More Kentucky colonels have worn a string tie than ever smelled powder on the field of battle. Yet it is also true that Kentucky has fostered a martial spirit. When rumors of war have reached the hollows and the hills, the local stalwarts traditionally drop the still-rake, damp down the furnace, shoulder Old Daisy and rendezvous at Lexington, inquiring courteously of the local constabulary, "Whereabouts is Matamoras?"

Kentuckians have always rejoiced in titles, especially if they suggest valor. A retired attorney-general of the state, a lawyer by trade, is not offended if known merely as "General"; nor does an inspector-general for the Louisville and Nashville Railroad reject the same form of address. It is a fixed fact in Kentucky culture, as Lawrence S. Thompson puts it, "All attorneys, all Democrats and certain respectable Republicans are entitled to have Hon. prefixed to their names in formal reference."

Any resident and many non-residents of the commonwealth, if presentable and personally popular, engaged in some legitimate occupation such as politics, and who have the right connections, can hope to acquire a military title from Kentucky by prerogative of the governor. This has held true from the earliest hour of the state when Governor Isaac Shelby put aside the cares of his office long enough to commission his son-in-law, Charles S. Todd, the first non-fighting Kentucky colonel.

Under the constitutional powers conferred upon the executive branch of the state government, and legislative authority given under the Kentucky statutes, Kentucky governors have at times in the state's history created colonels en masse. This army is not expensive to maintain. It gets no salaries and furnishes its own rations. The necessities of the public service have produced in our times such distinguished military figures as Fred Astaire, Bing Crosby, Jack Dempsey and "the entire University of Kentucky football team that finally licked Tennessee." The governor also has the power, and on occasion has not hesitated to use it, to commission a Rear Admiral of the Green River Fleet. By 1932 the colonels had become so numerous that they had to organize. Now they flourish under the imposing name of the Honorable Order of Kentucky Colonels. There is no official uniform—unless it is a quart of bourbon. The members have a good time during Derby Week. They ogle the arriving celebrities like Walter Cronkite, the newscaster, Bill Mauldin, the southpaw cartoonist and Jonathan Winters of Jack Paar show fame; and indeed, as already indicated, many of the colonels are upper-echelon celebrities themselves. They tour the horse farms and visit hospitable whiskey plants to see how bourbon is born. They watch the strutting drum majorettes in the annual Pegasus Parade on the day before the day before the Running for the Roses. They drop in at the Jim Porter Tavern for a succulent mint julep. This cloister, named after the authentic "Louisville giant" of a hundred years ago who kept a house of entertainment, still posts what are alleged to be his "Rules," including this warning: "Gentlemen imbibing foreign and alien spirits other than Bourbon whiskey may be requested to pay in cash."

On Derby Day Eve, the Colonels under their commander-in-chief, currently Kentucky Governor Bert Combs, and their den mother, Mrs. Anna Friedman Goldman, Secretary and Keeper of the Great Seal, turn out for their annual banquet. There is a television personality on hand from the National Broadcasting Company to act as master of the revels. In a julep-and-roses atmosphere the Derby Festival Queen offers a toast in authentic bourbon and the proceeds of the affair, which add up to substantially more than walking-around money, aid the twenty-five worthy causes in which the Colonels are interested. Next day, at the running of the Derby, the colonels listen with nostalgia to the band playing "My Old Kentucky Home" and sip the juleps which are handed about in the grandstand while watching the race and the crowds.

Once during Governor Albert B. (Happy) Chandler's administration there was a rhubarb when the attorney-general cantankerously ruled that all 17,000 colonelcy commissions expired with the term of the governor who issued them. The late W. C. Fields issued a dignified statement in which he declared "I stand on my record." But, being a good soldier, he pledged compliance. That is, he observed the ruling by signing his name thereafter as Col. W. C. Fields, Retired. But deep in his heart he and thousands like him cherished the wisdom of the old American adage which asserts "once a captain, always a captain." A month later justice triumphed. While the governor and lieutenant governor attended a baseball game in Cincinnati, the acting governor, the Honorable James E. Wise, a man of compassion, promptly reinstated all the colonels, issued a few new ones, and restored the admirals, too, whose commissions by then honored the names of nearly every lake, river, creek and dry branch in the commonwealth. When the Colonels get together, the softened accents of genuine Kentuckians mingle strangely with the speech patterns and phonetics of Brooklyn and Hollywood. While it is not true that almost anyone can be a Colonel, the converse *is* true—that a Colonel can be almost anyone, from Stephen Foster, who was posthumously honored, to the Commissioner of Internal Revenue, the head cataloguer of the University of Kentucky Library and Colonel Shirley Temple, who is also a Texas Rangerette.

Far back now in our national history the militia colonel on the settlement line was an authentic figure, an on-guard man. After the wars were over he donned his clawhammer coat and became a character in fiction. Now we have come the full distance. The Colonels are organized, like a labor union or a burial-benefits society. They represent a harmless whimsy and lend pre-race color to the Derby Festival, that boisterous week in Louisville which is a kind of American *Oktoberfest,* except that it is built around bourbon instead of beer, horses instead of zithers. Any number can play—New York admen and glossy people from the entertainment industries who would shudder at the idea of sucking corn juice from a fruit jar and never heard of black-eyed peas or fatback. But we cannot do without the Kentucky colonels. They provide us with humor and a touch of poetry. They liberate us from things as they are, make it plausible to believe that there is yet a crossing into a Kentucky of the imagination, where the dogwood blossoms all year around, taxes are low, the whiskey always prime and all men are as they would like to be.

Chapter 6

THE DARK AGE
OF AMERICAN DRINKING

SHREWD and readable Anne Royall, who earned her living in the second quarter of the last century by traveling widely in the United States and publishing accounts of her observations of men and manners, wrote repeatedly of encountering everywhere among the ordinary people a firm determination to enliven all huskings, housewarmings, christenings, hay mowings, eyegougings and dull Sundays with immoderate drafts of American whiskey. In Washington City, two hundred workmen were employed on the construction of the Capitol of whom, she estimated, "there are perhaps not half a dozen sober men," while the premises swarmed with "abandoned females" who sold whiskey by the drink in the passage between the Senate chamber and the House. In Connecticut the lady reporter found that in the Land of Steady Habits one of the steadiest was "the too free use of spirituous liquors." Other states and sections presented a similarly solid front of loyalty to hot waters. Of the South, Mrs. Royall wrote: "I am afraid my brave Tennesseans indulge too great a fondness for whiskey. When I was in Virginia it was too much whiskey," and adds, "The Ohio story was the same: too, too much whiskey."

In Maryland, where rye whiskey was worth about twenty-eight

cents a gallon, the dram shops were open on Sunday until the
middle of the century. The theory was that it was better to have
the men drunk there than at home. Southerners generally were
classified as either "slingers" or "eleveners." The former were
drinkers who upon awakening believed that a slug of sour mash
with mint and sugar—the sling was a close relative of the mint
julep—was necessary for taking the chill off the morning. In the
mythology which surrounds the Kentucky colonel, three slings
and "a chaw of terbacker" made a very satisfactory "breakfast
of champions." "Eleveners" were sissies who didn't resort to the
tickler until eleven o'clock in the morning. A tickler, it should
perhaps be explained, was a bottle of narrow shape, holding a
half-pint; just enough to tickle.

When Sut Lovingood, the irrepressible comic roughneck of the
George W. Harris sketches, comes loping down the mountain
somewhere near Knoxville, calling "Hey, Ge-orge!", the author
says, "He brought up near me, banteringly shaking the half-full
'tickler' within an inch of my face." Sut then added a few illuminating remarks about the cold-mix compounded whiskey he was
drinking, speaking in a wild East Tennessee dialect which I have
modified slightly in deference to the unaccustomed ear of the
present generation:

"What am yu gwine? take a suck, hoss? This here truck's *old*.
I kotched it myself, hot this morning frum the still worm. . . .
I put that ar piece ov burnt dried peach in myse'f tu gin it color—
better nor ole Bullen's plan: he puts in tan ooze, in what he sells,
an' that haint handy, he uses the red warter outen a pond jis' below
his barn;—makes a pow'ful natral color, but don't help the taste
much. Then he correcks that wif red pepper; hits an orful mixture, that whisky ole Bullen makes. . . . He's pisent nigh onto
three quarters ov the b'levin parts ov his congregashun wif it,
an' tuther quarter he's got intu stealing an' cussin. . . . Haint
he the durndest sample ov a parson yu ever seed enyhow?"

Just when and how alcoholic beverages and the evangelical
churches came to a parting of the ways suggests a fascinating
study which has not yet been undertaken. For the greater part
of the period under discussion here—the first half of the nineteenth century—the general attitude toward a dram was tolerant: "Well—ahum—I don't object, Brother Stanley, a toddy

tones up the digestion and induces more refreshing sleep."

In the days before an influential church could bar distillers from membership, two Kentucky church members who devoutly believed in following St. Paul's admonition to Timothy could hold the following colloquy just before the big revival meeting:

"How much 'sperits' did you git?"

"Ten gallons," the brother replied.

"Jest sech stinginess as that will spile the meetin' and kill the church. I got twenty gallons myself an' you are jest as able to support the gospil as I am, if you wuzn't so dog stingy."

Red liquor accompanied the westering Americans in their occupation of the North American continent. At approximately the same time that Lovingood was pursuing his exuberant and unsteady way among the knobs of the Tennessee mountains, a gold rush guidebook provides a realistic estimate of what the comfort of a gold miner called for. Assuming that a party of four was crossing the Great Plains to the diggings, the recommended allowance was one-half barrel of whiskey. Since the added weight was 175 pounds, the position of whiskey as a necessity is evident.

Mrs. Frances Trollope, the English novelist, in her unflattering middle-class British reactions to American life, divided American men into two classes: "literary men," by which she meant a rough approximation of the English gentleman; and chewers and drinkers. The categories in her view were mutually exclusive. She found the American male a striking physical specimen, often even handsome, but "always redolent of whiskey" when she met him in the public room of a Pennsylvania inn, sat near him at the play when Mr. Forrest brought *Hamlet* to Cincinnati, or anywhere the shirt-sleeved "peasant" extended his "hard, greasy paw" and wafted in her direction the breath of liberty, onions and whiskey.

If these scattered samplings seem to indicate that a whole nation had gone on an extraordinary binge, one can hypothesize some of the factors: cheap, untaxed liquor, lack of social outlets, chilly houses, grinding physical labor, a totally rough environment. Since salt was the principal means of food preservation, the salted meat which was eaten three times a day contributed importantly to the thirst which shocked humanitarians and reformers of the early nineteenth century into action.

For those with scruples there were hundreds of well-spiked proprietary medicines to choose from. The prescribed dosage approached the modern cocktail in potency. But thanks to the "medical dodge," one could moisten the clay while maintaining membership in the Good Templars. One class of medicines known as bitters often contained rye or bourbon whiskey as their active medical principle, as with the highly regarded Greeley's Bourbon Bitters which bore the illustrious and reassuring name of the great editor and temperance advocate. When one notes that in the early 1850's six hundred thousand men signed the pledge of just one of many crusading groups, the Washingtonian Society, it is evident that alcoholism was a social problem of massive dimensions.

The heavy drinking, in turn, loosed upon the land a legion of oratorical, reformatory gentlemen with a carpetbag, an extra shirt and a manuscript. They stumped the lyceum circuits with a set of conventional arguments, parlor tricks done with simple chemical apparatus, ghastly charts depicting alcoholic horrors, a supply of pledge cards and titillating descriptions of sin.

The anti-liquor forces also employed the printed word in a ruthless and tendentious effort designed to scare "inebriates" into the middle of next week. It is a vast and hair-raising literature, based upon the ethic that righteous ends may properly be accomplished by dubious means. Drinkers, they said, were "peculiarly subject to rheumatism, inflamed eyelids, headaches, bleeding at the nose, sores and ulcers, affections of the stomach and bowels, and premature trembling of the hand and head." They were also reported, in a grisly bit of science fiction, to be subject to spontaneous combustion from within. The *American Temperance Magazine* and the Reverend Jonathan Kittredge of Lyme, New Hampshire, a lurid whiskey pamphleteer of awesome mendacity, cited cases, always said to be "well authenticated," in which some unfortunate character who liked a nip of distilled waters was literally roasted alive from internal fires.

The alcoholic excesses of a hundred years ago also brought forth the temperance novel. These tracts in fictional form flailed away at the drinking problem with Bible quotations, scientific data of doubtful validity and all the devices of literary sentimentality. The titles favored by this sub-literary genre now convey the charm of lavender and old lace, as in *Elsie Magoon: or, The Old Still-House in the Hollow*. It is difficult not to linger over some of the characters, too, often insufferable little prigs who wear the badge of the Band of Hope and have all the answers, such as Fritz, a little German boy who lived not far from the wicked city of New York. Why was it wicked? The author knows and tells: "Because so much whiskey is sold there."

Much of the whiskey distilled before the Civil War was so heavy that it was scarcely drinkable and indeed was never intended to reach the consumer. It was a semi-finished article which moved through the commission houses to a rectifier, most likely located in Cincinnati, which brewed more lager beer than any other American city, handled more whiskey than any other mart in the whole world and made the barrels, stills and rectifying columns which the distillers required.

The rectifiers used the heavy distillate which came off the farms, often rather on the low side as to proof, for extending or blending with grain spirits (see "blend" in Glossary). Or the heavily flavored country whiskey might be redistilled and stripped of its flavor elements to make neutral grain spirits. The principle of reducing bulk and increasing value involved in turning corn into whiskey also, according to Charles Cist in his valuable, statistic-studded *Cincinnati in 1859*, "induces the conversion of whiskey into alcohol, which, condensing nearly two barrels into one, saves one-half the expense of transportation, to various distant markets."

The beverage which came into being when spirits were colored and flavored with additives was known to its familiars as "rectified." The word appears in the vocabulary of the immortal Captain Simon Suggs of the Tallapoosa Volunteers, that master of provincial roguery who sprang, bottle in hand, from the luxuriant imagination of John J. Hooper. Suggs was hurrying along the street in Tuscaloosa eager to get into a faro game, when his attention was caught by a window displaying liquors. He swept it with a practiced eye. "Thar's koniac, and old peach, and rectified. . . . That light-yaller bottle . . . that's Tennessee! I'd know that anywhere! . . . What a power o' likker they do keep in this here town; ef I warn't goin' to run agin the bank I'd sample some of it, too, I reether expect."

A meal at a house of public entertainment cost a quarter without whiskey or thirty-seven and a half cents *with*. An account book of an old inn in Potosi, Missouri, sets forth clear evidence that the patrons preferred the thirty-seven-and-a-half-cent deal. Running a doggery was a good way for a man with political aspirations to keep himself in the public eye, meanwhile getting his personal liquor at wholesale prices. Many who hoped to feed from the public trough availed themselves of this method of advancement and refreshment.

The moderate or occasional social drinker seems not to have existed. Men drank to excess or not at all. This sharp cleavage makes the per capita consumption of distilled spirits all the more impressive. Rising gradually from the level of about two and a half gallons in the closing years of the eighteenth century, the figure reached an all-time high in 1860 of three and a quarter gallons. Statistically everybody is included: women, children, slaves, Indians, John B. Gough, the temperance orator, who made a profession out of describing his feats in tippling traps, the man who took one glass of elderberry wine on New Year's Eve, as well as the hero of the old ditty:

> He is not drunk who from the floor
> Can rise again, and drink once more,
> But he is drunk, who prostrate lies,
> And cannot drink and cannot rise.

Since an average is an arithmetical mean, the drinking population somewhere, possibly in California, was doing even better. In San Francisco there was a barroom for every one hundred inhabitants. Here beer and bourbon fought a homeric battle for the throats of the thin line of patriots who balanced on the city's brass rails. In Albany, New York, the Dutch demonstrated that they had hard heads by putting away ten gallons of the American schnapps for every inhabitant. Sadly, Samuel Dexter, president of the Massachusetts Society for the Suppression of Intemperance, observed, "The pocket-flask is grown into a case-bottle, and the keg into a barrel." And all the while the settlements pushed west, the population doubled and redoubled, and the drovers, traders, boatmen, exchange brokers and one-gallus land agents, the quarter-race crowd with their dirks and their thirst, could agree as they raised a glass of the ardent, "Yes, sir, we *air* an Almighty people."

When a barrel of whiskey moved to the retail trade, the shipper often sent along a few decanters or fancy bottles which the buyers could fill and set up on their back-bars. Hopefully, from the point of view of the consumer, the bottle on the bar contained the whiskey in its original integrity as it came from the spigot. This was, necessarily, an act of faith in the taverner. There was no method of control. Or a man could own his own bottle. Many of these early flasks, hand-blown of course, were extraordinarily handsome and came in a variety of interesting shapes. A bottle was a valuable possession and all liquid commodities—flavoring extracts, syrup, vinegar, eau de cologne— were decanted from jugs, carboys or barrels into the customer's personal bottle. A bottle could even be valuable enough to be mentioned in a will. Charles Carroll of Carrollton, for instance, the Maryland signer, and a man of wealth, included among his bequests "18 doz. Quart and 2 Doz^n Pint Bottles."

In the years of expansionist sentiment before the Civil War, when the American destiny seemed manifest, the young glass industry made the eagle scream in a variety of delightful designs which reflected the popular temper and topical interests of the day. Fancy flasks which would slide down into the pocket of a greatcoat, now known as "commemoratives," celebrated the Gold Rush, the opening of new territories, the visits to the United States of La Fayette, Kossuth, the Hungarian patriot, and Jenny Lind. Letters molded in relief wished "Success to the Railroads." There were fanciful shapes, cornucopias, log cabins, corncobs, hats, shoes, canteens, violins and bull fiddles. They came in a charming range of colors, from pale green to almost black-green, swirled or plain. Up to 1840 George Washington was shown in uniform. Later flasks show him in a Roman toga. General Zachary Taylor, Old Rough and Ready, the hero of Buena Vista, didn't have to wait fifty years to get his toga. He made it the year after he was elected President. There are many bottles with Taylor associations. One bears a representation in the glass of a cornstalk. The legend says, "Corn for the World."

"To adorn common whiskey bottles with the likeness of our great," remark the scholarly McKearins, George S. and Helen, in their writings on early American flasks, "did not belittle the man or the country in the eyes of the citizens who bought the flasks, filled or unfilled." The number of such whiskey bottles still in existence suggests again the extent of use of alcoholic beverages, while the pictorial flasks with their ingenious designs, the McKearins say, "would seem to indicate a state of keen competition between glassmakers and also between purveyors of hard liquor."

Not all of the bottles dedicated to recording our history depicted national heroes or dealt with great events and elevated themes. Followers of harness racing might wish to tote their spirits in the Flora Temple flask. Flora Temple was the champion of the trotting tracks in 1859; her time, 2:19 ¾, as shown on the bottle. One handy little tickler carried the description, "The Traveler's Companion"; another inquired, "Will you take a drink? Will a duck swim?"

A Philadelphia distiller named E. C. Booz, often mistakenly taken for the eponym of the modern term "booze," had his name, address and the date 1840 blown into his dark brown-and-green quart container. Booz bottles were shaped like little houses, with a sharp peaked roof. An original is now worth up to $150— empty. The date blown in the glass does not, of course, necessarily date the bottle. This bottle was, though, historic in that Booz, by placing his name on a consumer package, took a step toward identifying, in the modern sense, the goods with their origin.

The popularity of the historical flasks slowly declined after the 1870's when whiskey firms began to distribute their goods under trademarked names. The eagle pint, the busts of General La Fayette, the log cabins and canteens which the early glass houses turned out, associating American whiskey with fervent moments of national pride, gave way to packages clearly denominating a brand. A man who liked whiskey that sits up in the glass thereafter carried a bottle called Mellwood or Sunnybrook instead of that "molded moment" preserving the recollection of how, at Buena Vista, Old Rough and Ready turned to Captain Braxton Bragg of Battery C, Third U.S. Artillery, and commanded, "A little more grape, Captain Bragg."

Citizens with bottles who appeared at those raucous capers

called militia trainings in the 1840's and 1850's, citizens with
bottles who marched in procession on Independence Day, bring
back the memory of an America which was young, bumptious,
inclined to shoot its cuffs about its internal improvements, manufactures, natural resources; the wisdom of its statesmen and the
bravery of its soldiers.

After cresting in 1860, the alcoholic flood receded in the post-
war years as the result of many circumstances, including ups and
downs in the economy, the increasing costliness of the "bottle
fever" and the development of a new, effective strategy on the
part of the aggressive prohibitionists. The evangelical churches
abandoned the idea of promoting temperance through the appeal
to the conscience of the individual and made a sharp change of
direction into the field of political action. Total abstinence backed
by statute and the police power became their goal. The new
methods got results. By the 1890's, half the area of the United
States had been dried up. Whiskey was no longer cheap after
the imposition of the federal excise tax. So productive of revenue
was this measure that it celebrated its centennial last year. Like
bourbon whiskey, the internal revenue levy gives every indication
of being with us as long as our institutions endure.

Never again after the Civil War was Congress able to escape
from the tangled and perilous fiscal, philosophical and political
problems associated with its partnership in the distilled spirits
industry. Tempers and voices rose in debates which were sometimes exciting, sometimes illuminating, sometimes quite funny,
often dull enough. The interminable dialogue over the proper
place, if any, of spirituous beverages in our society was the subject of investigation by countless Congressional committees which
tinkered with the excise tax for years and finally went whole hog
for constitutional Prohibition to advance a particular social philosophy. Originally, Congress had had no thought of assuming
a moral stewardship over the individual citizen. The government's position was simply that it had a big war on its hands
and needed the money.

Chapter 7

WHISKEY IN
THE CIVIL WAR

IN troubled times men seek the solace of religion or strong
drink, or both. When the northern volunteers started out for
camp in 1861 some turned to their Bibles and meditated upon the
ends of man. But the majority were in more festive mood. As
soon as home was well out of sight, one sergeant of the Second
Massachusetts wrote to his mother, "the band boys handed
around the whiskey bottle." Army life brought many soldiers into
contact with spirituous liquors for the first time and their experiences during "the quadrennium" undoubtedly widened the demand for hard liquor in the years that followed.

Experienced southrons took their liquid comfort with them
when it was possible. Farwell Gould, a Confederate hero from
the Ozark Hills, rode into battle at Pea Ridge with a jug in his
arms because, as he said, "there wasn't no safe place to set it
down." Among all the ingenious theories which have been advanced to explain and interpret the causes behind the War, the
most novel came from a Kentucky puritan, William Taylor
Adams, the beloved "Oliver Optic" of an earlier generation, who
wrote an incredible number of books for boys. Adams blamed the
War on whiskey which he said turned sober men of Union sentiment into cheering secessionists.

The northern armies probably drank more liquor per capita than the Army of Virginia. That was not due to greater capacity but to more reliable sources of supply. The federal troops had more money, hence more whiskey. They spent more time in travel, were more often stationed in large cities. And when money ran short, they were sometimes able to acquire their supplies by other means. One jovial Chicagoan recorded in his diary an account of an incident in New Orleans where the "Boys cleaned out a Bar up town, any amount of Whiskey, Rum, Gin, Brandy and Wine in camp."

Daily whiskey rations had been abolished in the U.S. Army in 1830. But field commanders could still give out whiskey as special issue, usually one-fourth pint, at their discretion. A young fifer with the First Massachusetts Infantry who had been shocked to see whiskey advertised in Boston because back home in respectable Fitchburg liquor was sold only on the sly, poured his government ration on the ground like a good Son of Temperance. But when he stood reveille at 4 A.M. in the snow at Falmouth, Virginia, and the order came "Fall in for rations," fifer Bardeen changed his mind and drank his portion. After that, "when the commanding officer gave out whiskey I yielded to his better judgment."

The quality of this "commissary whiskey" left much to be desired, according to one soldier-journalist who described it as composed of "bark juice, tar-water, turpentine, brown sugar, lamp-oil and alcohol." Officers could purchase liquors. But the private soldiers got a lawful drink only when they drew the ration.

Private stocks of whiskey appeared among the men who were inclined to take a chance on anything that wouldn't eat its way through glass. Some commanders confiscated and destroyed any ardent spirits they could find. Sutlers and peddlers, if caught selling liquor, were punished. One was drummed out of a New York regiment with a dozen bottles dangling from his neck. It seems highly unlikely that the common soldier tasted very much genuine bourbon when one notices the nicknames the men bestowed upon the available beverages: "Tanglefoot," "Nockum Stiff" and "Rotgut." Unusual punishment was sometimes meted out to drunken soldiers. Three men were on one occasion sentenced to

march in whiskey barrels for three days. Punishment for drunkenness on guard duty was mandatory, but social drinking when
off duty, if it led to nothing more serious than minor brawls, was
dealt with lightly.

Drinking habits varied in different regiments, naturally, according to the background of the men, whether German, Irish,
Yankee, recently assimilated immigrant, city or rural. The Germans clung to their beer, a preference noted in a song the Army
sang in a spirit of good-natured caricature:

> When I comes from der Deutsche Countree,
> I vorks sometimes at baking;
> Den I keeps a lager beer saloon,
> Und den I goes shoe making;
> But now I was a sojer been,
> To save der Yankee Eagle:
> To schlauch dem tam secession volks,
> I'm going to fight mit Sigel.

The characters of the officers and the influence of the chaplains
were also factors which affected liquor consumption. Regiments
noted for sobriety might fall off the wagon if the provocation
was unusual. The forty-eighth New York Regiment led by Colonel James M. Perry, a prominent minister, was known as Perry's
Saints. But while stationed on Tybee Island in June, 1862, a
severe storm blew ashore a large quantity of beer and wine. The
Saints accepted this stroke of fortune as clear evidence of the
divine will and acted accordingly.

Medically, alcohol rivaled quinine as the sovereign remedy,
and the boys were usually well impressed with the part played by
the whiskey in any cure which they observed. Whiskey also enjoyed a high reputation in cases of "a siege of flux," or the
"Tennessee Quickstep"—diarrhea—and if whiskey wasn't available, Radway's Ready Relief would do, which also provided the
anodyne of alcohol to ease the condition of men who were badly
fed, badly sheltered, overworked, and living under the sanitary
arrangements of the Dark Ages.

Sometimes the Army did some manufacturing. The Colonel
of the Ninety-fifth Illinois "turned out fifteen gallons of Rotgut
. . ." for a Christmas celebration in 1864. New Year's Day was

usually marked with drinking, the unauthorized discharge of fire-
arms and perhaps a tent or two were set afire. As one New Jersey
sergeant put it, "New Year's don't come but once a year & tents
are cheap." Recognized army types included the bummer, whose
basic objective was pillage, and the forager, not a natural thief,
but a man who liked his little luxuries, including whiskey, and
exhibited great resourcefulness in satisfying his needs. There
was, too, the confirmed alcoholic who could always buy, beg or
steal whiskey, would drink anything on which he could go into
orbit. Men of this stamp were little missed in case they died, were
dishonorably discharged or went "over the hill." A New York
soldier, known as Whiskey Bill, could always elude the guards
and find a barroom somewhere. A scamp from Vermont who got
a safe berth as a hospital worker and does not appear to have
done any fighting while he was in the army, became a successful
whiskey entrepreneur, and instructed his son back home in a
letter:

"I want yo to Send me 10 Galones of hye wines or Elcoll
[alcohol] I want it to sell i can git fore dollars a pint for it
yo can put it in tin canes [cans] And pack it in Saw dust have
the canes made so you can cork them tight And put them in A
good Stout Box fille the canes full so it wont ratle now Send it
as Sun as yo git this leter And Send . . . me the coss of it canes
And all . . . And when yo Send it Send me A letter the Same
time . . . be cufule And pack it so it wont wratle for they are
gitin very strick . . . if I can git it heare it will bring me good
too hundred dollars the minet I get it if yo cant git hy wines
git what yo can eny thing that is licker when yo Send it Direct
it to Doctor Sawin Just as yo have the rest." *

The ingenious author of this letter came to a sudden end.
Before his enlistment expired he fell off a hospital boat and
drowned.

The most famous anecdote of the Civil War period involving
whiskey is undoubtedly Lincoln's whimsical remark about the
brand of whiskey General Grant drank. The incident occurred
when Grant was under attack for mismanagement of the battle
of Shiloh. After the end of the Mexican War, Grant had lived

* From *The Life of Billy Yank* by Bell Irvin Wiley, copyright © 1951, 1952 by
The Bobbs-Merrill Company, Inc.; reprinted by special permission of the publishers.

the monotonous life of a junior officer in lonely, dreary frontier posts. He liked liquor and a little whiskey showed on him. Rumors to the effect that Grant drank to excess arose periodically, although the officers around him during the Civil War testified that liquor had never affected his official acts. Modern historians who have weighed the evidence regard the case against Grant as not proved. At any rate, after Shiloh the newspapers hammered on the question of his drinking. Henry T. Blow, a Representative in Congress from Missouri, went to Lincoln about the reports. Lincoln cut him short: "I wish I knew what brand of whiskey he drinks. I would send a barrel to all my other generals."

Grant never defended himself against the stories. But there was lively speculation for many years as to what kind of whiskey the North's most successful general might favor. Colonel Isaac Stewart of Washington provided an answer to the question. Sitting in the Astor House in New York City in the 1880's with a congenial group of Grand Army comrades, Colonel Stewart recalled the days when General Grant was opening up the Mississippi River. Stewart stoutly defended his chief against the charge of being "a drinking man," but did recollect one occasion on which the general—but let the Colonel tell it as he remembered it:

"I think it was on the night of February 23, '63, down at Vicksburg. We were all pretty tired and sat in the cabin of the river steamer, the *Magnolia,* waiting for the morning. My stateroom was next to the General's, and I was thinking of turning in when the General said to McPherson [Major General James Birdseye McPherson, commander of the XVII Army Corps]: "See here, before we go to bed let us have a nightcap. Stewart has got some prime Old Crow whiskey around here somewhere.' I went to my stateroom and brought out the bottle. The General filled a goblet—not a little one, but a good big goblet—to the brim with that Old Crow whiskey, and he tossed it off. It was a whopping big drink and the only one I ever saw the General take during all the years I was with him."

The soldiers of the South got their whiskey in the streets and back alleys of towns, from sutlers and from bootleggers who employed other soldiers as agents. Peddlers circulated discreetly with a canteen and tin thimble used as a jigger glass. An Irishman of the Second Tennessee Volunteers was caught taking a pull from the barrel of his gun. He had filled it up at a nearby grocery. Confederate pickets usually had tobacco to trade for northern whiskey. The central government at Richmond exerted such pressure as it could against the sale and use of busthead beverages, but it was never very successful in controlling the liquor situation.

The small country stills of Kentucky, manufacturing from fifty to five hundred barrels a year, had gradually increased in size so that at the outbreak of the War their storage rooms contained large amounts of grain which both Union and Confederate forces bought or confiscated for food. In the autumn of 1862, Governor Joseph E. Brown of Georgia pointed out to the legislature that the South could get no more "Western whiskey" from the Upper South because it was cut off by the enemy. The Confederacy needed alcohol for chemical, mechanical and industrial purposes and as a solvent in the manufacture of medicines. A ration of whiskey was allowed in the army under circumstances of protracted fatigue, and whiskey was a regular component of the Confederate Navy ration. The military doctors relied upon whiskey for the treatment of rheumatism, neuralgia, fevers, syphilis, gonorrhea, measles and the dirt diseases. Quinine was the recognized treatment for the ever-present malaria. It was scarce as French brandy, both being subject to the blockade. Various native barks were tried as substitutes for quinine—dogwood, poplar, willow; two pounds of bark macerated in a gallon of whiskey. And sometimes they just left the barks out.

The market price of rectified—blended—whiskey in the Confederacy rose rapidly from twenty to twenty-five cents a gallon in the winter of 1860–61 to thirty-five dollars a gallon in the fall of 1863, an indication of the supply situation. State by state, by executive order or legislative enactment, the southern states ordered a strict prohibition for the civilian population, not as a social measure, but as a necessity of food conservation. The issue was regarded as bread versus liquor. Meanwhile the Confederate government entered into contracts with distillers for the manufacture of whiskey to meet the needs of the military establishment.

The slaves and free Negroes found prohibition no novelty.

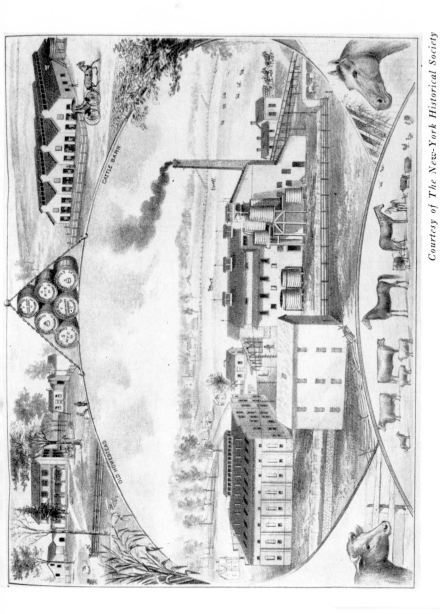

Courtesy of *The New-York Historical Society*

A sketch by an unknown artist of the Edgewater Distillery and the prosperous farm buildings of the proprietor, Thomas Jefferson Megibben.

Courtesy of the Landauer Collection New-York Historical Society

At Churchill Downs. Left to right, John G. Carlyle, Cleveland's Secretary of the Treasury; U.S. Senators Joseph C. S. Blackburn and J. Proctor Knott; also the distiller John G. Roach, a leading personality along Whiskey Row in Lousiville.

They had been legally denied liquor since the eighteenth century to assure efficient labor and because of that ancient plantation nightmare, the fear of a slave insurrection. Strict regulations required a retailer of liquor to take an oath that he would not sell or give spirits to slaves. The first offense was subject to a fine, the second carried a jail sentence. But the "grogshops," as Frederick Law Olmstead noted in his travels in the cotton states, purchased stolen goods from the slaves in exchange for whiskey much watered down and made stupefying by an infusion of tobacco. Nor could the slaves be prevented from drifting off to secluded woodsy cabins where drink was set out for them, even when the effort at control included the fear of beatings. One distiller located in Cynthiana, Kentucky, making an obvious pitch to the field hands, filed for copyright in 1860 a label for "Star Whiskey, Very Fine Old Bourbon Whiskey." It depicts a dark-skinned consumer framed in a six-pointed star, carrying a carpet-bag filled with bottles in one hand, a decanter of Star Whiskey in the other. A balloon streams from his mouth saying, "It 'Zacly Suits Dis Chile!"

Invoking the sacrosanct principle of state rights, most of the southern states resisted the efforts of the Confederate government to acquire stocks of whiskey. Georgia, from which the commissary general hoped to obtain 250,000 gallons annually, unhelpfully passed a law requiring all distilleries to be located at least twenty miles from a railroad or navigable stream. The Secretary of War tried to get the law suspended where it affected distilleries producing for the army, but the governor was much more interested in asserting the supremacy of the laws of the state of Georgia and in conserving the grain supply for native Georgians; and he took a disenchanted view of whiskey, anyway.

South Carolina imposed heavy fines for distilling from grain except for hospital use. The railroads were pressured to refuse whiskey as freight, and the women of Statesville, North Carolina, anticipating Carry Nation by fifty years, knocked in the headers of whiskey barrels and spilled the essence of the corn right into the street. The governor of Alabama ordered every still in Alabama to shut down. Officers of the militia were authorized to seize the stills and take the liquor to the nearest courthouse, where the politicians and functionaries of local government made sure that no drop of liquor ever traveled in violation of the law to the field hospitals or fighting men. Virginia joined the march toward prohibition belatedly but made it good and strong by imposing stiff penalties upon any distiller who fulfilled his contracts with the Confederate government. The Georgia statute was amended endlessly to stiffen penalties and to include potatoes, dried fruits and molasses as well as cereals. In the final dark days of the Confederacy, when Sherman was already in Atlanta, the legislature was still tinkering with the prohibition law.

Enforcement involved difficulties which were never satisfactorily resolved. One Georgia colonel not only refused to support the law, but even ran a still himself. The men who held licenses to manufacture whiskey for the central government were probably citizens of average honesty. But whiskey would bring from fifteen to twenty times the contract rates on the black market. Paying three or four times the market price for corn, the contractors could still make a killing. Many distillers manufactured more whiskey than their contracts called for. Often they deliberately turned out such a poor article that the inspectors rejected it, because the real profit was in disposing illegally of the substandard liquor.

When whiskey was scarce in the southern armies, the ordinary Johnny Reb was inclined to blame the situation upon the insatiable thirst of the army doctors. A skit which appeared in *The Camp Follower,* an army newspaper published at Augusta, Georgia, in 1864, dealt with this subject in the manner of the catechism:

"What is the first duty of a surgeon?"

"Under the names of drugs and medicines to purchase a full supply of good liquors."

"What is the second duty?"

"To cause all private cellars to be searched, and all the good brandies found there to be confiscated, lest the owners should smuggle them to the soldier, give them away and make the whole army drunk."

"What is the third duty?"

"To see that he and his assistant drink up all of said liquors."

The suspicions expressed in this satirical trifle were not without a basis in fact. One Confederate surgeon wrote in his memoirs that following the receipt of spirits he and his fellow medics usually succeeded in "drinking up every drop . . . before morning."

Devoted drinkers applied endless patience and ingenuity to accumulating enough baldface to get a small bun on. After Appomattox, the wartime acts of the southern states restricting the manufacture and sale of liquor were repealed. By the late 1860's, with normal grain crops being harvested again and a revival of commercial activity, the internal revenue laws of the United States were effectively applied in the new South. Yet they were widely resented as being patently a Yankee trick. Out of the bitterness arising from the military occupation and a natural taste for easy money and hard liquor, the idea arose that the manufacture of wildcat whiskey was a peccadillo, perhaps, but scarcely a crime.

The old-time distillers, their clothing dusted with corn meal and smelling of still beer, could not have said for certain whether the yeasts of the air belonged to the animal or the vegetable kingdom. But they were thoroughly schooled in the practical aspects of fermentology and understood that the addition of just the right kind of these magical cellular organisms to saccharin liquids was all-important to the manufacture of good whiskey. No wonder, then, when a troop of marauding northern cavalry swept through a Bluegrass county, one family distiller fastened a rope to his yeast jug and hid it in the well. A blue-coated sergeant rolled up the windlass and asked what was in the jug. Disgusted when told that it contained yeast, he was about to bash the jug on a rock when the entire household pounced upon him, the master and mistress of the castle, the daughter and faithful Cato, who together wrested the heavy copper can away from profaning hands to save the antebellum spores of *Saccharomyces cerevisiae* for a better day. Thus the heritage of one of the nation's finest old bourbons was preserved for the enjoyment of future generations.

For thousands of veterans the end of the Civil War came in 1895 when the Grand Army of the Republic held its first Encampment south of the Ohio River. In that year, 30,000 Union soldiers gathered in Louisville, with only four fatalities, to march in parades, listen to speeches about brotherhood, relive their memories and attend the free barbecue and the balloon ascension at Riverside Park. Whiskey was present in generous quantities and exerted a pacific effect in helping the men who had worn the blue and the gray to find common ground. The manufacturers of I. W. Harper contributed to the healing of old emotional wounds by producing for the event a handsome decanter shaped like a soldier's canteen, filled with the famous Nelson County bourbon which bore the Harper name.

Louisville was overflowing with some 300,000 extra people, not only the "boys," but the ladies of the Women's Relief Corps, the Sons of Veterans, assorted pickpockets, confidence men, midway barkers and various broad-minded young ladies recently arrived from Chicago, Cincinnati and New Orleans. They extended a frolicsome welcome along Green Street in the spirit of southern hospitality as understood by Elsie Livingston, Miss Daisy, Miss Louise, Madame La Roy (French), Señorita Alfareta (Spanish) and Sallie Scott (Creole). The addresses of these frail lovelies were set forth for the convenience of veterans "on pleasure bent" in a curious little handbook entitled *GAR Souvenir Sporting Guide* (1895), easily obtained in any Louisville saloon.

Despite the happy spirit which prevailed at Louisville, it is natural that misunderstandings should sometimes occur after a few rounds of drinks. Vance Randolph has collected the engaging story of a get-together in an Ozark saloon, "jammed with GAR men," his informant said, "a-bragging how they won the war." There came a rude interruption when three young punks made off with a Union soldier's wallet. The local *Clarion* came out the following Thursday and told how the rogues were "confederates."

As a result of this publication the local southrons nearly mobbed the editor. It took the best efforts of the mayor to calm down the situation. He reminded the angry citizens that he had ridden with Jeb Stuart, "and you all know I ain't no Republican." Confederates, he pointed out, had been spelled with a lower case *c*, so the newspaper "didn't mean no disrespect to the Southern Confederacy." Everybody went home satisfied. The newspaper editor gratefully brought out a bottle "and him and the mayor took a drink . . . and him and the mayor took another drink."

Chapter 8

GOLDEN YEARS
OF THE BOURBON
ARISTOCRACY

A FEW of the antebellum whiskey-makers survived the destruction and confusion of war, such as the Dants, the Wathens and the Beams. The majority disappeared from the distilling scene because of death and wounds, because the old homestead was in ruins, because the distillery had burned down or because the family capital had been put into Confederate bonds. Speculation in whiskey and whiskey properties had risen to dizzy heights. Ownership of existing blocks of whiskeys, rights to old and honored names, sites of distilleries, all changed hands rapidly under the pressures and opportunities of new times.

New firms began the manufacture of whiskey, but always with respect for tradition—"upon the old copper-distilled plan" as the commercial announcements of the period often expressed it. Men who had been stock raisers, lawyers, judges, horse dealers, bankers or commission merchants came forward as distillers, men named Atherton, Stitzel, Miles, Sutherland, Thompson, McBrayer. They controlled or had access to capital. This was necessarily so since whiskey was taxed by the United States government after 1862, and during the first years the payment was due at the time the high wines were pumped into the cistern. This rigorous provision in the revenue law was later eased so that a bright young man could start in at the bottom as a beer runner, learn the business, start up on his own, capture a piece of the market and live to be described admiringly in regional biographical works as a "self-made" man who had more money than Carter had pills.

M. V. Monarch started up near Owensboro in 1867 making a barrel a day, absorbed other Daviess County properties producing a dozen brands of sour mash with the old-style bouquet and finish. Monarch also produced a quick-aged whiskey with the arresting name Kentucky Cyclone. By the 1890's, M. V. Monarch was described as "king of the whiskey trade in Kentucky." Handsome, courteous, generous, both wealthy and honest, Monarch lived a full and exemplary life, marred only by the fact that he turned Republican to vote for James G. Blaine. A brother, Thomas J. Monarch, was a loner who went his own way "all out of tune with modern ideas and in touch rather with things of long ago." Still another brother, Richard Monarch, distilled under the Glenmore name, while his Kentucky Club was recommended as having "the most delightful influence on the nervous system." Kentucky Club was, says one old account, "whiskey such as your grandfather used to drink."

Distilling dynasties propagated whiskey labels by a kind of cellular division. The name McBrayer was associated with various trade names, particularly the "J. H. McBrayer" and the "W. H. McBrayer." John H. McBrayer was a veteran of the Mexican War who led a gallant charge at Buena Vista as Captain of a company known as the "Salt River Tigers." The Captain started making a superior whiskey in Anderson County in 1848. William H. was a Presbyterian elder, a merchant and mule trader. He also practiced law and politics and was called "Judge." After serving for two terms in the Kentucky Senate, Judge McBrayer began to give serious attention to a little still he owned on the banks of a stream in Anderson, that mother-county of famous distillery brands. Mrs. McBrayer christened the business Cedar Brook—a name suggested by the dense growth of cedars along the cliffs bordering the creek. Clashes over the commercial rights to family names often led to asperities and court proceedings. "Other whiskeys called 'McBrayer,' " runs an indignant statement from the Cedar Brook Distillery, "have been thrust upon the public by avaricious competitors who sought to infringe upon the brand, but the original and only genuine W. H. McBrayer has never been manufactured by any other. . . ." Similar joustings have occurred over such names as Pepper and Dant.

The bourbon makers held to the Old World custom of a family following a calling. Sons followed fathers and passed on to their sons the old formulas and methods, the sense of vocation, the underlying assumption being that skill in handling a set of stills could be transmitted through the genes. Perhaps there was something to the idea. Thomas Monarch, sire of those previously mentioned, was a distiller who emigrated from Maryland to Kentucky. He had five sons. Four out of five became successful distillers. And even today, in the era of large corporations operated by professional administrators, an executive of a distilling company will mention that his great-grandpappy had a still at the forks of the creek and it is assumed that four or five generations in contact with the fermenting tubs counts for something more than the ability to arouse a meeting of district salesmen or to understand the regulations of the Alcohol and Tobacco Tax Division of the Internal Revenue Service.

Although average daily production figures rose slowly, the time had already passed, by the 1870's, when a country distiller, hearing of a better supply of cold, limey water, could load his whole distilling equipment into an old wagon and move to a new location. The grist mill operator who did some distilling as a side-line in an open-faced shed was passing from the scene. Substantial names appeared, their prosperity guaranteed by the certainty that the country was growing and that human nature and the law of fermentation would keep the bourbon flowing—names like Bixler, Ripy, Lillard, Medley, McCullough, Chinn, Thixton, Sherley and Saffel. The self-made man with a good formula and a way with yeasts was in a way to become a Kentucky gentleman and a guardian of the agrarian tradition, presiding as a graceful host at the sideboard while his guests toasted the Confederate heroes who had laid down their arms in 1865 not defeated, as they put it, but plumb exhausted from beating the bluebellies.

Production of bourbon in Kentucky in 1881 was 31,869,047 gallons, which gave the distiller of that period every reason to believe that his daughters would marry up and his sons would carry on. One whiskey-maker gratefully named his son Granville Bourbon. Another called his favorite horse Duke of Bourbon. Hamilton Clark Applegate's Old Rosebud, a three-year-old gelding, carried the name of the family whiskey. He won the Derby, too, setting a new track record.

There was much marrying and giving in marriage among the bourbon elite. William Sutherland married one of the Miles girls. There were dynastic unions between Medleys and Wathens. John J. Roach, a Virginian, established himself in Louisville as a wholesale grocer, whiskey merchant and founder of the Old Times distillery which barreled Old Log Cabin Sour Mash. His son, John G., followed him, while a daughter became by marriage a Wathen. E. W. Bramble married Mary Lorraine, a daughter of Thomas Jefferson Megibben, whose Edgewater and Old Lewis Hunter whiskeys were known as far away as New York City. Bramble entered the firm and acquired a reputation as a good "taster." Megibben was an Alger hero, the ambitious, honest hustler who made good in the Ben Franklin tradition.

Born in Ohio of Pennsylvania stock, Megibben became a still hand in Ohio, moved to Kentucky, became chief distiller of a Harrison County distillery and bought the business. Megibben made money out of the war speculation in whiskey and put up a lordly mansion about the size of the Cynthiana courthouse on a high hill overlooking the Licking River. Called Monticello, the big house looked across Cynthiana, then a flourishing town with three distilleries, five wholesale whiskey houses, seven churches and nine barrooms. The Megibben dining room is still remembered, with its massive, heavily carved sideboard, built with capacious liquor cabinets at either end. Also remembered is the adventure of Megibben's little daughter Mattie, who was asked to bring a toddy upstairs to a business associate of her father's. Mattie did not arrive, but was later found asleep on the stairs, the toddy inside her. As a man who owned 12,000 barrels of sound, mature bourbon, had sat in the legislature, was past president of the Latonia Racing Association and could pay $25,000 for a Shorthorn heifer, Megibben was clearly entitled to be called, and was called, "the Honorable."

At the time of his death in 1890 in his sixtieth year, T. J. Megibben was a patriarch in the Old Testament style, rich in sons, daughters, honors, land, tents and sheep. He was the most important distiller in Harrison County, owning all or part of six distilleries, shipping his bourbon all over the United States and exporting to Europe. He was the largest landowner in the County, maintained a stable of fifty thoroughbred horses and one hundred trotters and roadsters. His "tent"—Monticello—was three stories high, contained twenty-seven rooms. A Victorian landmark built of brick imported from England, each brick individually wrapped, the interior was ornamented with hand-carved walnut and mahogany, the ceilings frescoed by an artist brought over from Italy. The library was well-stocked with food for the mind—Gibbon's *Decline and Fall*, De Luxe Edition, the *Complete Works of Henry Wadsworth Longfellow*, De Luxe Edition, the writings of Jefferson Davis and Alexander H. Stephens on the War Between the States, McGuffey's *New Sixth Reader* and a stray copy of the *Cincinnati Enquirer* for June 24, 1887.

The son-in-law, Bramble, carried on the firm and the old way of life after the founder's death. He too was not unhonored when he had joined the ghostly company of those who have passed this way and gone to their long home. For when the new Baptist Church was built in Cynthiana, Bramble's widow donated a pipe organ with a plate attached to it which honored "the Glory of God" and the memory of Bramble.

When the contents of Monticello were dispersed at an auction sale, down to the last bon bon dish, etched shot glass and hand-painted hair receiver, the collection was found to include one quite odd item, an A. B. Dick Co. mimeograph machine with paper feeder. This obviously calls for explanation. During a number of years after Mrs. Bramble's death, the old residence built on a whiskey fortune had been occupied by a hell-fire evangelist. His was the whirring mimeograph machine which rolled out alarms and tocsins—"Liquor people getting strangle hold on national and state government," the Methodist publicist, a minor league Billy Sunday, shouted, "For Heaven's sake . . . wake up!" The bourbon aristocrats had enjoyed their brief hour upon the stage. The curtain fell and rose again to reveal the Coming

Man—a Prohibitionist.

The first attempt to apply the methods of mass production to the manufacture of whiskey was a dismal failure. A group of New England promoters, incorporated under the name of the Hope Distilling Company, in 1816 put up a mammoth steam-powered factory on the then edge of Louisville, with advanced materials-handling machinery, power-driven rakes to stir the slurry, stills weighing ten tons and brought over in sections from England. The theoretical put-through was 1200 gallons a day and five thousand hogs were fed upon the stillage. With Louisville a leading whiskey market and the popularity of the beverage rising, the enterprise should have prospered; but it didn't. It failed because of business politics, unfaithful agents, shortage of working capital, destructive litigation. The little log stillhouses which mashed in small tubs and distilled over open fires made better whiskey than did the monster. At least the folks who drank the whiskey thought so.

The term "distiller" was applied equally to the owner of a still or to the man who was in charge of operations. Often the owner and master distiller were the same man. The occupation was not a learned profession. One Bourbon County distiller wrote how as a young man he "set in with a gentleman by the name of Jas. Hutchinson in the distillery business, which I had learned from my father and was Complete master of. I averaged him three gallons of whiskey to the Bushel of grain that he furnished me the first season, which pleased him so that he Enlarged his Distillery. . . ." One of the best master distillers could neither read nor write. He didn't know an ester from an aldehyde. He had, however, an uncanny sense of just when to draw the beer off. He knew grain, and could produce his own yeast. He kept to his standards by taste and smell and could confidently ask a buyer to rub a few drops between his hands, gently inhale and catch the redolence of apples, a sound test for a sound bourbon.

The judgment of some of the old taste-testers bordered upon the miraculous. They have been known to name the county, the exact valley, the creek bottom, in which an aromatic bourbon was made. What they knew came not out of books but out of bottles. Such a man was important in establishing values. Musty grain, for example, could be detected only by the human palate. William S. ("Bill") Barnes could take a sip and tell who made a whiskey and how old it was. "Pat" Lanphear had so keen a whiskey sense that when a dealer once asked him what was wrong about a barrel that had gone "musty," and a laboratory chemist couldn't tell him, Lanphear sniffed, tasted and announced:

"Only thing the matter with this whiskey is that it has undoubtedly been under water."

Investigation confirmed that the barrel had been stored in a basement that had flooded.

As a tour de force, George G. Benz once tasted seven different whiskey samples of different ages and mashes from seven different distilleries. All were unlabeled. Benz called off without an error the names of the distilleries which made each sample. He stated further whether it was sour or sweet mash in each instance, and evaluated the quality of the whiskey.

Perhaps the most remarkable man to enter the whiskey industry during the post-Civil War years was Colonel Edmund Haynes Taylor, Jr., who was born in Columbia, Kentucky, in 1832. He was a grand nephew of General Zachary Taylor whose aide told the Mexicans at a ticklish moment "General Taylor Never Surrenders," a declaration which was molded into many a whiskey flask and did the old General no harm in his successful campaign to become President of the United States.

Colonel Taylor was a man of education and cultivation, plus all the Taylor grit and stubbornness. He represented a sharp break with the tradition of distilling as a simple manufacturing operation. Taylor had the instincts of the merchandiser. To modern eyes he would have looked quaint enough, sitting at his roll-top desk clad in formal striped trousers, wearing a high silk hat and disposable white lawn string ties. Taylor was actually an early example of the professional executive. He was able to project himself into all phases of business—production, finance, sales promotion and, beyond that, to render important services to the industry.

Taylor placed the emphasis upon "pure goods" and made his Old Taylor, Hermitage, O.F.C. (the initials for Old Fire Copper) and Carlisle brands a standard of bourbon quality, his barrels commanding about twenty cents more on the gallon than other whiskeys. And every tumblerful of the Old Sinner which emerged from the Taylor warehouses had a beautiful bouquet about its person and was sold long before it was released. The Colonel had a firm hold on the concept of the uniform product and the consumer package, and labored long and fruitfully for the passage of the Bottled-in-Bond Act which would compel the seller to state on the label what was in the bottle.

Until the late 1890's, a distiller's brand might be six-year-old whiskey in one locality and three-year-old goods in another, both bearing the same label. A cafe-owner or barkeep could purchase a barrel of the best bourbon and do with it as he pleased. Once the proof gallon tax was paid and the barrel withdrawn from the warehouse, the supervision of the whiskey by the federal government ceased. After hard lessons learned in the panic of 1893, after much debate, a bottled-in-bond bill backed by, among others, Taylor and John G. Carlisle, fiscal expert and Secretary of the Treasury, passed Congress. President Cleveland, in the last hours of his second term, signed the bill into law.

Colonel Taylor, who lived to be ninety years old, was a bridge between the old ways and the new. He had known Dr. James C. Crow, Oscar Pepper, Judge William B. and John H. McBrayer and W. F. Bond. He remembered the uneven gravities, the unreliable temperatures and attenuations. (*Attenuation:* reduction in density, a thinning which occurs in the distiller's beer as fermentation advances.) Taylor discarded the uncleanly wooden beer still. His beer was a creamy liquid, rich in yeasting power. His fermentation was faultless. One can still hear the voice of this aristocratic Kentuckian down through the years as he raised it against "carelessly made whiskeys, whose aim is quantity and whose objective is"—what perfect nineteenth-century English!— "mere chaffering for cheapness."

Most whiskey plants of the last century looked something like a sawmill. For steam, there was a boiler house and a tall, thin, black smokestack. Such a frill as landscaped grounds was not thought of, except by Colonel Taylor. He thought of everything, including what inevitably we now call public relations. The Colonel built pergolas and pools. He had turrets, too. The Old Taylor Distillery on Glenn's Creek, near Frankfort, looked like a medieval castle with thick stone walls, arched windows, red slate roof, towers and crenelated battlements, stone bridges, a sundial and sunken rose garden. Over his spring, Taylor erected a spring-house with Roman columns, sheltering the water gushing from the birdseye limestone in what amounted to a shrine. This structure is still there and looks about the way it did in the Colonel's heyday.

Perhaps it was wildly romantic—or was it?—this setting of a Rhenish castle in the Kentucky landscape, surrounded by grounds groomed like a gentleman's estate. Tourists and picnickers gladly came to look at the water, sniff appreciatively the aroma from the distillery and accept complimentary "tenth pint" bottles of Old Taylor. They were not likely to forget the experience. And that satisfied Edmund H. Taylor, Jr.

During the 1870's the old pot still evolved into the three-chambered charge still which gave a semi-continuous process. A further step was the introduction of the continuous beer still, or stripping column, which was adapted from the "patent" still invented in 1831 in England by Aeneas Coffey. The small fermentors gave way to the large. There was more machinery and instrumentation. The crude malt made from corn was superseded by barley malt made by reliable maltsters which became a business in itself. Stillhouses were redesigned to accommodate the columnar still which rose to a height of four stories. More warehouses were constructed for holding larger inventories. The cattle sheds, where the stillage from one bushel of corn fed one head for one day, each animal chained to the trough, were extended; likewise the pigpens until, according to a reporter for the New York *World,* who toured the region in 1872, "for more than a mile before you reach one of these immense Bourbon County distilleries" the nose announces that pigs are present.

The investment which these developments required, and the rising burden of federal taxation, put those small distillers who were unwilling or unable to follow the trend in a difficult position. With an up-to-date plant costing more than a thousand-acre blue-grass farm, the distillers who worked in horse mills in the quiet hollows off the railroad had to discount the age of technology in some fashion. They fell back on a nostalgic theory of whiskey quality. The world, they said, was getting away from the sound values of the good old days and the "old-fashioned system" of making bourbon. So receptive was the drinking public to the theory that the smaller concerns were the real guardians of whiskey quality, that many distillers who were undercapitalized competed quite successfully by selling tradition as part of the product.

One colorful character, J. B. Thompson, proprietor of the Old Fort Spring Distillery at Harrodsburg, which made Old Jordan Bourbon, did an amusing switch on the usual story-line and burlesqued the clichés of whiskey promotion. He said he did not claim to make Old Jordan as the pioneers did, with no machinery, out of damp, moldy, rotted corn, using crude malt and stills that scorched the mash. Nor, he said, was the formula picked up in the Garden of Eden by Adam. It was not known to Rameses I, or graven on stone by the mound builders in curious pictographs. As a matter of prosaic fact, he bought the formula from a man named P. H. Jordan.

Thompson made no claim that he had inherited from his grandfather the knack of producing a superior sour mash whiskey. In fact, he continued, none of his ancestors was versed in the distilling art, though many "were rated as fairly good consumers." Daniel Boone, Simon Kenton, James Harrod and the other legendary heroes and Indian fighters of the Kentucky Valhalla died, Thompson admitted, without ever tasting a drop of his Old Jordan, "a sad and melancholy fact," he lamented, "which entitles them to the sympathy of all."

To finance rising costs and larger investments, the distillers had to borrow more and more money. This resulted in the development of a financial instrument peculiar to the liquor industry, the warehouse receipt. A warehouse receipt pledged as collateral specific barrels of whiskey in a government warehouse. The contents of each barrel, unlike most commodities, was constantly rising in value, according to age, the percentage of small grain used, the quality of the original distillation, the district of origin, and the demand for particular blocks of whiskey. Banks would loan up to eighty per cent on this type of paper which was readily negotiable. Thus the distiller got his money out of the distillate in his warehouses and could manufacture more whiskey. The receipts were generally regarded as a prime investment. Yet they were not completely without risk. Every once in a while it came like a clap of thunder along Whiskey Row in Louisville that some jobber or commission merchant had been loading the banks with forged receipts. This possibility of fraud is reflected in an old advertisement of Flexner Brothers, Louisville engravers and stationers, which offered for sale receipt forms which the firm stated could not be counterfeited.

As late as the 1930's there was an active market in warehouse receipts. For a brief, frenzied period after Repeal there was a mad scramble for this commercial paper on the part of unsophisticated buyers who wanted either a barrel of whiskey or a whiskey speculation. Boiler-room salesmen, recruited from the bond business, sold receipts to the general public for what turned out sometimes to be non-existent whiskey. It had "evaporated" in one sense of the word or another. The value of the receipts may also have been eaten up by unpaid warehouse charges. Or the whiskey may have been in the wood so long that it was senile. The salesmen did not mention the federal, state and local taxes involved, or the fact that after Repeal, under the Code of Fair Competition for the Distilled Spirits Industry, the buyer couldn't obtain actual ownership of the whiskey unless he held a permit to distill, rectify or bottle. In various states the attorney general's office also said no. They had prohibitory laws of their own and took the legal position that a warehouse receipt covering a specific barrel of whiskey was not a security but was to be construed as a sale of the whiskey itself. Any hopes entertained by a Missourian or an Iowan, for example, of acquiring a supply of bourbon through the purchase of a warehouse receipt at the time the United States was whiskey-poor, went glimmering as a result of these legal rulings.

Warehouse receipts still exist, but their importance has diminished as the power of the manufacturer has increased. Whiskey is a big business now, and a consumer-oriented business, like the food and tobacco industries. Today the large distilling companies are able to generate the financial strength they need through cash flow and bank loans made on statement.

The American philosophy that acquisition of tangible property is the ultimate purpose of life, under which a man works for his calling, rather than the reverse, was ameliorated among the whiskey families who entertained the hedonistic thought that it was important also to attend race meetings, enjoy the game of politics and sometimes sit and rock with a frosted glass in hand. They expected the market to seek their excellent whiskeys, although occasionally as a daring gesture to a new order in business management they sent a sample to one of the great national expositions. Judge McBrayer took the highest award at the Philadelphia Centennial with his Cedarbrook, and the Old Times distillery people sent their fine table whiskey to the World's Columbian Exposition in Chicago in 1893. In fact, they operated a small still in a log cabin right at the fairgrounds, next to the cliff dwellers' exhibit.

As the ribbon of time unrolled, the orders of society in the land of bourbon seemed fixed and secure in their privileges, duties and emoluments. There were problems of a temporary sort, of course, such as William Jennings Bryan and the silver question; and alert George Garvin Brown, successful distiller and devout Christian gentleman, understood more clearly than did most of his confreres in the industry just what it meant when the Woman's Christian Temperance Union entered Kentucky as a branch of the Women's Missionary Union. Temperance was once more on the march, pitting against the wealth and political influence of the whiskey interests the combined power of the women, the Protestant churches and the little girl so indoctrinated by her anti-alcohol schoolbooks that she could not look at a glorious sunset without reflecting that it was the same color as her papa's stomach after he took his highball.

Dr. Eliphalet Nott, noted temperance orator and president of Union College, had looked into the use of alcoholic beverages recorded in the Bible and become convinced that the wine served at Cana was unfermented. George Garvin Brown, equally sincere in his Presbyterianism, reached an opposite conclusion, and produced a tract of his own, fighting fire with fire. In *The Holy Bible Repudiates "Prohibition,"* (1910), Brown collected and published at his own expense all the verses from Genesis to Revelation containing the words "wine" or "strong drink," with interpretive comment emphasizing the thought that the Christian revelation includes the temperate use of alcoholic beverages.

"I have been a whisky merchant and manufacturer for forty years and believe now, as I always have believed," Brown declared, "that there is no more moral turpitude in manufacturing and selling an intoxicating liquor than there is in manufacturing and selling any other product, of course realizing that man is responsible to God for his every act and that the conditions surrounding every individual act must be taken into consideration in determining whether it be right or wrong. This applies to every business and condition in life."

Less prescient than Brown, most distillers failed to read their future, secure in the belief that there were some things that were permanent in this changing world—good land, good family, the Democratic Party, White Supremacy and Old Line Sour Mash whiskey. Surely, for a time, the path of a bourbon baron lay in pleasant places, with his Southdown sheep and blooded cattle scattered over his broad acres, the smoke rising above the trees around his stillhouse, the modest cottages clustered beside the warehouse, visible evidences from the castle set on a hill that all was for the best in this best of all possible worlds.

Chapter 9

DRINKING DOWN
THE NATIONAL DEBT

UNDER the Constitution of the United States, Congress has power to levy every kind of tax, direct and indirect, at a specific rate or ad valorem; that is, in proportion to value. The only limitation placed upon this taxing power is that direct taxes shall be uniform throughout the United States, and that they shall be apportioned among the states. In practice, the national government obtained its revenues before the Civil War chiefly from customs duties levied upon foreign commodities rather than from internal imposts. From the time when President Jefferson's administration repealed the taxes which had provoked the Whisky Rebellion, with the exception of four years, from 1813 to 1817, spirits in the United States were free of any federal excise tax until 1862. Even the intemperate poor could drink the fiery domestic distillate which was often sold as "brandy" but was actually cheap whiskey.

During the many years when the federal government relied chiefly on import duties for revenue, the manufacture and sale of American liquors was under the control of the states. The national government was concerned with alcoholic beverages only in these ways—collecting the customs duties on foreign importations, the regulation of the whiskey business in the District of Columbia, in western territories not yet admitted to the Union, in the army and navy and in the trade with the Indians. We have already glanced at how the War of the Rebellion drew liquor into the fiscal history of the United States. Despite the deep feeling against taxes on consumption, Congress found it necessary to pass an internal revenue act "to support the Government and to pay interest on public debt." This law became effective July 1, 1862. After that, for time out of mind, Kentucky representatives and senators, Ohioans from the great whiskey center of Cincinnati, legislators whose constituents included the important distilling interests located in Peoria and Pekin, Illinois, tilted against the dry members from Iowa and Michigan. Their divergent views on the proper place in American society of the juices flowing from the alcohol still have been spread over hundreds of closely printed pages of the *Congressional Globe* and its successor, the *Congressional Record,* while the public printer turned out a stream of special committee reports, House documents and records of Senate hearings.

Since the time of Charles I, liquor has been regarded by legislators as an eminently suitable source of revenue. It is a luxury. It does not figure to any great extent as a raw material needed in the manufacture of other products. It is widely used for social purposes. The demand is inelastic; that is, strong and steady. It caters to an habitual taste. Yet it is not necessary to health or efficiency. When the American government was forced to look for new ways to raise money, the tax on drinkable alcohol gave every promise of producing the money. And such a tax fitted in neatly with the wise counsel voiced by Colbert, the celebrated finance minister of Louis XIV, who is reported to have said "the act of taxation consists in so plucking the goose [i.e., the people] as to procure the largest quantity of feathers with the least possible amount of squealing."

At first the tax was fixed at twenty cents a proof gallon. That meant a gallon of 100-proof spirits as defined in the United States —231 cubic inches of alcoholic beverage at sixty degrees Fahrenheit. The law was repeatedly amended and altered by Congress from that time down to the death of the legal liquor industry in 1920. The uncertainties of legislative action gave the whiskey business a highly speculative character. The first impost was followed by two quick jumps in 1864, going to sixty cents and later to a dollar and a half. On January 1, 1865, the rate rose further to two dollars per gallon. The tax now equaled an advance of 1000% on the cost of manufacture, an open invitation to illegal distillation. At the same time the lawful distiller became a kind of conduit for the collection of the tax, finding himself in the extraordinary position of dealing more in taxes than in liquor.

Congress created a "bonded period" in 1868 which permitted a delay of one year in the payment of the excise tax. This was granted as an indulgence so that the producers might have a reasonable time to find a purchaser before being compelled to tax-pay their whiskey. This period was extended to three years in 1879, to eight years in 1894 and the tax force-out was raised to twenty years in 1958. As one tax increase followed another, there was a drop in demand for foreign liquors which had to pass the U.S. frontiers. About 1885 corn, a cheaper grain of greater alcoholic yield, displaced rye and bourbon became clearly the national favorite among what are now defined as straight whiskeys.

As the taxes were increased, Congress refused time after time to make the increases retroactive. That is to say, they did not include existing stocks. Thus the whiskey already in existence and taxed at a lower rate automatically advanced in price by at least the amount of the tax increase. Before the new charges took effect, the distilleries operated at capacity to build up heavy inventories. Even new plants were rushed to completion so as to catch the rise, then closed down when the market for whiskey reached the new level and stabilized. Editors, bankers, clergymen, legislators and canny citizens generally purchased blocks of whiskeys at about eighteen cents a gallon on which they realized fortunes. During one speculative spree the industry distilled and stored at least forty million gallons, equal to a year's supply for the whole United States.

Solid information relating to fortunes made out of information leaked from the committees of Congress is understandably scanty. Stories and rumors floated around about various prominent personalities of the day who benefited from knowing what was going to happen. Much of "Tom" Megibben's wealth was acquired during this speculative era. He owned several warehouses filled with mature whiskey on which the tax had already been paid. The windfall made him a millionaire and paid for his estate, Monticello.

Up to 1894, Congress virtually legislated for the benefit of the holders of whiskey stocks rather than the United States Treasury. In that year for the first time, an increase in the rates was applied to whiskey already in the warehouses. Although the federal excise helped to dry out the heavy drinker because of the increased cost of alcohol as a propellant, the temperance forces were displeased because the revenue law gave liquor a new standing. The United States was now a partner in the business. Horace Greeley, Henry Ward Beecher, Wendell Phillips, Gough, the sensational temperance lecturer, and Neal Dow, father of the "Maine Law," the first state prohibition law, all called on President Lincoln to register their protest against taxing drinking alcohol. But within a few years a quarter of the federal government's revenue was coming from beverage alcohol, rising to more than fifty per cent of the total income between 1876 and 1909. The law had many side effects. It drew the liquor interests closer together, hastened the centralization of distilling, put the manufacture and distribution of liquor into national politics. Experience in the United States and in other countries has shown that taxation is a powerful instrument for the control of liquor consumption. Taxes can reduce the total. They can shift consumption from one economic class to another. They can rearrange the patterns of usage. The alcohol tax is the prime instance in the modern state of the regulation by law of personal habits which are adjudged to be good or bad according to the consensus of the community. The whiskey trade has had many occasions for meditating on Chief Justice John Marshall's famous dictum in *McCulloch v. Maryland,* "the power to tax involves the power to destroy."

When the United States took charge of the manufacture of all alcoholic drinkables, there came into being an army of officials, inspectors, gaugers, government aides called "storekeepers," guards and intricate regulations as to the seals, stencil plates (after 1868, the still-familiar stamps), locks and keys of distillery buildings and mountains of paper work. The gauger measured out the amount of grain for distilling, saw that the composition of the mash was strictly adhered to. A government man was on hand when the whiskey barrel was filled and burned the history of the distillate into the barrel head on what was called the stamp or "government end." When a barrel of aged whiskey was withdrawn from the warehouse, the gauger applied a "wantage rod" for determining the ullage—the empty portion of the cask, due to evaporation and absorption. The storekeeper was under strict orders to admit no one to the warehouse, not even the owner, except in his presence. And, says an old gauger's manual, in substance—don't give the key to anyone!

Recognizing the problem of illegal distilling, Congress dropped the tax from two dollars a gallon to fifty cents in 1868, the year of the first bonding act. At this time, also, the barrel stamp was devised as an improved technique of tax collection. Whiskeys were known as "one stamp" or "two stamp" goods. One stamp simply stated the date the tax was paid. Whiskey so marked usually went to a rectifier for blending. When two stamps were affixed to a package, information was added as to who made the whiskey and when. This whiskey moved directly from warehouse to retailer. There were severe penalties, so long as the revenue agents were in charge of it, for tampering with stamped whiskey.

A test case which occurred in the '80's showed that the consumer did not get much of a shake in those days. Internal revenue agents seized three barrels of whiskey at the *estaminet* conducted by Pat Mallon on Avenue D in New York City. A violation of the revenue laws was claimed because Pat's barrels were partly filled with water. So the contents did not conform to what the stamps called for. It was conceded that the packages had been properly tax-paid and correctly stamped. In view of that, the judge ruled, no injury to the U.S. government had resulted when the saloonist cheated his patrons with watered grog. Mallon won the decision.

The postponement of the tax under the bonding law stimulated the aging of whiskey and so produced a better product. Meanwhile, the U.S. Treasury was sitting pretty. It had physical possession of the whiskey. It also had a first lien on the distillery, the warehouses and could if necessary levy on the distiller's private estate. Another way to postpone taxes was to ship American whiskey to Europe under an "Export law" and bring it back when the market conditions were more favorable. The whiskey remained in bond during its Grand Tour and paid no import duties when it returned home. The liquor benefited from the ride and there was a gain in proof of from two to five per cent. William Foerster

& Company, for instance, advertised to the trade in 1894: "Superior whiskey storage in Hamburg, Germany," with "Small outs owing to good care."

"Outs" or "outage" refer to evaporation, leakage and soakage into the staves. In eight years the shrinkage amounts to about thirty-six per cent, leaving approximately thirty-two gallons of liquor in a barrel with a rated capacity of forty-nine wine gallons. Individual barrels vary somewhat in this respect. This is a general standard. In 1880, Congress excused the industry from paying taxes on liquor which had disappeared. This was known as the "Carlisle allowance" because of the effective championship of the bill by the then Representative, later Senator and finally Secretary of the Treasury, John G. Carlisle, of Kentucky, a hard money man and a good judge of bourbon whiskey.

A story has been handed down that Carlisle, known to be a poor card player, was engaged at the noble game of poker with President Grover Cleveland, Senator Don Cameron of Pennsylvania, and Henry Watterson of Kentucky. Carlisle drew four cards. At the showdown he held four kings.

"Take the money, Carlisle, take the money," exclaimed the President. "If ever I am President again you shall be Secretary of the Treasury. But don't you make that four-card draw too often."

Cleveland was President again and Carlisle was appointed Secretary of the Treasury.

The debate over the Carlisle outage bill produced some lighter moments, including quotation of the line penned on the excise by the English poet, William Cowper, who wrote of his country, "Her cause demands the assistance of your throats." A snide theory was advanced on the Republican side of the House that whiskey was the "natural beverage" of the Democratic party. To this canard, Hiram Casey Young, of Tennessee, a proponent of the shrinkage clause, and one who thought the sour mash distillers should pay only upon what the barrel gauged at the time of withdrawal, responded in this vein:

"Forming my opinion from frequent declarations of my Republican friends, I had concluded, before the commencement of the discussion which has been had upon this bill, that the subject of whiskey was peculiarly under the charge of the Democratic party.

. . . But it must be admitted, I think, that Republican gentlemen have in the discussion evinced an acquaintance with the subject so thorough and intimate that it could hardly have been acquired otherwise than by the closest relations and most frequent contact."

To this the staid *Congressional Record* adds the stage direction, "Laughter and Applause." But Omar Dwight Conger, a Michigan Republican, rose to insist that any familiarity he had with whiskey was due to the many years he had spent in close contact with Democrats. "If I have not been able to feel their influence," he said, "I have certainly smelt their breath."

Benton McMillin of Tennessee got in a thrust by remarking that if the whiskey tax was, as some Republicans had said, a contribution, since no citizen was required to drink whiskey, perhaps in the future when a man wished to treat a friend, he should invite his companion to have a drink by asking him if he cared to "make a voluntary contribution to the support of his government."

The distillers of sour mash suffered in the financial panics of 1870 and 1893. Sentiment developed for marketing whiskey in bottles which would be corked, sealed, sold under proprietary names, with a guarantee of integrity from the United States government. The Committee on the Judiciary of the House of Representatives investigated the whiskey market, recommended legislation to protect the public against counterfeiting and adulteration and Congress passed a bottled-in-bond bill. Its signature into law by President Cleveland in 1897 has already been noted. Chapin & Gore, a Chicago firm handling Kentucky whiskeys, quickly cased in glass some four thousand barrels of Old Hermitage Bourbon which they had exported and reshipped back to this country. Old Hermitage thus became the first American bottled-in-bond whiskey. Secretary Carlisle's features are, or should be, familiar to all who appreciate bonded whiskeys, for an engraved portrait showing Carlisle in three-quarters face has appeared on the green strip stamp which overlays the cork or cap on all bottled-in-bond whiskeys released since 1897.

The strip stamp over the top of the bottle stated, and still does, the year and season of distillation and of bottling, the proof and the age, which must be at least four years. The presence of the stamp is evidence that the liquor is the product of one distillery and one season, that the whiskey has been continuously under the

supervision of the government and that the package is full measure. The stamp constitutes a guarantee that the whiskey was bottled at 100 proof and that nothing has been added after distillation except water. The presence of the stamp is not an indication
of the grade of grain used, or the strain of the yeast, the cleanliness of the plant or the skill of the distiller. Yet the green stamp
has always enjoyed a popular reputation as the sign of whiskey
quality.

After receding to a low point in 1868, the federal tax on liquor
gradually rose to $1.10 and stayed at that figure until 1917, when
it began to soar. The taxing power gave the industry new con-
figurations, because the government could not economically patrol
the farmer-distiller who mashed only a few bushels in a day. The
consumer who could not afford tax-paid bourbon turned to "green"
blockade whiskey. The hillmen of Dixie had always manufactured
a native fluid from their corn patch. But now inquisitive snoopers
prowled the hills "to spoil the sport," Henry Watterson wrote,
"and dull the edge of patriotic husbandry."

For the sometimes melodramatic story of tax-free "moon,"
often marked by the crack of a rifle and a splash of blood on the
ferns, turn, if you will, to the chapter which follows.

Chapter 10

MOONSHINE
AND HONEYSUCKLE

EVERY so often for a generation after the end of the Civil War a fellow who lived back on the ridge would come into town to liquor up and enjoy county court day or to renew his mortgage. And he would hear about how there was some kind of new federal law against "makin' " under which some of the boys had been "penitentiaried." This was hard to swallow especially, as was often the case, when the blockader had fought to preserve the U.S. government, which now said that he could turn his corn into hogs but not the white mule which his neighbors needed for their stomach trouble.

Among unreconstructed rebels a legalistic argument was widely approved which asserted that there really hadn't been any general government since the South withdrew from the Union. They recognized only the authority of county and state. The real motivation lay, of course, in the fact that there was easy money to be made in running an illicit distillery. Community opinion was divided upon the subject of making and drinking moonshine whiskey. In the gradations of sin as it was measured among the foot-washing Baptists, there were worse offenses than "stillin' and drinkin' "; such as not observing the Sabbath.

"Them boys," a woman in Aurora, Missouri, said indignantly,

"was a-sellin' *field whiskey* right on Main Street, an' it a Sunday!"

A member of Congress from Memphis, Tennessee, in discussing in the House the proper method of apportioning the liquor tax, admonished a colleague from an East Tennessee district who opposed the tax:

"But does not my friend know . . . that there is less tax paid and more whisky drank in his district to the square mile than in any other similar-sized territory in the United States (Laughter). . . . Now, I dislike to tell it, but I believe it is susceptible of proof that a large majority of my colleague's constituents have not allowed an hour of daylight to pass since they were three years old without testing the quality of some character of exhilarating liquid, and that they never had a drink of good whisky except when they came to Memphis to be tried for violation of the revenue law or upon some other business. (Laughter)."

In an economy where crops were often measured not in bushels but in gallons, the whiskey tax disturbed an ancient way of life. Along the hog-back ridges that fan out south of the Cumberland River, near the Kentucky-Tennessee line, where the original settlers were free Negroes, with some admixture of white and Indian blood, the children played, not cops and robbers, but moonshiners and revenuers. They learned by doing—to carry water or stir the hot mash. And at eventide they joined their elders in a dipper of homemade mountain dew. A teacher in a one-room frame schoolhouse in Cumberland County, in addressing his scholars at the end of the day, was once heard to say:

"Now, chillun, tomorrer we is goin' to take up mixin' in the mash."

The term moonshiner referred to a person, usually but not necessarily operating in the southern states, who manufactured spirits, probably from grain, but possibly from sugar, by moonlight—secretly—to evade the excise tax. The profit opportunity related directly to the amount of the tax. The moonshiner learned to think more kindly of the federal tax on spirits as he observed that it was in practice a subsidy of his business by the government in Washington. The "free" 'stiller's operating costs were low. He used crude, inexpensive equipment and the cheapest materials.

The processes were essentially the same as those employed by the legitimate industry. There were, of course, no refined techniques of quality control and no interest in by-product recovery. The moonshiner prepared his coarse meal or chicken middlings in an open barrel. Sugar was added to hurry up the fermentation, for speed was essential to the illegal distiller. Except for a touch of malt, the grain base was all corn; no rye was used. After the low wines were doubled, the high wines were run through a blanket, a charcoal filter or an old felt hat to knock off some of the rough edges. Bottling was a hand process. The local baldface went into fruit jars, five-gallon tins or old soft drink bottles from which was derived a popular name for woods whiskey—Soda Pop Moon. The distiller was not overly concerned about cutting out the heads and tails and he was in no position to age his product. His was strictly a jug business, his premises cluttered with filth and the indescribable litter which traditionally accompanies the manufacture of illegal whiskey.

Usually the moonshiner possessed just one still. After the mash was singled, he ran the low wines through the same still for doubling. The stills sometimes had pet names. A big one, standing shoulder-high, is displayed in the Museum of the Kentucky Historical Society, and bears the affectionate nickname "Old Yellow." It was operated in 1896 in Estill County, Kentucky. The Filson Club in Louisville displays a still which was captured in Perry County while in place over the furnace, and smoking hot. Sometimes, in their brushes with the law, the woods distillers worked a wily game on Uncle Sam. When an old still and worm were about burned out, if the equipment was operated by a group or community of perhaps twenty neighbors, one of the partners would let himself be captured in the act of making a run, the other nineteen appearing as willing witnesses against him. The moonshiner would be put away for six months or a year. The witness fees and mileage to the nearest United States district court would purchase a new apparatus—at public expense. The prisoner had better room and board than he knew at home and returned to the bosom of his family healthy, well-rested and ready to resume his career.

The stillhouse could be merely a crude arbor of brush. Or it was sometimes built solidly of logs, with one door, no windows, and chinked or daubed with clay to keep out the weather. In a corner stood a rough bedstead with several quilts and blankets for the use of the man who slept at the still when a run was made. There was also a skillet and coffeepot, an axe for cutting firewood, a rifle in the corner to discourage unwanted visitors, and a little jug of panther sweat to keep off the seed ticks. Corn liquor was regarded as a specific for the bloodsucking, mite-like insects, according to a doctor who practiced in the Ozark region of Missouri. "It ain't safe for a teetotaler to walk through the timber," he declared. If there was nothing to drink near the still but branch water, the mountaineer followed it with a draught of his moon which had a reputation as an antiseptic—"it kills the bugs."

The real character of illegal corn whiskey may be appraised from a caution issued by Irvin S. Cobb, the Paducah *Schriftsteller* and connoisseur of genuine bourbon. Cobb warned his reader not to drink moonshine while standing on rocky ground because he might get cut and bruised when he fell down. The usual practice was to shake up the bottle before taking a belt. This distributed the fusel oil and aldehydes evenly throughout the liquid and the sight of the bead on the distillate gave a man confidence to take a chance. But the effects of wildcat corn have produced a whole cycle of folk tales.

A stranger, gazing at a fifty-foot streak cut through the woods up hill and down, looking as though the landscape had been shaved, asked a loafer near a 'shiner's cabin what it was. It was, of course, the right of way for a power company transmission line. But the native assured him solemnly, "One of them big fellows from Arkansas took a drink of Tom's whiskey here, an' that's where he tore down the brush, a-runnin' to the creek for water!"

Royal E. Cabell, Commissioner of Internal Revenue back in the 'teens, told a true story about a kind of liquor described as "squirrel whiskey."

"What kind of liquor are you selling, Mose?" the judge asked an old Negro who was up before him on a bootlegging charge.

"Judge, I am selling squirrel liquor."

"What kind of whiskey is that?"

"Well, Judge, that is the kind of licker old man Jones makes up the holler at his still, and when a rabbit get three drops of it he will sit up on his hind legs and spit my hound puppy in the face."

"That is pretty powerful liquor, Mose; but why do you call it squirrel whiskey?"

"If you go out on a cool morning and take your gun and sit down under a hickory tree and wait for a squirrel, and you take along your tickler of that licker and take three or four drinks and presently, when you see a squirrel up on a limb, you forget all about the gun and clam up the tree and catch that squirrel yourself."

In 1894, Kentucky had 584 registered legal distilleries, of which 433 were then in operation, making mostly sour mash bourbon, although there was a small production of fruit brandies and some rye, gin and cologne spirits. There is no way of knowing how many wildcat stills were turning out "Yack Yack Bourbon." But in this same year, 499 suits were commenced or pending in Kentucky for violation of the internal revenue laws, and it was estimated that the revenue agents were seizing hardly a tenth of the moonshine stills which were pouring out untaxed raw spirits. For the country as a whole about eight thousand persons were arrested in one year, 1881, for being connected with frauds upon the revenue.

This is a reminder that whiskey produced without the blessing of the United States government was not a phenomenon peculiar to Kentucky. In the days when the Reverend Sam P. Jones, the great evangelist and reformed drunkard, was lambasting alcohol in Alabama and Georgia, the native stills of the Piedmont were turning chopped corn into a fiery spirit which added to the variety of life back in the mountain coves. In faraway Alaska the people of Sitka, restive under a territorial prohibition law, were consuming a hundred barrels of molasses a month, not all of it for pouring on flapjacks. In West Virginia, the Carolinas, Arkansas, and even in the fastnesses of Brooklyn, New York, there was a clandestine liquor industry. Manhattan had its cellar workers, too, and the whiskey made in the remote areas of Long Island was transported to New York in milk cans and sold as the product of Kentucky. In ice cream parlors the password was "sarsaparilla," the cost, a dime.

Most businesses have tax problems. The moonshiners were happily free of these. But they had others. Their chief concerns were how to avoid the officers of the law and how to distribute the product flowing from their stills. With their taste for seclusion, moonshiners did not generally favor internal improvements like graveled roads or turnpikes. There was usually a path which they used to travel to work, although the Roper boys of Van Buren County, in Arkansas, slid down to the job on a grapevine. Arrangements for service were well understood locally. At a point one or two hundred yards from the stillhouse, a sign was posted on a tree to the effect that anyone who required a jug of arbor whiskey should stop at that point, holler three times, place his money and container at the root of a designated tree, and retire for a few minutes of reflection. When he returned the money was gone, the bottle was full and the buyer could swear with good conscience that he did not know who produced his relaxer.

The highland people were temperate. They tapped the jug regularly; but they knew when to stop. The story is told of a man in Knott County, Kentucky, who turned off a whole quart of moon before putting aside the tin cup.

"Won't you have some more?" he was asked.

"Nope," he answered. "It might fly to my head."

Distribution arrangements included peddling from a wagon. A man in butternut clothes was driving a team of mules hitched to a canvas-covered wagon filled with corn fodder. On a road in North Carolina he encountered three U.S. marshals.

"Howdy, neighbor."

"Howdy, gentlemen," said the driver courteously, touching his hat. "Powerful fine weather we'uns are hevin'!"

"Yes," agreed a marshal, who carried a Winchester rifle slung over his shoulder. "Can you tell me where we can get some whiskey? We are strangers in this section, and dry as a herring."

"Gentlemen," said the wagoner earnestly, "whiskey is mitey hard to git. Thar's so menny uv these hyar dep'ty marshals 'round that we'uns are 'fraid to tech the pesky stuff. . . . I hev got a leetle moonshine hyar, and I run a pow'ful risk in conveyin's hit; but hit's only a few gallon that I use for my stomach's sake. . . . I'll let you hev a little."

The artless confession threw the officers off the scent. They filled their flasks, for which the man would take no money, and he continued on toward Asheville with five barrels of illegal distillate under the cornstalks.

Before World War I, most moonshine whiskey did not travel far. But country stills did supply nearby towns. If a traveling salesman were to say in the hearing of a hotel bell captain, "Oh Lord, my God, ain't there no help for the widow's son . . . ?" he was likely to receive a jug labeled vinegar and maybe an assurance from the sheriff himself that it was the real stuff. Vance Randolph tells of one such drummer who got a quart of good corn, hollered happily for ice water "and before sundown he says everybody in town is Nature's noblemen and Polk County is the garden spot of all creation."

Another man in a similar fix was instructed to go out on the street where he would find a Negro standing on a corner with a shoebox under his arm. He approached the lounger and asked:

"Do you know how I could get a quart of whiskey?"

"Boss, I reckon I could rustle up a quart for two dollars. But you will have to have enough confidence in me to give me the money first."

The stranger handed over the bills and the Negro said, "You just hold my shoes a minit and I'll be right back."

So the thirsty visitor stood and he stood until he decided that his faith in mankind had been misplaced again. Finally, he looked in the box. There was his whiskey.

National Prohibition made the manufacture and distribution of crooked liquor into a giant industry. The rustic with his little pot still was succeeded by the syndicate "alky cooker" of Chicago, Detroit and other urban centers. The wagon peddler gave way to the long-distance trucker. The speakeasy took over the functions of the "blind tiger." The operations of the gangsters of the Prohibition era were brought under effective control by 1937 through the re-establishment of the legal distilling industry and the maintenance of taxes at a low level, two dollars per gallon for the federal excise and about sixty-six cents, on the average, for the state levies. New techniques of enforcement placed a close check on the flow of materials used in the manufacture of spirits, such as sugar, molasses and corn meal. Increases in taxes during

This large pot still, standing as high as a man's shoulder, was captured from a moonshiner. It is now in the museum of the Kentucky Historical Society, Frankfort.

Dashing General Orville E. Babcock, who was indicted for his activities in guiding the "Whiskey Ring."

World War II were not followed, as usual, by an increase in bootlegging because the racketeers were hampered by wartime shortages of sugar, copper tubing, sheet metal and automobile radiators which, placed in cold, running water, were often used to condense the alcoholic vapors.

When a "temporary" tax boost to an historic high of $10.50 per gallon was adopted in 1951, and sugar and copper were already decontrolled, the mobsters swung back into production. The illegal sector of the liquor industry found it possible to absorb the costs of equipment seizures and heavy fines and still manufacture, in the decade ending in 1960, almost one fifth of all the distilled spirits consumed in the United States. Today, the greater part of this production originates in the southern areas where cooking corn grits is deeply ingrained in the habits of the people. Here economic necessity presses hard upon low income groups. Here public opinion tolerates the practice celebrated in an old song which should be sung with scoops and slides in the mountain style:

> I'll go to some holler
> I'll put up my still
> I'll make you one gallon for a two dollar bill.

An ingenious wrinkle in the bourbon-producing section is called "barrel dogging." This procedure involves "sweating" bourbon out of tightly closed barrels by steaming the barrel. After three or four hours of heating, the whiskey is tapped out and filtered to remove particles of the char and any foreign matter. The proof is often quite high, the color likewise, and the whiskey is good. No equipment is needed except some jugs, firewood, an old felt hat for the filter process and a location where smoke drifting above the treetops will quickly be absorbed into the atmosphere. The yield is from a pint to a gallon of very dark, genuine bourbon. There is little risk of arrest because it takes only an hour or so of illicit labor—just when the whiskey is being tapped, strained and bottled. All other acts such as hauling barrels or building a fire are perfectly legal.

Determined moonshiners in the old days could often stand off a small army. But more often than not the woods distiller put his faith in mobility and his ability to do a mile in four minutes over rough terrain. The arrival of federal men in the vicinity was announced by the cry, "Fi-i-i-ire in the hole!" the traditional warning of the moonshiner. Or perhaps there came the hoot of an owl, the crowing of a rooster. Even the little children knew how to sound the signal horn that could be heard for miles; and they early understood its importance. Quickly the fires were banked. The mash was abandoned; the still toted up the creek and hidden in a fence corner under the wild pea vines. Thus, when the posse arrived there was nothing to see and nothing to hear except the murmur of the stream as it sped past the boulders and debouched into wimpling pools.

All strangers were assumed to be with the "revenue," which often put a lumber buyer, mule dealer or folklorist collecting ballads in a situation of potential danger. The officers were skillful at assuming disguises. One would traverse an "infected area" as a peddler of Yankee notions. Another posed as a canvasser selling a repair item called "iron cement." Some purported to be tinkers and fixed teakettles. The revenue men were interested in local gossip, smoke and a characteristic smell which their educated noses could identify instantly. And they watched the stock. Horses loathe the smell of a distillery, but cattle and hogs are passionately fond of still slop. Many a free 'stiller has been betrayed by his own livestock snuffling around the building where the still was concealed.

The moonshiner has usually been treated romantically in literature. Those who know the species scoff at this idea. "The confirmed moonshiner is incurable," asserts Lawrence S. Thompson. The wildcatter may have learned how to weave chair bottoms during several sojourns at the state penitentiary, "but he always goes back to the worm and the mash-rake."

Especially notorious around the turn of the century was the Gibson family which followed its ancient calling in Jackson and Clay counties in Kentucky. There was, first, Harrison Gibson. He had five sons, Jack, Brownlow, Hanney, Fleming and Henry. And sometimes Joe Stamper and William Madden, who had married two of the Gibson daughters, were housed in the same cell block as the old gentleman. Mesdames Stamper and Madden were equally as skilled in the art of "doublin' " as their husbands. Harrison Gibson estimated that the Gibsons, in the years they had moonshined it together, had made not less than 50,000 gallons of corn liquor. Their whiskey factory had enabled them to live comfortably and they had accumulated a tribal competence of between $40,000 and $50,000 in cash. In a reminiscent mood one day at the county jail, Harrison Gibson remarked:

"Yaas, I think I am the real king of the Kentucky 'shiners. I am nigh on to sixty years old, and I have been making the stuff ever since I was a boy thirteen years old. I have made enough of it to float that battleship that blowed up. . . .

"Now, I brought them boys up," the old man continued, "to make whisky. When Jack was but nine years old I took him to the still with me. Within three days that boy understood the biz thoroughly and could make 'doublins' to fare-you-well. When he was eleven years old he was as good a 'shiner as his pa. . . . I made the other boys learn, too, Brownlow, Hanney, Fleming and Henry wuz right up to snuff before they were fifteen years old. . . . My gals took their medicine, too. I made 'em all learn. . . . My old woman understands 'shinin' just as well as I. All my sons are raisin' children, and I'm going to see that they all follow the business of their grandpap or know the reason why. We'll all be out again soon, and we'll make enough corn juice to flood Kentucky."

The artists of the mash rake who were caught have produced some vivacious moments during their appearances in various courtrooms. When a judge asked to see the record in one case the prisoner spoke up:

"Judge, my record is puffect—in court nine times, sent to the 'pen' nine times."

In the United States District Court at Nashville, Tennessee, an old Baptist preacher expressed great surprise that a minister of the gospel should have been hailed into court "for making a little liquor for medicine." He explained:

"I just made two runs last fall and one run of peppermint in Jahnywary, and in them three runs I didn't make over thirty gallon in all, and it was for medicine, too. One of the gals in the neighborhood was sick with the breast complaint, and another one was down with yaller janders, and I wouldn't of made the runs if it hadn't been on their account. Now, them's the facts, as God is my jedge."

The audience in the courtroom applauded. The preacher got a hundred dollar fine and costs, which he peeled off a seven hundred dollar roll and paid on the spot.

One must guard against the fancy that these mountain bootleggers were Robin Hoods operating in some kind of Sherwood Forest. Place names such as Kettle Hollow and Shooting Creek are reminders of the life-and-death struggle between the forces of the law and the corncrackers. There was gunfire and the hum of high-powered bullets clipping the buds off the dogwood. Occasionally there were pitched battles. About half the time the moonshiners escaped. But the still, worm and vats were, if found, invariably destroyed. If the still could not be found, the expedition was, as the revenue men termed it, a "water-haul." It was a grim game, played for keeps. Susan Vanmeter was a dashing young widow who wouldn't bother to carry a squirrel home unless she had shot it through the head. She fired upon a revenue agent in defense of her admirer, John McIntyre, but to her disgust she only splintered the fence in front of his face. As she told the judge, she would have fetched him, only she was using the no-good gun. John had the good one down at the still.

The southern highlanders have made many songs about the loneliness of life and the consolatory bottle. There was a group gathered around the potbellied stove in Clabe Kazee's store on Horse Branch. Clabe was squirting tobacco juice into the spit box, and he crossed his knees, tilted his chair back and made a ballad for Jean Thomas. Miss Thomas, a former court stenographer, sought out the Kentuck scop and gleeman of mountain balladry with such devotion that she became famous as "The Traipsin' Woman" and wrote a book about her experiences published under that title. So while Kazee got ready, Buck Tipton unlimbered his battered guitar to "second on the box." The song was called "Crabtree Still" and celebrated an event which Clabe Kazee was at pains to explain. "You understand this taken place acrost the river. Not here on this branch." Well, in the story told by the song the sheriff came snooping up on the ridge and the bullets "went zickety split." A distiller named Chuck was hit, and George and Charlie landed in jail. The ballad sets forth the morality of the distilling communities:

There's one thing they all done wrong,
Stayed on Goose Point one day too long.

Later Clabe said rather sheepishly to his audience around the store that he didn't "hold with drammin' " and would sing a piece with "nary drap o' licker in it." Everybody laughed and he sang a song he learned off of Lije Littleton, a neighbor.

In the days when the rifle was a necessary tool of the moonshiner's trade, a revenue agent was, so an old story goes, scouting for a still in the hills when the bark of a hound dog attracted his attention to a slatternly shack on a mountainside, nestled among the grapevines and second growth brush and weed trees. Scrambling up to the door, he encountered a young boy.

"Hi, mister."

"Is your father around, sonny?"

"Nope. Pap's up thar makin'."

"Makin'?"

"You know—'shine."

"Up where, did you say?"

"Yander," pointing toward the steep hillside.

"Is your mother at home?"

"Ma's up there, too, helping pappy."

"Sonny," said the officer, "could you use fifty cents? All you have to do is to take me up there where I can talk to your father and mother."

Silently, the boy held out his hand. The agent demurred.

"No, no," the government man objected. "Not now, but later —after we get back."

"I'll take the money now," said the boy. "You ain't coming back."

Chapter *II*

THE GREAT
WHISKEY STEAL

A SHODDY episode in the moral history of whiskey became a matter of public knowledge in the mid-1870's. In this affair the United States Treasury was raided by its own high officers as well as minor functionaries who got their pinch, too, as a result of a cozy arrangement with large distillers in various urban centers who turned out "crooked" whiskey.

The federal excise tax on liquor had no more than gone into effect than a suspicion arose that distillers and rectifiers were cheating on their payments. Increasingly, during the administration of Andrew Johnson, rumors were flying around Washington of organized "rings" which were violating the law. Chicago, Peoria, Milwaukee, Cincinnati, Indianapolis and New Orleans were mentioned as centers of fraud. St. Louis, after General Grant's inauguration in 1869, was especially under suspicion as the headquarters of a network of bribery, coercion and defiance of the law. The appearance of New Orleans on this list may seem odd, in view of its geographical remoteness from grain country. Yet the savings which accrued through evasion of the tax were so great that it was possible to transport grain from the Middle West, manufacture the whiskey in New Orleans and still undersell upriver distillers who ran a legitimate business.

The whiskey frauds are a reminder that the North, as well as the South, had reconstruction problems. The rapid progress of industrialization, the new economic power exercised by financial freebooters, the scramble for wealth by speculation, the philosophy prevailing among many politicians that public office existed for private gain, all signaled a general lowering of civic and business ethical standards. This was the era of Boss Tweed in New York City, of the Gold Corner and Black Friday, of high-level public servants trading favors for a share in railroad construction contracts. The veterans of the victorious armies, it seemed, having but recently saved the Union, were now to enjoy the privilege of looting it.

On March 4, 1869, the inauguration of General U. S. Grant as President of the United States was celebrated at a brilliant ball, awash with medals, uniforms, gold braid and old Grand Army comrades who were soon to take over the machinery of government. Once installed, they acted in several capacities, as government officials, as party satraps and as adventurers preying upon the public purse. A notable personality in this concourse was a stout, ruddy, black-eyed brevet general named Orville E. Babcock. Babcock was a graduate of West Point who had served as aide-de-camp to Grant. He received the post of Superintendent of Public Buildings and Grounds in Washington. What was much more important, he became Grant's secretary, presiding over the anteroom leading to the President's office, receiving or rejecting visitors, managing patronage, participating with relish in Republican party intrigues. General Babcock, who had performed many delicate missions for Grant during the War, became in civil life a prime mischief-maker, the center of various cabals of spoilsmen in attacks on the State Department and the Treasury, placing squibs in newspapers to influence the course of stock prices, attempting to control Cabinet appointments, undermining the authority of administrators whom he tagged with the fatal name of "reformers."

Babcock was deeply involved, for example, in a callous and harebrained scheme to grab the Caribbean republic of Santo Domingo and made a secret trip to the island to pick out a good coaling station for the United States Navy. He also looked over the Dominican natural resources which might provide opportunities for private exploitation. Fortunately, the plot aborted, although President Grant was greatly engaged by the idea. As subtle as any medieval bishop whispering behind the arras, Babcock diverted and managed his chief and proved his devotion to the President's satisfaction by constant warnings against designing and wicked men. With his flowing mustache and imperial, his good manners and soldierly appearance, his fastidious dress, his dash and daring, his quick intellect, General Babcock was no ordinary operator, but a man of capacity who almost made it as one of the really great rogues of history.

Babcock might have gone far, says Matthew Josephson in *The Politicos* (1938), "were it not that his immoderate appetites for clothing, drink and fornication—all to be satisfied at the cost of the public Treasury—led him to ever more brazen adventures and needless risks."

It was through Babcock that the Whiskey Ring was able to operate a systematic fraud that riddled the revenue service and reached into the White House. The Treasury men out in the field and the distillers believed, not unnaturally, with Babcock so deeply involved, that the President was at least aware of the game if not an actual participant. There was an understanding that the proceeds from the tax shakedown were to be applied to the re-election of President Grant. This, too, gave plausibility to the idea that the President was privy to the arrangements. Some portion of the money collected did go to shore up Republican positions in closely contested elections. But increasingly, since greed feeds on greed, the graft was simply whacked up as personal plunder.

On the ground in St. Louis, the headquarters of the Ring, was Babcock's opposite number and a bird of the same feather, a brevet brigadier general, John A. McDonald. McDonald was from Missouri, a small, wiry man with no education but plenty of nerve. He had been a "steamboat runner" on the levee at St. Louis; that is, he drummed up trade for the line he represented. His wife taught him to read and write after their marriage and he developed marked gifts for leadership, recruiting volunteers so successfully at the beginning of the War that he got the post of Major in the Eighth Missouri regiment and during hard campaigning attracted favorable attention. After the War,

General McDonald exploited his military background and political connections as an agent pushing war claims against the
quartermaster department of the Army. He also bought up
vouchers against the government as a personal venture. As
McDonald's horizon widened, he came into some relation with
President Grant.

When Congress overhauled the revenue law in 1868 it created
supervisors in charge of districts to check on the collectors and
reduce the possibility of fraud. A senator from Arkansas wrote
to the new President that his state needed an honest man to
watch over revenue matters. General Grant looked around.
And there was the man of the hour, John A. McDonald. With
the strong endorsement of generals Sherman and the audacious
Babcock, of James B. Eads, the famous Mississippi River engi-
neer and other St. Louisans, McDonald was commissioned
Superintendent of Internal Revenue in the autumn of 1869 for
Arkansas, Kansas, New Mexico, Texas and Indian Territory,
despite urgent protests from Senator Carl Schurz of Missouri
and other liberal Republicans that McDonald was a person of
ill-repute and unfit for the office.

Around the beginning of 1870, Missouri was added to the
new Superintendent's responsibilities and he established his
headquarters in St. Louis. There he flourished as the chief
federal official in the city and a sort of proconsul for Grant
in political matters. By the next year, 1871, McDonald had
the whiskey racket rolling, with himself the center pin of the
plot. The method of operation was for the U.S. officials to allow
the distilleries to run a specified percentage of their output untaxed. The money was split fifty-fifty, or, some investigators of
this tangled period say, it was more in favor of the government
men than the distillers, say about sixty-forty. And sometimes
when the need for diamonds and champagne or a rustic retreat
in the Wisconsin woods was pressing, there were special assess-
ments. In any event, the clique had discovered that the whiskey
still was a veritable money machine.

The Ring included, in addition to McDonald and Babcock,
William Avery, the chief clerk in the Internal Revenue office
at Washington, McDonald's immediate subordinates, C. W.
Ford and Colonel John A. Joyce, who was both a pimp and a

poet, and various other figures on the middle western political scene, as well as the owners of ten or more large distilleries and rectifying plants in St. Louis. Reluctant distillers were harassed and entrapped in technical violations or systematically black-mailed until they saw the point of joining.

When agents came out from Washington who were open to a proposition, they were handed sums of money ranging from $5,000 up to $10,000. There were pleasant melon-cuttings, in which cash was put up in packages and tossed over the transom into hotel rooms. If honest agents started on an investigation, a warning telegram preceded them: PUT YOUR HOUSE IN ORDER. Then the distilleries ran straight until they got the word again, perhaps a jocular message: EVERYTHING LOOKS WELL. SEND ON REPORT. FEEL HUNKEY. McDonald, the link in St. Louis with a mysterious higher power in Washington, spread the doctrine that "the old man knows." Impressive corroboration of this idea occurred when the Secretary of the Treasury shifted McDonald to Philadelphia and the Ring was able to get the President to revoke the order.

There is no evidence that President Grant ever knew of these shenanigans. McDonald's influence with Grant can be adequately explained on political grounds. The Republican party in Missouri was dangerously split. The "liberal" Republicans, led by Senator Carl Shurz and former Senator B. Gratz Brown, were opposed to the harsh Reconstruction policies, to the Dominican adventure and to General Grant. And they wished to repeal a provision in the Missouri state constitution which disenfranchised all who had taken part in the Rebellion. Grant needed McDonald because McDonald was for Grant for a second term, a third term or until hell froze over. He represented the chief hope of "stalwartizing" the state. "Stalwarts" were the beneficiaries of the spoils system. They opposed civil service reform, waved the "bloody shirt"; i.e., fomented sectional hostility between the North and the South for political purposes and were willing, as *The Nation* said in a contemporary explanation of Stalwartism, "to let 'the boys' have a good time with the offices."

An admirer of the competence in chicanery of Jay Gould and Jim Fisk, McDonald organized his own monopoly in the spirit of their piracies. The alcohol stills operated at night, which was

a violation of the law. Storekeepers would allow two quick
fermentations in the time the law prescribed for one. Distillers
were permitted to keep books to show only a fraction of actual
production. Barrels of whiskey were sent to rectifying establishments and "dumped," meaning emptied into the common cistern,
without dispatching to the revenue collector a "dumping notice,"
as regulations required. At the rectifiers' the gaugers refrained
from canceling stamps on lots ready for shipment. One trick was
to duplicate shipments by a double use of stamps, or by failing
to enter one transaction. All this added up to a slush fund of
about $3,000,000 annually. A gentleman known as "Con"
Megrue, an ex-revenue agent who was experienced in the business of illegal distillation, was brought on from Cincinnati to
collect the swag. Saturday was payday. Every Saturday night
Megrue received the money due for the week. He kept one-
fifth, passed on a similar amount to Colonel John A. Joyce and
a fifth to McDonald. A newspaper publisher and the small fry
got the rest.

The ostensible purpose of the collections was accomplished
when Grant was re-elected in 1872. A new fund was started at
once to elect Grant again. Meanwhile the Grant appointees
purchased lavish homes, rented luxurious suites in the best hotels,
enjoyed discreet suppers with ladies of the evening. This was
the age of diamonds. Sparklers twinkled from tie-pin, ring finger
and shirt stud of authentic millionaires, of the sporting gentry,
of all manner of quacks and speculators. The cut stones flashed
a message of solvency and reassurance. In addition to being re-
markably pretty, they had these solid advantages—they could
not be levied upon in bankruptcy proceedings and they were
highly portable in case a quick getaway to Texas or Canada was
indicated.

On one occasion when General Babcock visited the "boys"
in St. Louis they presented him with a large diamond shirt stud
weighing almost four carats at the substantial cost of $2,400.
But General Babcock, who knew his diamonds, was not amused
when he discovered a flaw in the stone. He complained bitterly
to Joyce that "the little thing we gave him was a fraud." So all
hands chipped in to make amends to "our Washington friend,"
as McDonald expressed it, and the defective sparkler was ex-

changed for a finer one. And at Christmastime, caught up in the spirit of the season, they sent Babcock a box of the finest cigars. When he opened it, he found, laid across the Havanas, a thousand-dollar bill.

Nothing was too good for the President's secretary when he visited St. Louis; for he was the watcher in the watch tower, the inside man who shot the Ring vitally important telegraphic messages: PUT YOUR HOUSE IN ORDER. YOUR FRIENDS WILL VISIT YOU. Or, in happier vein, THINGS LOOK ALL RIGHT HERE. LET THE MACHINE GO. On one occasion when Babcock was in St. Louis arrangements were made by Colonel Joyce for his diversion involving the co-operation of the most beautiful lady in the city, one Louise Hawkins, who had been first seduced at the age of fourteen in a small town on the Illinois Central, but had made a brilliant career as a demimondaine in St. Louis. Joyce fixed up an assignation for the General with the glamorous Lou, known also to her clientele as "the Sylph," at Freund's Restaurant, Fifth and Pine streets, directly after dark. The Sylph was described appreciatively by McDonald:

"Her form was petite, and yet withal a plumpness and development which made her a being whose tempting luscious deliciousness was irresistible. Most beautiful of face, with eyes of deepest azure, in whose depths the sunbeams seemed to gather, and the fires of love from flames of flickering constancy, seemed ever and anon to melt into love itself. . . . She was the essence of grace, distilled from the buds of perfection, and with a tongue on which the oil of vivacity and seduction never ceased running; she was indeed a sylph and siren, whose presence was like the flavor of the poppy mingled with the perfumes of Araby."

After General Babcock met *la Hawkins*, his St. Louis contacts often received telegrams from him signed "Sylph" in warm remembrance of a memorable instance of St. Louis hospitality. When letters were exchanged, the letterhead was cut off and the signatures pseudonymous. "Just keep our kettle boiling," one such letter ran, "and don't let anything interrupt the good cause of patriotism."

The largesse of the Whiskey Ring even included the President. McDonald furnished the White House table with gifts of choice game, fruits and other delicacies at a cost, he estimated, of nearly one hundred dollars a week. When President Grant and a numerous entourage, including Secretary Babcock, spent ten days in St. Louis in 1874, staying at the recently opened Lindell Hotel, McDonald (salary: $3,000 per year) paid the hotel bill. And according to his own account he did more. General Grant had a passion for fast horses. McDonald, as he remembered it later, put at the President's disposal a pair of roadsters and a fine buggy. When the President got out on Gravois Road, headed toward a farm he owned, he pulled in the reins and touched the horses up a little with the whip. To his delight he got four minutes out of them. So McDonald impulsively presented the team and the handsome and ornamental buggy to the Chief Executive, together with a complete outfit including two blankets for each horse and gold breastplates engraved with the President's name, all of which was sent to Washington a few weeks later in a chartered railroad car. The bills were receipted in Grant's name. Later, when McDonald's feelings about General Grant had undergone a sea-change, he placed this transaction in as unfavorable a light as he could.

On the same visit, McDonald also wangled for the President the award of a blue ribbon to a colt that Grant was showing at the St. Louis Fair, an important annual event in the Mississippi Valley. General Grant, who had a genius for making mistakes, accepted these extraordinary attentions with nonchalance. The only sour note came from a St. Louis *Globe* reporter, obviously not a member of the Whiskey Ring, who wrote of the horse show award, "The ribbon was given as a compliment to the President and not to the animal."

In June, 1874, the Secretaryship of the Treasury was filled by the appointment of Benjamin Bristow, a tall, lean, honest Kentuckian with a passionate conviction that others in the public service should be honest, too. Bristow set into motion a plan designed to trap the St. Louis racketeers. First an around-the-clock watch was established to check on the amount of grain that was moved into each distilling establishment and the quantity of liquor moved out by Bevis, Frazier & Co., Bollman & O'Hara, McCartney & Company and other firms which were violating the law. The observers were changed each day to make identification difficult. When the stakeout was detected by the distillers, the investigators were beaten by goons and roughed up by the local police.

Another prong of the inquiry involved tracing shipments of liquor out of the city under the pretext of collecting commercial statistics. One special revenue agent named Yaryan, who was trusted by Bristow, with the help of a small clerical force, checked railway and steamboat bills of lading for all whiskey shipped, noted the shippers' names, the consignees, the number of gallons, serial numbers of the government stamps. The data was compared with the sworn returns made to the district collector's office. The discrepancy, after allowing for the spirits consumed within the city, represented the extent of the fraud. The examination began March 5, 1875. The government forces were ready to spring the trap by May and the tenth of the month was set as the day for the raids. The ring heard something, became uneasy. But McDonald insisted there was no cause for alarm. At the last minute a warning telegram went to St. Louis: THE PLAGUE IS ADVANCING WEST. ADVISE OUR FRIENDS TO LEAVE THE CITY. The message came too late.

Special agents carried out simultaneous seizures with complete surprise in St. Louis, Milwaukee and Chicago. They acquired as evidence 1,200 barrels of illicit whiskey and the ledgers and office records of sixteen distilleries and sixteen rectifiers. Later there were further seizures in other cities, made on the basis of the information turned up in St. Louis.

President Grant at first gave vigorous support to the attack upon the whiskey conspiracy. Later he became increasingly reluctant to face unpleasant disclosures about his appointees.

"Well, Mr. Bristow," the President remarked to the Secretary of the Treasury just after the raids, "there is at least one honest man in St. Louis on whom we can rely—John McDonald. I know that because he is an intimate acquaintance and confidential friend of Babcock's."

"Mr. President," replied Bristow, tight-lipped, "McDonald is the head and center of all the frauds."

The prosecution was successful in obtaining grand jury indictments against 176 defendants—distillers, rectifiers, wholesale dealers, revenue supervisors, gaugers, storekeepers, collectors, their deputies and several private parties. Newspaper headlines flashed across the country. Columns were filled with facts and speculations about the whiskey scandals which competed in public interest with the rumors about the fate of Charley Ross, child victim of the famous, and unsolved, kidnapping of the time; and the blow-by-blow reports of the trial on lurid charges of the great divine, Henry Ward Beecher.

W. D. W. Barnard, a St. Louis wholesale druggist, wrote a long letter to Grant while the grand jury was conducting its inquiry, in which Barnard reported that the defendants were openly boasting that the President would not let them suffer. They had told the prosecuting attorney, the letter said, "that you [Grant] could not give them up, or Babcock would be lost." This letter was forwarded to Bristow, docketed on the back in Grant's hand, "Let no guilty man escape."

The first whiskey ringer to hear the turn of the bolt was Colonel Joyce, who made a florid speech in court when he was sentenced on November 13, 1875, comparing his fate with that of Galileo, Tasso, Columbus and Napoleon. Joyce prophesied that the demand for clean government would subside, for he discerned "the flood even now is settling into its former bed, where the crystal waters shall again reflect the green foliage, the oak and the sycamore, and the gentle breezes and birds of spring shall make merry music in the aisles of a generous nation."

The strategy of those implicated was to drag the scandal to the White House door as their best chance of getting off, and to arouse Grant's suspicions that Bristow's zeal was inspired by personal political ambition. The hot pursuit of his dapper secretary convinced Grant that there was a plot against him. By August it was generally known that the indictment of Babcock was impending. But the President accepted Babcock's explanations and clung to him only the more stubbornly as the chase closed in. Meanwhile many of the distillers had pleaded guilty and paid their fines, relieved no doubt to be out of the wretched business. McDonald was convicted on November 23, 1875, and drew a sentence of three years and a fine of $5,000. Joyce was at the gate of the prison at Jefferson City on April 16, 1876, to welcome his former superior to his new abode.

When the news came that the grand jury at St. Louis had returned a true bill against General Babcock, the political effect of his prospective exposure became a subject of anguished meditation in Republican party councils. The elections were less than a year off. The energies of the prosecution began to flag noticeably. Babcock received all kinds of overt help. Favorable interpolations mysteriously appeared in some of the evidence. Detectives representing Babcock stole vital material from the office of the government attorney. Nevertheless, many interesting telegrams were read into the record. Many communications appeared in Babcock's handwriting, including a dispatch to McDonald which became famous: I SUCCEEDED. THEY WILL NOT GO. I WILL WRITE YOU. SYLPH. This was interpreted as a warning that a sudden descent of honest revenue agents on the St. Louis distilling industry had been countermanded.

General Babcock was resourceful in his own defense. He won delays while calling loudly for speed and vindication, made grandstand plays, demanded, although unsuccessfully, a military trial, used every legal trick in the bag. His trial was viewed generally as a trial of the inner organization of the Republican party. The special counsel who knew more about the conspiracy than any other man was removed. Witnesses were refused leniency if they turned state's evidence, an obvious intervention in behalf of Babcock. Most extraordinary of all—the President announced that he wished to testify as a witness for the defense in a criminal prosecution brought by the government he headed. With great difficulty, he was dissuaded from dashing across the country to make a personal appearance in the St. Louis court. Instead, his deposition was taken in Washington in an impressive setting witnessed by two members of his Cabinet, with Chief Justice Morrison Remick Waite serving as notary. Grant testified that his secretary had explained everything to his satisfaction. The President, suspicious of honest men but credulous when among rogues, had swallowed the theory advanced by Babcock that the whole affair had been blown up as a political stunt to win the Republican presidential nomination for Secretary Bristow.

With the full weight of the presidential office thrown into the scales on his side, and since none of the whiskey thieves had peached on him, General Babcock was acquitted on February 24, 1876. The band from the government arsenal serenaded the former soldier on the night of his triumph and his admirers made up a purse of $10,000 as a slight token of their esteem. With the Republican palace guard under heavy obligation to the members of the Ring for their silence, none of those who went to prison served his full term.

The American public generally received Babcock's "vindication" with skepticism. After the trial, Babcock returned boldly to his usual desk. Grant and his secretary were closeted for a long interview. When Grant came out, his face was set. The next day General Babcock locked his desk and departed, not for the penitentiary where the *New York Tribune, The Nation* and the *Springfield Republican* thought he belonged, but to assume new duties as Inspector of Lighthouses. In the lighthouse service Babcock was, presumably, safely removed from temptation. He never again sat at the President's elbow and was, in fact, soon indicted for his exploits in connection with another "ring" known as the District of Columbia Ring which was caught fabricating evidence against an innocent man on a charge of burglarizing a safe. The mustachioed *intrigant* passed from public view after that and was drowned at Mosquito Inlet, Florida, on June 2, 1884. Although the manipulators of the whiskey frauds were successful to some degree in blunting Bristow's efforts against them, the Ring was shattered beyond recovery by the indictments, prison sentences and public sense of revulsion.

When McDonald was clapped in the bridewell, despite Babcock's impassioned assurance, "they will never turn a key on you," the unfrocked Supervisor of Internal Revenue remained uncommunicative about the affairs of the Whiskey Ring. He was playing for a pardon and quick release. Meanwhile he was quite snug in his small apartment at Jefferson City. He had $12,000 in cash with him in his cell, enjoyed various privileges and little touches of luxury. He could sleep the sleep, if not of the just, at least of a man who was no tattletale and hoped to be rewarded for his silence. Friends came to see him, including a member of the Grand Jury who kept his friend filled in on the secrets of the jury room.

McDonald gradually lost his faith in men as he continued to

languish in prison for the balance of Grant's term. He was released on January 26, 1877, soon after Rutherford B. Hayes
was inaugurated. When Hayes failed to get along with his party,
the Stalwarts began to boom Grant for a third term. Just at
that juncture, McDonald published a curious, rancorous book,
known as *Secrets of the Great Whiskey Ring* (1880). It was
ghost-written. McDonald undoubtedly furnished the material.
When President Grant was being cross-examined after making
his deposition in behalf of Babcock, the attorney referred to
General McDonald as an ignorant man.

"I would not call him ignorant exactly," President Grant said
by way of correction, "he was illiterate"; but, he added, "had
seen a great deal of the world."

McDonald's account of the Ring, which may have been issued
as an anti-Grant campaign document, attempted to tie the President directly with "this history of official corruption whose conception occurred in the mash tub." The evidence is always indirect, a matter of the construction put upon letters, dependent
upon reports from Babcock of conversations with Grant, or
assertions which McDonald made upon his "honor." At the
party convention in Chicago in 1880 Grant's hopes were frus-
trated by a coalition which agreed upon Garfield. McDonald had
the grim satisfaction of knowing that there was to be no third
term. His book, with its asserted "Chain of Evidence," may
have influenced the balloting at the convention.

Although Grant had a grafter in his Cabinet and another
in his anteroom and could allow himself to appear in public as
a guest of Jim Fisk, his personal honesty has never been successfully assailed. Energetic and slothful, reckless and plodding,
humble and imperious, sensitive and obtuse, U. S. Grant as
President had an uncanny ability for getting into scrapes. At the
time of his death the *New York Tribune* said: "The greatest
mistake of his life was the acceptance of the presidency."

Near the end of his career, the General was asked whether
he had anything to regret.

"No," he said, "nothing but being deceived in people."

Yet history has not treated Grant unkindly. His eight inept
years as Chief Executive have been largely blotted out by the
memory of his achievements as a soldier and the heroism of

the haggard invalid at Mount McGregor, writing his *Personal Memoirs* in a race with death, occasionally glancing out the window, bowing stiffly to the crowds which gathered in front of his house.

Chapter 12

THE HIGHWINE TRUST

THE sacred word "trust," as used in the seventy-first Psalm, and as applied by the courts to the protection of widows, orphans and all who are weak and dependent, acquired a new and disturbing meaning in the last two decades of the nineteenth century when the trust became a subtle legal shelter for commercial combinations or cartels aiming at monopoly. The device of the trust came into general use after the Standard Oil Company had developed it as a means of eliminating competitors. Whiskey quickly followed the lead of oil, and the "Whiskey Trust" in the late 1880's and early 1890's became a public issue and an object of popular odium.

The story begins with taxation. It has been shown in an earlier chapter how the liquor industry, tipped off to coming increases, engaged in a frenzied production of alcohol and whiskey. The result was over-built capacity, large stocks and falling prices. The economy was expanding, yet in some respects the market was contracting. The high taxes lowered per capita drinking and made the product too expensive for many industrial uses, such as the manufacture of varnishes, furniture polish, solvents for medicines and "burning fluid" for illumination. The trust device offered a way to control the market. It worked well in a number of other industries.

"We thought," said distiller Charles C. Clarke, of Peoria,

Illinois, "we could make better profits and create a more stable business by organizing into a trust. A trust agreement was drawn up, which was a copy of the Standard Oil trust agreement, but changed to suit our business."

The essential feature of the agreement was that shares of stock in corporations which formerly competed were placed in the hands of trustees who thereafter operated the combination as a single unit.

The nickname "Whiskey Trust" was a misnomer. "Highwine Trust" came nearer to the mark. The combine manufactured commercial spirits from Illinois corn. A part of this alcohol was refined further to produce a completely neutral product for making eau de cologne, essences or blending into what the trade then knew as "staple" whiskey. The Trust made some straight whiskey, but not very much.

In most respects, then, the interests of the Trust were antagonistic to those of the bourbon distillers whose straight and bonded whiskeys competed with the blended article. They were separate geographically, too. The distilleries whose product required aging gathered largely in Pennsylvania, Maryland and Kentucky. The Trust members were located north of the Ohio River, especially in Indiana and Illinois. The members of the Trust were the big wheels from a volume standpoint. The distributors and wholesalers whom the Trust attempted to control through a system of illegal rebates, handled about two-thirds of the beverage alcohol consumed in the United States.

Before it set up the formal trust, the spirit industry experimented with loose arrangements called "pools." Pooling was forbidden by specific statutes and was also illegal under common law. The whiskey pools were based upon a "gentleman's agreement" to limit output and fix prices. But it always turned out that there was someone in the club who wasn't a gentleman. One of the earliest efforts, organized in the 1870's, was known as the "Peoria pool," promoted by H. B. ("Buffalo") Miller. Another Peorian, decidedly *not* a member of the club, assured the pool of an exciting existence. In those days, a distiller with access to capital, who was willing to pay a bonus for fast work, could erect a distillery and be stripping the alcohol out of corn mash in ninety days. Such a man was Edward Spelman, of

Peoria. This talented operator built one distillery after the other so that the pool would have to buy them in.

Another try at pooling developed out of a general industry meeting in November, 1881. Output was reduced on a voluntary basis, and prices raised. Profits were large for a time. But all the pools suffered from a built-in weakness. Being illegal, they were unenforceable. Men who would conspire against their customers would scarcely keep faith with each other. Some scoundrel always ran over his allotted output, or undersold his associates, preferring to shade his price a cent a gallon and make a sale at the expense of his pledged word, rather than prosper along with the prosperity of others.

The pool cracked wide open in May, 1882; but another was launched in the fall of that year. It was renewed yearly until 1887. The managers never found any sure means of enforcing the policies of the syndicate.

In the spring of 1887 the leading manufacturers of alcohol turned their stock over to nine trustees who were to run the business in the pattern that was developing in oil, sugar, copper, tobacco, beef and steel. The trust mechanism "spread like a disease," in the words of a New York State Senate Investigating Committee. Known as the Distillers' and Cattle Feeders' Trust, or colloquially as the "Octopus," the syndicate gathered in more than eighty plants, conducting its affairs from a headquarters at 205 North Jefferson Avenue, Peoria, Illinois, a four-story "Steamboat Gothic" mansion built by a pork packer and once the home of Robert G. Ingersoll, the orator and Great Infidel of the lecture platform. The writer who is tapping out these lines, once a Methodist child and son of that middle border located where the *Chicago Tribune's* writ ceases to run and the St. Louis *Globe-Democrat* takes over, can testify to the depreciative atmosphere surrounding the word "Peoria" as uttered in genteel downstate Illinois homes in the early years of this century. Among us Epworth Leaguers, "Peoria" was very nearly a swear word; except that we didn't swear. But Peoria meant sin and Ingersoll's free-thinking. It meant saloons. In Peoria the corn mash bubbled, hot as the fires of hell, while the stills poured out The Serpent in such establishments as the Great Western, Woolner Brothers, the Globe, Clarke Brothers and others.

The Highwine Trust, called by a modern student, Ernest E. East, "one of the largest and most notorious combines in the industrial history of the United States," could fix the quotations on spirits and whiskey. It would lower the price to force independent distillers into the organization. Later the price would shoot up and the Trust would reap a harvest. When to bring a distillery into the group and when it was cheaper to crush it out of existence always presented a nice problem, if not of ethics, then of practical judgment. The Trust managers, if they thought at all beyond their ledgers and stock tickers, were pleased to align their business philosophy with the new scientific doctrines of biological evolution. John D. Rockefeller, Sr., expressed the idea by a pretty analogy:

"The American Beauty rose can be produced in all its splendor only by sacrificing the early buds that grow up around it."

The Trust closed down most of the distilleries it acquired, operating only ten or twelve which were best-located as to markets and freight rates, or which were able to extract a particularly high yield of alcohol from a bushel of corn. In Peoria, for example, where the monopoly controlled twelve plants, there were a number of special advantages. The syndicate had access to an unlimited vein of cold water. There were an estimated 13,000,000 tons of coal within eight miles of the county courthouse. Peoria maintained an active grain market and was served by thirteen railroads and good water transportation. There may also have been technical advantages. For at Peoria the Highwine Trust turned out 4.535 gallons of alcohol per bushel as against the national average of 4.24+. The modern industry gets a yield of about five gallons today. The combination could also count on lower management costs and lower sales costs through the operation of a single sales force.

The Trust could jiggle two markets, the market for their product and the market for their securities. The trust certificates kept swinging back and forth and up and down. Among the speculators involved were Nelson Morris, the Chicago meat packer, who had an arrangement for feeding thousands of cattle at the Peoria distilleries; James R. Keene, turfman and plunger, who managed various commodity pools; Thomas Fortune Ryan, the Traction King; and William C. Whitney, former Secretary of the Navy in the Cleveland administration, and also known as a powerful and adroit member of "the Ryan crowd." Dexter T. Mills, a Boston distributor of spirits, told Clarence W. Barron, the financial journalist, that the Distillers and Cattle Feeders' Company would have been a good investment if "run for itself," but with its orientation toward Wall Street "it is only balloon speculation."

The organizer and promoter, the diplomat, the handler of men, the Svengali of the Whiskey Trust was Joseph B. Greenhut, its long-time president. Greenhut was born in Austria and brought to Chicago as a child. He served in the Union Army in Hooker's Corps, rose to Captain, and arrived in Peoria with a net worth of about fifty dollars. Greenhut found his metier in manipulating stocks for the benefit of insiders, and later removed to the Eastern seaboard with a fortune reputed to be ten million dollars.

Among the arguments used by agents representing the Trust to convince reluctant independents were the profits to be realized from a distilling monopoly, profits from the probable increase in value of their trust certificates and the persuasive effect of a charge of dynamite. Two packages of explosive were thrown on the roof of a vat room of H. H. Shufeldt & Co., a stubborn Chicago holdout. There was considerable damage but no arrests. The *Chicago Tribune* aired the charge that the Trust was responsible. Later George J. Gibson of Peoria, socially prominent secretary of the Trust, was arrested by federal officers for the attempted torpedoing of the same distillery with an ingenious device, a kind of infernal machine designed first to start a fire and then to shoot a projectile through a wooden vat of alcohol which would presumably destroy the building. Gibson was indicted in the Criminal Court of Cook County, Illinois, for procuring gunpowder with felonious intent, for attempted arson, attempted destruction of property and conspiracy to commit murder. The corporation official was trapped by an incorruptible revenue agent who had been offered up to $25,000 for placing the Rube Goldberg machine under the vat in Shufeldt's cistern room.

Gibson resigned his position with the Distillers' and Cattle Feeders' Trust, but received a vote of confidence from the board

of directors at the time of his departure and lived forever afterward without visible means of support. The Company insisted
it was not involved. The case was just something the management read about in the papers, probably the work of "anarchists."

"We have heard of it so much it has come to be a kind of
chestnut with us," President Greenhut told a Congressional
Committee engaged in investigating the Trust in 1893.

A wily and reluctant witness, Greenhut, when asked about
his knowledge of trusts in general, said that he attended only to
his own business—"I do not know what is in existence." Asked
specifically about the Sugar Trust, he said he knew "only what
I have seen in the newspapers, and I suppose what you read in
the papers must be true; so I judge there must be a trust." Had
the question been directed to how the various glucose plants in
the Middle West had ended up in one big family, the President
of the Highwine Trust could perhaps have given a more responsive answer, since he was its organizer.

Gibson was never tried on any of the charges against him.
Distilleries which were not members of the Trust had a rough
time of it around 1890. One at Peoria had a disastrous fire
after the insurance companies received a mysterious message
to cancel their policies. Two smaller plants at Pekin, Illinois,
burned to the ground. One Pekin distiller who had been financially
ruined by the Trust wrote out an account of the ruthless methods
of the syndicate. An officer of the Whiskey Trust with literary
tastes paid him $50,000 for his manuscript, which is a very decent
price for a one-book author, and a manuscript which, in fact,
never saw the light of day.

The profitable operations of the Trust brought new competition into the industry faster than the combine could eliminate it.
The Trust found itself floating on a sea of difficulties, exacer-
bated by successful government action against it under the
Sherman Anti-Trust Law for restraint of trade. Dissolved by
the Supreme Court, the Trust became a rose under another
name, the Distilling and Cattle Feeding *Company*. Trustees
became directors. The trust certificates were exchanged for
shares of stock, composed of "nine-tenths water," the *New York
Commercial Bulletin* informed its readers. The Company maintained that henceforth it was not subject to the Interstate Com-

merce Act or any other act of Congress because it wasn't engaged in interstate commerce. It was just an Illinois corporation
with no agents outside the state. The Company's drays delivered
the liquor to a local freight station. The consignee took it from
there.

Company troubles included an unsatisfactory price level after
the depression of 1893, company officers speculating in the Company's stock and the burden of properties which the Company,
or the old Trust, had acquired and virtually thrown away. Rent
and taxes were paid on abandoned plants year after year. Men
were paid for staying out of the business. Charles C. Clarke,
of Peoria, as one example, went into the Trust, but later became an independent producer of rye whiskey. An old sign announcing the presence of Clarke's Pure Rye is still in place above
the etched glass windows of a Third Avenue barroom in New
York. One liquor merchant with strong nerves went short of the
Distilling and Cattle Feeding Company stock, then cut the price
of spirits to depress the stock on Wall Street.

The Trust, as it was still universally called, went into and
out of receivership a number of times, accompanied by slight
changes of its corporate name and the sloughing off of incon-
venient financial obligations. The records of the original Trust
disappeared completely. General John McNulta, on one occasion
receiver for the Company, had to cut open two safes to get at the
records which revealed, among other things, that officers had
used corporate funds to protect their personal accounts with
brokers while they sold Company stock on margin. The Whiskey
Trust was legislated against in Illinois. Its complicated affairs
were spread upon the official record of the Judiciary Committee
of the House of Representatives. There were exhaustive, and
exhausting, hearings conducted in 1899 before a Commission
set up by act of Congress to find out what Trusts were all about.
Sometimes the Whiskey Trust was the American Spirits Manufacturing Company. Sometimes it was the Standard Distilling
and Distributing Company; or it might do a dissolve into the
Distillers' Securities Corporation, a holding company incorporated under New Jersey's hospitable laws. But always it was
monopolistic in its operations and usurped powers not conferred
by its charter. And the stock went up and down. It is no exag-

geration to say that the resentment which the public felt toward the Trust for its arrogance, its tactics of bribery and political lobbying and its association with the chain saloon system, tended to strengthen the anti-whiskey vote which brought on Prohibition.

Despite all the legal in-fighting, intimidation and a notorious system of rebates, the declining prospects of the Trust were shadowed forth in this statistic: between 1880 and 1890 a thousand distilleries of grain were licensed to operate. The point is: it was just too easy to get into the business of making alcohol. This assured the blenders ample supplies at very close figures and made hardy perennials of such newspaper headlines as WHISKEY WAR IS RESUMED, or STRENUOUS TIMES IN THE WHISKEY TRADE. The Trust was still selling a raw material in bulk to distributors who owned valuable trademarks and were in touch with the consumer. It was time to integrate and sell branded goods in a consumer package, as the National Biscuit Company and other pioneer grocery manufacturers were doing at the beginning of this century. But the Trust did not read the lesson. Dividends were suspended by 1913.

During the years of Prohibition, transformed into U.S. Food Products Corporation, the old outfit made yeast, vinegar and cereal products, went through the wringer once more and came out as the National Distillers Products Corporation in 1924 under the astute leadership of a man with no whiskey background whatever, Seton Porter of the famous engineering firm of Sanderson and Porter. National Distillers acquired priceless stocks of mellow bourbon and many important brand names during the years of despair. Porter organized himself into a rescue squad. As a financial physician he administered numerous blood transfusions. As a *curé* he pulled a miracle—the moral regeneration of the disreputable old Trust. As a prophet he saw, almost as soon as did Mr. Lewis S. Rosensteil over at small but scrappy Schenley Products Co., a rainbow in the sky. It spelled R-e-p-e-a-l. Through his gift for foretelling, Porter was able to greet the Twenty-first Amendment to the U.S. Constitution cheerily, for National Distillers owned over half the aged whiskey in the United States. Thus today's National Distillers Products Corporation, now a leading merchandiser of top-drawer, aged bourbons, through a complicated line of descent, is the reputable offspring of the roguish old Highwine Trust.

The bourbon makers also tried their hand at combination. Thomas H. Sherley, a Louisville capitalist with interests in the New Hope Distillery Company, the E. L. Miles Company and the Belle of Nelson label, compiled exhaustive data on production and finance as it affected the small distiller. A plan was devised. From it came the Kentucky Distilleries and Warehouse Company, a combination of fifty-nine distilleries which followed the old-time pot still methods of manufacture, and controlled one hundred and thirty-five brands. These interests a generation later found their way into National Distillers. Thus at long last two basically different conceptions of American whiskey, one which tried to make straight and bonded whiskeys the standard, the other which believed in the lighter, blended product became, by merger and corporate marriage, compatible members of the same family.

Chapter 13

WESTWARD THE JUG OF EMPIRE TOOK ITS WAY

R ED liquor accompanied the westering Americans in their
occupation of the North American continent in such
bounteous quantities—by bottle, jimmy-john, cask and barrel—
that Mark Twain once suggested the line stamped on the back
cover of Bancroft's *History of the United States,* "Westward
the star of empire takes its way," would better reflect the American experience if rendered "Westward the jug of empire . . ."

Bullwhackers, traders, trappers, hide hunters and soldiers,
sod busters, gold seekers—they crossed the Mississippi, left behind the old civilization of the eastern forest region, settled the
short grass plains, pushed on to the land of mesquite and buffalo
grass, lugging with them at great labor and expense their ruby-
hued comforter. Wagoners of prodigious thirst, who could train
on whiskey and then move two tons of merchandise four hundred
miles in a month's time; miners whose pack horses carried pan,
pick, shovel, flour, salt horse and red-eye; mountain men and
government surveyors: they all liked plenty of whiskey, agreeing
with the semi-legendary Mike Fink, who declared, "I'm not the
kind of man that's satisfied with washing his mouth out." They
took their whiskey straight the same as they did their quinine.
As one leathery old Texan said, mixed drinks were to be rated

with featherbeds, "the pleasure of payin' taxes" and other doubtful blessings of civilization.

And so the whiskey wagon jounced along, crossed the desert
and threaded the passes of the Rockies and Sierras to the western ocean; and always, as Bernard De Voto wrote, "the honey
bee flew ahead of us and there was a hooker of the real stuff at
a day's end." Whiskey made life endurable for men who lived
with loneliness, ate beans, salt meat and gulped coarse coffee,
slept in the wet with teeth chattering from ague, and who woke
up, like as not, to find a small, companionable rattlesnake sharing
a blanket. And so the tin cup passed around the campfire. After
the fried beef and biscuit the stopper came out of the jug and
the stories began to flow:

"I'd been hyar afore, tradin' liquor to the Utes."

Or:

"Did I ever tell you of how I run five Injuns several miles,
when I had no other weepin than an old single-bar'l shotgun
loaded with bird-shot? . . . It was in '72 when I was haulin'
government stores from San Antonio to Fort Concho."

Or:

"I jist fetched old Ginger up and drawed a bee line on his
cratch, and, stranger, I giv him sich a winch in the stomach that
he dropped straight in his tracks; he did! in five jumps I riz his
har. . . ."

In the flickering light of the campfire, bourbon softened the
edges of a harsh environment, lent emotional color and lift to
the booted and buckskinned group. Ranchers, railroad contractors, U.S. marshals and mountain men shared the faith that
whiskey was of the highest therapeutic value in a long list of
emergencies; that it strengthened the heart, improved respira-
tion, cured hydrophobia even more effectively than a madstone.
Whiskey was indicated for chills and fevers, general debility,
kidney ailments, malaria and palpitation. "Topeka," observed
a Kansas City newspaper, "is about as sickly a town as is in the
country, or that whisky fever is as much an epidemic as it is in
any Kentucky village running a prosperous sour-mash distillery."

This much is certainly true: after a good pull the patient was,
in doctor language, "symptomatically improved." If the keg was
empty or the patient had scruples about taking his liquor plain,

Paine's Celery Compound offered an agreeable sensation and respectability. So did Dr. Simmons' Liver Regulator, widely esteemed as the cowboy's friend. The Indian braves thought highly of Dr. Sweet's Infallible Liniment. Taken externally, it was said to grow hair, if followed by internal applications to clinch the roots. The Commissioner of Internal Revenue was grieved to learn that the medication in Hostetter's Bitters was so minimal and the cutting edge of the alcohol so keen that the bitters were being sold by the drink; and so the question arose as to whether Hostetter should not be paying the regular tax on beverage alcohol.

"Us kids heard," remembered Carl Sandburg out of his rural Illinois childhood, "that you could get drunk on one bottle of Hostetter's."

When a westerner asked the bartender for "whiskey," he meant bourbon. If he got what he asked for, which was doubtful, it was, of course, barrel whiskey. All the drinker had to rely on was his taste, experience, the effect and whatever lingering faith he may have had in saloonkeepers. "Pure" whiskey could easily be extended and doctored. In southern California tequila masqueraded under the trade name of many a proud old bourbon. Raw and fiery, it burned hotly in the bellies of the men who painted their tonsils with it, leaving the celebrant, in the words of one master of cowboy lingo, "so shaky he couldn't pour a drink of whiskey into a barrel with the head out."

Most of the potions available deserved the names bestowed upon them—skull varnish, tarantula juice, Taos lightning, snake water, bug juice and dynamite. As the whiskey rocked and splashed around on the journey through the sagebrush and across the fords, the compounded article did not, alas, improve either with the passage of time or the motion of the pitching wagon. But it packed a punch, as is evidenced in a paragraph preserved in a scrapbook of yellowing clippings: "A man out in Kansas said he could drink a quart of Cincinnati whiskey, and he did it. The silver mounting on his coffin cost $13.75."

When a wagon train met an army detachment, a crude bar was set up across a pair of barrels. Whiskey following the railheads was first dispensed in tents, then in prefabricated buildings moved to their site on flatcars, with the barman often setting out the drinks before the roof was on. When Forsyth, Montana, for example, was the end-of-the-track town on the Northern Pacific, twelve saloon outfits were brought in in 20 x 40 sections, with bar, tables, piano and chairs. In a matter of hours the professor was spanking the ivories and a man had been shot in an argument over a dance hall girl. A railroad can in one month, wrote Alex. E. Sweet and J. Armoy Knox, in *On a Mexican Mustang Through Texas, from the Gulf to the Rio Grande* (1884), produce "a town of a hundred houses, where beer is sold, billiards are played, the gentle tiger is bucked, and the strange woman holds her court . . . where the bedbug luxuriates, and even the book-agent lurketh around. . . ." The town referred to was Luling, Texas, "a place where a drink of whiskey costs twenty-five cents . . . so moves the car of progress; so the 'star of empire westward takes its way . . .' "

Capacities were prodigious. We do not have to guess about this. Western historical societies still have old records and bar bills which demonstrate the need of teamsters, meat hunters, cattle barons, English remittance men, fading actresses, for shots of red liquor in numbers running from five to thirty-plus per diem. Big vices went with big heroisms. The frequency with which armed men unlimbered their howitzers suggests that they were not drinking the higher grades of bourbon. San Francisco had twelve hundred murders between 1849 and 1854. The homicide rate among the drinking population east of the Mississippi was far lower, due either to an effete population, poor marksmanship, better whiskey or, according to one hypothesis, because they did not keep their guns oiled.

The movie and television dramas to the contrary, "shootouts" were definitely discouraged. When the Masterson brothers, Jim and William B., the latter known as "Bat" among those whom he had not as yet shot, plugged the bartender of the Lady Gay Saloon in Dodge City, Kansas, they were arrested and fined ten dollars and costs. The Mastersons felt the weight of social disapproval in other ways, too. There was a complaint that some of the bullets passed through the premises of the Long Branch Saloon next door to the Lady Gay and even disturbed the regular conduct of business in G. M. Hoover's wholesale liquor warehouse, where kegs of genuine Kentucky Club were

Courtesy of Library of Congress

A dance house in Leadville, Colorado. Lady gamblers and geishas, a shot of Taos Lightning or good bourbon helped to make life tolerable at the diggings.

Courtesy of Brown-Forman Distillers Corporation

Two specimens of liquor advertising done in the turn-of-the-century manner. Stagy "gag" art or voyeuristic illustrations were used to catch attention.

endangered by the gun play. The *Ford County Globe's* account of the collision was definitely unsympathetic: THE FESTIVE RE- VOLVER. AGAIN ITS MUSICAL VOICE IS HEARD IN THE LAND.

The distillate which caused much of the trouble also extended mercy. When a cowhand in town for a whing-ding had seen the bottom of a tumblerful of Nebraska Needle-gun a few times, his marksmanship was apt to be erratic. Mostly, and despite the myths perpetuated on Channel 4, the cowpunchers usually reached the point where they could be carried out before they had committed homicide. And so they were carted off to the cooler. In this condition, as Dr. W. P. Burts, first mayor of Fort Worth, was pleased to note, they were not likely to run away.

Until the rise of the temperance movement, American citizen- soldiers marched and fought on alcoholic liquors which were issued to them as a part of their rations, although the quantities were modest. The New York Public Library owns a manuscript order dated October 2, 1776, at Fort Sullivan, directing the delivery to bearer of "Nine gills of fatigue rum for Capt. Daniels Company." Valley Forge was made a bit more endura- ble because the men got from a gill to a half-pint of whiskey, depending on the state of the supplies. Zebulon Pike, then a cap- tain with General Wayne during the operations against the Indians on the upper Miami River, wrote in 1794 a paper which still exists: "The bearer hereof is entitled to one quart of whiskey having made the best shot on the Left Wing." In the War of 1812 the men formed messes of seven soldiers under a non-commissioned officer. Rations issued to them consisted of meat, bread, salt, vinegar, soap and whiskey.

During the administration of Andrew Jackson, spirits were removed from the army ration, but George Croghan, inspector- general of the regular army, who visited the forts along the rivers of the "new West," found that where there is money, there is whiskey. At Fort Crawford the soldiers would carry into the post as part of their washing a blanket soaked in liquor and then wring it out. In the 1840's smuggling whiskey to the army was called "Running the Mail." The Mail Runners handled a villainous type of brain-warper for which they demanded and received as much as thirty-five dollars a gallon.

The usefulness of whiskey, or the tornado juice that passed

for whiskey, in cheating the Indian out of his furs, horse, gun and blanket, and for extinguishing Indian titles to desirable real estate, was so great that the whiskey trader was never brought under effective control. Fortunes were made out of Indian whiskey. The big-pawed, heavy-featured Scotsman, Kenneth Mc-Kenzie, once styled "King of the Upper Missouri," owed his fur empire to whiskey. "Liquor I must have," he said, "or quit any pretensions to trade in these parts." McKenzie integrated vertically; that is, he raised corn and set up his own distillery on the Missouri River, where the odor of the fermenting corn mash mingled with the stench of green hides and fur-bearing Indians.

Luke Short, the famous gambler, got his start when he filled a wagon with what was known as Old Pine Top and set up business in a thicket near the Red Cloud Reservation. Short occasionally had to kill an Indian to keep order, although he hated to do it, as that meant he had to face some nocturnal digging. Luke always loathed physical exercise. The military finally and firmly put him on the train for Omaha, but they never discovered his private cemetery. When he got back to Dodge City he had $60,000 in his pocket and every reason, as he stepped into the Long Branch Saloon, to make the hospitable gesture which he did: "Gentlemen . . . suppose we adjourn to the bar and take a little something just for old times' sake."

After January 30, 1897, liquor could be sold lawfully only to persons who were not Indians. But—what is an Indian, or when is an Indian? This interesting question was answered by the Supreme Court of Oklahoma Territory in *Keith v. The United States and Another*. The Court decided that the son of a white man cannot be an Indian. Since half-breeds were universally known to have white fathers, it made the law prohibiting the sale of whiskey to Indians a dead letter. The Hon. Hiram Price, Commissioner of Indian Affairs in the years 1881–1885, once raised a hearty laugh in Congress by the quaintness of his expression when he described the affinity of the red men with liquor in these terms: "Now the first Indian who learned to raise corn in this country, after he had raised his crop under the instructions of a white agriculturist, came to the white man and said: 'I want to know how to fix this corn so I can eat it out of a bottle like the white man.' "

One reason why the Indian was especially vulnerable to whiskey lies in what was served to him. E. C. ("Teddy Blue") Abbott explains this in *We Pointed Them North:*

". . . You take one barrel of Missouri River water, and two gallons of alcohol. Then you add two ounces of strychnine to make them crazy—because strychnine is the greatest stimulant in the world—and three plugs of tobacco to make them sick— an Indian wouldn't figure it was whisky unless it made him sick —and five bars of soap to give it a bead, and half a pound of red pepper, and then you put in some sagebrush and boil it until it's brown. Strain into a barrel, and you've got your Indian whisky; that one bottle calls for one buffalo robe and when the Indian got drunk it was two robes."

It would be inaccurate to leave the impression that the West was won without the assistance of *any* good bourbon whiskey. There wasn't anything better to be had than the drinks set out by Fred Locke of Las Vegas, who wore a Prince Albert coat, ascot tie with pearl pin, formal striped trousers, a high silk hat and was called, and no wonder, Lord Locke. His partner, Brooks, was also a gentlemanly fellow. They opened up in 1880 with four barrels of prime Kentucky bourbon and a clientele admitted by invitation only. Lyman Frisbie of Carson City, Nevada, advertised in the Carson *Appeal,* "Whiskey of the most humanizing and exalting character. . . ." Frisbie's is remembered in both song and story. The song includes the couplet:

> Thar's flounders in Frisbie's winder,
> Thar's speerits at Frisbie's bar . . .

And the story has to do with a sporting character named George Cogill, a wandering minstrel and barroom comic who amused the patrons and cadged drinks in Frisbie's place. Cogill was a man of great capacity. He could hold more whiskey than any thirteen members of the local Democracy of the Ninth Congressional District of Indiana. Cogill once spent a week in New York City where he looked at the Fifth Avenue Hotel but stayed at the Tombs and was put off the trains only eighty-three times on the round trip.

At the other end of the spectrum lay the Wells Fargo Saloon

in Junction City, Kansas, which practiced truth in advertising by announcing "The Worst Liquors, The Poorest Cigars, and a Miserable Billiard Table." Further west, Robert Ford of the ballad "the dirty little coward that shot Mr. Howard"—i.e., shot Jesse James—operated Ford's Exchange at Creede, Colorado, and was reputed to serve the worst drinks in the Rocky Mountain region. Much of the "overnight" whiskey produced in the cellar by local compounders was as deficient in proof as it was in the aromatic characteristics of genuine bourbon. It was an expression of approbation in the whiskey mills of the West for a customer to designate a drink as "sink-taller whiskey"; for it was believed that a piece of tallow floats in weak whiskey but sinks in high-proof spirits.

The great philosophic problem of evil is posed in a bit of doggerel written about the catastrophe of April 18, 1906, in San Francisco which left a whiskey warehouse undamaged:

> If, as they say, God spanked the town
>   For being over-frisky,
> Why did He burn the churches down
>   And spare Hotaling's whisky?

The saloon in the West was even more of a key social institution than its eastern counterpart. When a man lost his lodge pin, it was natural for him to publish a Lost and Found advertisement directing the finder to return the pin to his favorite saloon. "Bat" Masterson, ordering a nickel-plated .45 caliber revolver from the Colt's people in Hartford, Connecticut, asked that future correspondence be sent to him in care of the Opera House Saloon in Dodge City. And in Butte, Montana, when Molly Demurska, queen of the underworld, took the town marshal, Jack Jolly, to have and to hold, the knot was tied in the Clipper Shades Saloon, after which the happy pair were drawn through the streets on the town fire engine.

Barrooms were such prime news sources that the *Gold Hill* (Nevada) *News* not only paid an editor his salary, but made an extra allowance, known as "whiskey money," used to loosen the tongues of local citizens who knew where the body was buried. The editor himself, like all other deserving, steady drinkers, got a morning stiffener for free in any saloon where he was known

to spend his money. Some citizens inevitably abused this chivalrous gesture. "But," says Wells Drury, in *An Editor on the
Comstock,* "as a general thing . . . the respectable ones didn't
extend their routes to more than seven places."

Often the western drink emporium was the setting for worth-
while cultural activities and moral advancement. Artemus Ward
once delivered one of his lectures in a saloon. Horace Greeley
made a speech against drinking in the bar of the Denver House
which was heard with perfect good humor. The courthouse and
the barroom were one in the shack presided over by Judge Roy
Bean. Bean was a saloonist and a "character," but also a regularly elected justice of the peace. Bean held sway at Langtry,
Texas, as self-styled "Law West of the Pecos." He still enjoys
a measure of apocryphal fame as a sort of combined cut-up and
local *alcalde.*

"Hear ye! Hear ye!" Old Roy would intone in his "Jersey
Lilly" (sic) taproom and suggest a snort of his nectar before
the honorable court convened.

The proprietors of these western oases were constantly involved in legal controversies brought on by their inveterate dis-
regard of all regulations, especially the Sunday closing law. In
New Mexico Territory, working on Sunday was contrary to law,
and selling liquor was deemed to be work. But the traffickers in
liquor took the position that the law did not apply because selling
red-eye was a noble endeavor based upon necessity, charity and
mercy, which the enactment expressly recognized. Western society looked with tolerant wisdom upon the problems of the drinker
who had on more sail than he could carry. A man fell into a hole
in a sidewalk while under the influence of red liquor and the trial
court held that he was guilty of contributory negligence because
he was drunk at the time. Not so, said the Supreme Court of California. It held, "If the defendants were at fault in leaving an
uncovered hole in the sidewalk of a public street the intoxication
of the plaintiff cannot excuse such gross negligence. A drunken
man is as much entitled to a safe street as a sober one, and much
more in need of it."

There has been a curious connection between preachers of the
gospel and rum-selling in the annals of the American West. The
region in the last quarter of the last century was dotted with

saloons run by ex-clergymen from back East who for their own reasons had exchanged the cloth for the bar rag. Joe Stinson was educated for the ministry, but ended up running a brass-railed tippling trap in Santa Fe, open twenty-four hours a day, seven days a week, with a gambling layout in the rear. Tom Kline, likewise, came west to save souls, but went into the thirst business at Bland. Many ministers, of course, invaded the dim precincts with the sawdust on the floor and the combined aroma of all the drinks of yesteryear to bring the Word before it was too late. They were invariably treated with courtesy, even when the hosts were assailed as "fiends in human form." In encounters of this sort, the cup-bearers of the Demon Rum came off at least as well as the spade-tail preachers so far as basic good manners are concerned. When the man with the message appeared, the poker players threw in their cards, pocketed their chips and the bar was closed as the evangelist mounted the platform of the keno outfit. Such a visitor made a few remarks of a religious nature at the end of a bar in Macon, Missouri, in 1909. The proprietor and the bartenders stood with folded arms during the devotions, then joined heartily in singing "Jesus, Lover of My Soul." The ranks of the saloonkeepers included few professed skeptics. Once two clergymen preached so powerfully in Close & Patterson's Saloon in Las Vegas that they were able to baptize four gamblers and fifteen hurdy-gurdy girls who were led to the improvised altar by Lazy Liz and Nervous Nellie. A reporter who was present passed up the opportunity to be saved, but remained for the subsequent jubilation when the bar reopened.

It was often difficult to tell the preachers and the gamblers apart, as they were the only citizens wearing long, black frock coats, white shirts and string ties. A man who was both was called upon to eulogize the memory of Charles ("Riley") Grannan at the rear of a Rawhide, Nevada, gin mill. Grannan was a Kentuckian and an honest gambler who had won and lost more money on horse races than the average man saw in a lifetime. Now he was at rest behind a saloon. Services of a sort were held over the rough coffin by the Reverend W. H. Knickerbocker, a Methodist pastor who had himself drained the chalice of life. Routed from the gambling tables, the Reverend was asked to express the farewells to Grannan of the assembled mourners—

rough miners, faro dealers, bartenders, dance hall girls in silk kimonos. They listened respectfully as he said unto them:

"I feel it incumbent upon me to state that I now occupy no ministerial or prelatic position. I am only a prospector. I make no claim to moral merit whatever or to religious authority, except it be the religion of the brotherhood of man."

The compassionate and eloquent tribute to the gambler which followed is generally regarded by those fortunate enough to possess the full text as one of the truly moving funeral orations in our language.

The line was thin which divided off the recreational facilities of the old West into theater, concert hall, dance house, faro bank or whiskey den. Women were scarce in the proportion of about four girls to fifty men who paid half a dollar to dance with a damsel and a dollar a drink at the "water hole" when the caller sang out "All promenade to the bar!" With every five drinks purchased, the patrons received one snake free. The geishas scrounged for what they could get through commissions on drinks, or renting out their physical charms, or gambling. Some of the names of girls who ornamented the resorts of the old cattle trails are remembered: Rockin' Chair Emma, Jack-Rabbit Sue, Covered-Wagon Liz, Dodge City Kate, Ogallala Shorty. The Bull Run, a San Francisco deadfall, called their ladies "pretty waiter girls," known to their familiars as the Galloping Cow, Roaring Gimlet, Lady Jane Gray and Little Lost Chicken. Martha Jane ("Calamity Jane") Canary was viewed as part of the overhead in bars from Billings to the Rio Grande, most of which she boasted she had been thrown out of.

Few of the women gamblers who ran a square game—Kitty the Schemer, "Madame Moustache" or Haltershanks Eva—ever found it necessary to draw a gun. But the derringer was always handy in the reticule. "Faro Nell" could shoot the heels off a man's boots; or if he cared to hold up a glass of whatever liquid he might be using to ward off dehydration, Nell could knock it out of his hand from a distance of several yards.

"Poker Alice" Ivers, who spoke with a clipped British accent and took her whiskey neat, liked especially to skin a greeny on the Burlington Route because it was a granger railroad and carried passengers of a particularly rustic character. Sunday

"Poke Alice" read her Bible and meditated. She refused to throw a card on the Sabbath day and taught her girls their Sunday-school lesson in the parlor devoted for six days a week to highly secular frolics. The only time Alice ever shot a member of the U.S. Cavalry, using a .38 on a .45 frame, she asked the sheriff, after she had been deposited in the calaboose, for her favorite reading matter, the Holy Bible. A search revealed that the jail didn't have a copy, which so shocked the conscience of the jury that they rebuked the authorities by finding Alice not guilty.

It took "all kinds" of men and a variety of institutions to establish the outposts of civilization in the Great West—the farmer, the trader, the missionary, the lawyer, the newspaper, railroad, church and jail. But always, wrote Mark Twain, as he turned this progression over in his mind, whiskey arrived on the scene first, which he declared was a "solemn and beautiful" thought. The men who punched the cattle from Texas to Kansas, who spanned the high Sierras with steel rails, broke out the high-grade ore, logged off the big timber, built the lovely city of San Francisco, drank mescal and Taos lightning when they had to, but made bourbon the prestige whiskey of the West. And they found mint along the Sweetwater to grace the julep cup. Clear, cold mountain streams were diverted into man-made ditches between the tents and cabins down on the flats. Bourbon and ditch water, one and inseparable. Our people couldn't have civilized the West without bourbon and ditch.

At least, they didn't.

Chapter 14

A SOFA WITH EVERY CASE

THERE was little point in the distilling industry's arranging for a well-developed "Miss Bourbon" to smile prettily, wear a tiara and wave her jeweled scepter over a barrel of whiskey during all those long decades when American whiskey was without identity. Promotional gimmicks and advertising, therefore, were not an important factor in moving wet goods to the thirsty until the beginning of the present century. Advertising meant "business card" announcements of names and prices, novelties such as art calendars, bar glasses, match boxes, pocket diaries and similar give-aways which were passed out to the trade. Bar whiskeys carried the label of the house. One such paper label was embellished with a picture of a big elk in a wild, mountain setting and was imprinted "Fine Old Bourbon Whiskey from Grand Central Hotel Bar, Denver, Colorado." Drugstores retailed bourbon in clear glass bottles, as they did medicine. The quality of the medicinal whiskey vended in "dry" territory was the subject of comment by Bill Nye, the humorist and popular philosopher, who remarked soon after Kansas adopted statewide prohibition in 1880:

"If it is the great big burning desire of your heart to go into a town of 2,000 people and open the thirteenth drug store in order that you may stand behind a tall black walnut prescription case day in day out, with a graduate in one hand and a Babcock fire extinguisher in the other, filling orders for whisky made of stump water and the juice of future punishment, you will do well to go to Kansas. It is a temperate state, and no saloons are allowed here. All is quiet and orderly and the drug business is a great success."

Grocery stores handled bulk whiskeys from the spigot, like vinegar or kerosene. Fancy places like J. F. Conrad Grocer Co. in St. Louis stocked whiskeys of their own bottling. "Jug goods" or "case goods" was the term for whiskey put up in glass. They also sold "in wood" by the gallon. Stock labels were sometimes shipped with the barreled whiskey, double imprinted, as in "Old Crow Hand Made Sour Mash Bourbon Whiskey," with the further information supplied beneath, "Expressly for O. F. Haley Co., Fort Worth, Texas. See that Seal Over Cap is Unbroken." Exclusive deals were common. All the Old Jordan made in the 1890's went to W. H. Thomas & Son, Louisville; all the Cedar Brook made by W. H. McBrayer was contracted for in advance by a sole agent—James Levy & Bro. at Cincinnati. The problem of finding the consumer rested with the distributor, not the manufacturer. Obviously, under this system, labels were of uncertain value as a guide to the consumer.

There was a running controversy which grew hotter as the century ran out over whether much of the liquor that reached the public was really whiskey at all. This rhubarb, of which more later, got an airing in Congress in 1896. It was developed during committee hearings that a little over two million gallons of whiskey was then being sold annually "in its original integrity," while 105,000,000 gallons were used for mixing purposes in beverages which contained from three gallons of aged whiskey to each twenty gallons of grain spirits, down to practically no whiskey at all. This grade of goods involved some rather simple work in the basement with ethyl alcohol, concentrated Essence of Bourbon, prune juice, a dash of fusel oil and a mysterious something in a bottle labeled "Body and Age Preparation." In a matter of minutes a liquid came into being which was widely offered as Old Bourbon. Such whiskey was, naturally, a good deal cheaper than the aged product.

"It is an admitted axiom that quality recedes as cheapness advances . . . the ancient Bourbon flavor has departed," mourned

Edmund H. Taylor, Jr., "and the stomach groans under the dominion of the new ruler." Gradually and at first timidly the industry experimented with bottled goods as its hope and protection. The Bottled-in-Bond Act of 1897, referred to earlier, was a powerful stimulus to trends already in the making. Bonding of whiskey in the wood was almost forty years old at the time. The new feature was distillery *bottling* under government supervision. Yet even the bottle wasn't absolutely new. George Garvin Brown, who found his warrant for distilling the "good creature" in the Bible, put his bourbon in bottles around 1870 and named it after the great Confederate cavalry leader, General Nathan Bedford Forrest. But the name came out for some reason now lost to history with only one "r," as Old Forester. A few other fine table whiskeys were available in glass before the 1897 Act, among them Quarter Century, a bourbon distributed by J. T. Weller; Old Guckenheimer, a rye; also Old Crow; and Hunter's Baltimore Rye.

In order to develop consumer packages, a way had to be found to achieve close tolerances in the diameter of the neck of the bottle. The bottle neck for new marketing techniques was quite literally the neck of the bottle. This difficulty was overcome when in 1903 Michael Joseph Owens, inventor and glass manufacturer, brought out the first fully successful automatic glass-making machine. It produced "small mouth ware" in astronomical quantities. Figures tell the story of the shift to the consumer package: in 1903 the Kentucky distillers bottled 400,000 gallons of bourbon. In 1913 the figure had risen to 9,000,000 gallons. After the bottle was standardized, department stores became an important outlet for family whiskeys, and it was a common, and pleasant, sight to see a store window filled with Green River, Clarke's Whiskey, Hermitage and Old Tub at a dollar for a full quart.

The necessity for establishing brand names with the consumer having arisen, the distiller found himself involved with new frauds and abuses. In the year Old Forester made its bow, only 121 trade marks of all kinds were registered under the U.S. Trademark Act. Only sixty-two trade mark cases had then been decided by the American courts. Gradually the conception gained ground that the owner of a label whose value he had created was entitled to protection against imitators—an idea expressed in the oft-quoted assertion of Lord Langdale: "A man is not to sell his goods under the pretense that they are the goods of another man."

The value of trademarking as it applied to whiskey was observed by the U.S. industry when Hiram Walker & Son successfully entered the United States market. Hiram Walker was a sixth-generation Yankee from Massachusetts who sold flour, feed and whisky in Ontario. Walker exemplified in his career the copybook maxims and homely virtues and built a whisky barony at Walkerville. Like all distillers, "Mr. Hiram" owned cattle. One of his cows became famous in American lawbooks in connection with the legal principle of mutual mistake. The cow bore the aristocratic name of Rose of Aberlone. She had a problem; she couldn't conceive. Mr. Hiram regretfully sold her for beef to a man named Sherwood. Then, at the last minute, Walker learned that Rose was about to become a mother. He refused to deliver the cow. Sherwood sued. Walker finally won out for Rose in the Supreme Court of Michigan and the case went into the textbooks. It has been celebrated in delightful verses by Professor Brainerd Currie of the University of Chicago who tells in rhyme the tale of Rose's shame and subsequent triumph and the legal tangle which still plagues the weary law student; for, as Professor Currie poetized:

> . . . even the reluctant drone
> Must cope with Rose of Aberlone.

But enough of cows. The Walkers, Mr. Hiram and his son, "Mister Ed"—Edward Chandler Walker, 1851–1915—introduced Walker's Club Whisky into the United States in 1882. This distinctive Canadian whisky—note the spelling of whisky in Canada—was so well liked that some of Kentucky's finest citizens got worried. They pulled on their Congress gaiters, packed their valises and took off for Washington to argue that people who enjoyed Walker's Club Whisky might think they were drinking the national drink, made in Kentucky. So there ought to be a law, they told such sympathetic elder statesmen as Kentucky Senators James B. Beck and John S. Williams and the rising younger Kentuckians in the House, J. Proctor Knott, John G. Carlisle and

Joseph C. S. Blackburn. Walker thereupon added to his label the word "Canadian," which clearly identified the place of origin and the ownership. Thus the now famous name, Canadian Club, was born. This tactic hastened the growth in the United States of Canadian Club and contributed to the education of the bourbon distilling interests. They noted down a useful datum: when a distiller wished to find markets far from home, the way to become favorably known was to develop a trademark.

There were legal metes and bounds placed upon a man's fancy when he dreamed up an alluring trade name. A label could not convey false information. A whiskey could not be associated with the labor movement, for instance, by calling it "Knights of Labor Whiskey" when it had no connection with the organization or its members. The same rule applied to lines of endeavor as disparate as distilling and horse racing. Churchill Downs, Inc., successfully stopped a distillery company from adopting as its corporate name Churchill Downs Co. The court ruled that the borrower of a name borrows the good will that attaches to it.

A distinctive word can be protected, such as "Crow." Woe to a distiller or rectifier who launched a brand of liquor called "White Crow." He would undoubtedly find himself engaged in expensive litigation, since some eighteen hundred legal actions have already been brought in defense of Old Crow—trade mark cases, cases involving substitution, tampering or "cutting." The word "old," on the other hand, is not according to trade mark law descriptive of the age or an indication of quality. It merely points to "the kind"; that is, the word is simply a part of a mark indicating provenance of the merchandise.

This point is aptly illustrated in a favorite anecdote of the dean of Kentucky distillers, Mr. Julian J. P. Van Winkle, Sr., who distills good stories as well as good bourbon. Between races at a county fair, according to "Pappy," a little merchant carried a basket up and down the rail, shouting *"Hot* pie . . . get yo' *hot* pie!" A hungry customer bit into one, then spluttered, "Hey, boy! This pie ain't hot!"

"I know it, boss," grinned the youngster. "Dat's jess de *name* ob de pie!"

Since only lawyers and business executives understand that proprietary names are, under trade mark law, denominative only of "the kind," it is not surprising that the drinking public cherishes fond mental associations with such a cobwebby word as "old," or that more liquor labels start out with "old" than any other word.

Artists, semanticists and lay psychologists, sensitive to the latent poetry of life, have labored to produce trade names with tempting overtones. Among such efforts may be cited, for sheer virtuosity, Old Tub, Rebel Yell, Mountain Dew, and here's a cozy one, Chimney Corner Bourbon.

Building up consumer acceptance of a brand label meant also taking on a running battle with counterfeiters. "Beware of fraudulent imitations and refilled bottles," warned Jas. E. Pepper & Co. "All genuine barrels, cases and bottles (when unbroken across the stopper) bear this signature, 'Jas. E. Pepper.'" The signature was distinctive, protectable and had psychological value.

During an investigation of the whiskey market in 1893 by the Committee of the Judiciary of the House of Representatives, the following dialogue took place between Mr. Greenhut, whom we have already met (Chapter 12) and a member of the Committee:

Q.: Retailers sell them for seven-year-old Crow whiskey, and five-year-old, or sell them for anything they please?

A.: They sell them for anything they please; we have no control over them.

Q.: And you brand them any way they want; that is, you give them any fancy name they want?

A.: Yes, sir.

The imitation of labels by photographic processes, the duplication of corks and stoppers, the refilling of genuine packages with factitious liquids loaded court calendars with civil suits, applications for injunctions and claims of damage from infringements. Prosecution was costly. Juries were hard to convince. When the courts did enjoin the sale and award damages, the imitator could always start up again trespassing upon some other trademark.

Hiram Walker & Son was especially aggressive in seeing that counterfeiting or tampering with Canadian Club was a dangerous game. Walker had detectives patrol the retail outlets looking for bastard bottlings with a Canadian atmosphere. The Company advertised boldly to the general public, named the fakers and invited libel suits. Walker advertised on a billboard, for instance, in Joliet, Illinois, that a local hotel was selling some other Canadian whisky as Canadian Club. The hotel sued, but Walker won. One Charles Klyman of 232 East Kinzie Street, Chicago, was indicted for an even graver crime: he sold American whiskey as Canadian Club. The price he had to pay to escape the consequences is set forth in the following announcement.

JULY 25, 1898.   BONFORT'S WINE AND SPIRIT CIRCULAR.   192

A CONFESSION.

Chicago, Ill., June 3, 1898.

Messrs. HIRAM WALKER & SONS, Limited.

Being under indictment by the Grand Jury of Cook County, Illinois, charged with having put up and sold American whisky as your "CANADIAN CLUB" Whisky, the bottles, labels, capsules, etc., being imitations of yours, my wife has appealed to you to take into consideration her unhappy position and that of our young children. This you have consented to do upon the following conditions:—

1.—That in the public interest I shall not go wholly unpunished.

2.—That I shall solemnly pledge myself never again to be a party to the imitation of any goods whatever, whether yours or those of others, and should I violate this promise the present indictment against me shall be revived and prosecuted.

I accept these conditions without any reservation. I admit that I am guilty as charged under the Illinois Trade-Mark Act of having imitated your labels, capsules, etc. As some reparation I consent that this document may be published in trade journals, newspapers, etc., as extensively as may seem to you proper in your own interest and for the ends of justice; I promise to forever abandon all connection with the production or sale of goods to my knowledge falsely labelled or described; and I agree that should I fail to keep this promise the above-mentioned indictment against me may be reinstated.

Witness, RUSSELL WHITMAN.   (Signed)   CHARLES KLYMAN.

NOTE.—Mr. Klyman until lately carried on business at 232 East Kinzie St., Chicago, in his own name and as The Dr. Ancker Bitters Co.

"People of Chicago," Walker proclaimed on another occasion, "you are being swindled. A. M. Rothschild & Co. and Frank Brothers are selling fraudulent goods after being duly warned regarding them . . . we will promptly meet them in the courts of their own state. . . ."

The United States government also took part in this game of cops and robbers. A department store, grocery or bar was permitted to blend whiskey in quantities up to five gallons, as a convenience. If, however, the retailer compounded more than five gallons, the revenue agents were interested. For the store was then subject to a special federal tax.

In 1894, when the bonding period was raised from three to eight years, bourbon distillers hailed the postponement of the tax payment for five more years with enthusiasm, especially those with large holdings of maturing whiskey. Three years later, as has been noted, came the provision for distillery bottling. This arrangement, Colonel Taylor said happily at the time, "now transfers to a consumer anywhere on the globe a bottle of Kentucky whiskey just exactly as that whiskey was made and matured on the original distillery premises," with the green strip stamp "telling, under government imprimatur, all the essential details which might interest the consumer in the identification of a pure, unadulterated whiskey."

The U.S. Treasury has always made it clear that the designation "Bottled in Bond" does not necessarily imply superiority. But the innovation stimulated a happy chorus of advertising. "Uncle Sam says its All Right . . . . we dare not take a gallon of our own whiskey from our own warehouse unless it is all right," Hayner Whiskey pointed out. Old Sunnybrook decorated its advertisements with a picture of a soldierly looking government man wearing an official cap marked "Inspector" and pointed out, "The Inspector is back of every Bottle." A wholesaler handling, among others, such representative labels as Hermitage, Sunnybrook and Paul Jones, decorated its advertising with some ten different pictures of Uncle Sam in various pleasing poses, with the bold heading "Uncle Sam is Our Partner."

The general public responded warmly to the bonded goods. "If you want to catch bass in this country," a Douglas County, Missouri, man explained to a stranger, "you got to use a cork for bait, with a green revenue stamp on it." He meant to indicate by this that the wise fisherman gave the guide a bottle of good whiskey. Falmouth, a St. Louis brand, bombarded the grangers and stockmen of the Missouri Valley with such persuasions as these: Every drop tested by a government inspector. No chance of adulteration. Cut out the middleman (a favorite gambit with the Populists and Greenbackers). Four quarts for $2.75, and Money Back if Not Satisfied.

A characteristic feature of advertising in the 1890's and early 1900's was the coining of the catchy phrase or slogan. The technique evolved out of the necessities of billboard advertising which had to be short and pithy. Many of the apt phrases struck off in some moment of inspiration became a part of the language. Some acquired a good will worth millions of dollars. This is the period when Fletcher's Castoria introduced "Children Cry for it." George Eastman flashed out "You press the button; we do the rest." Schlitz Beer contributed "The Beer that made Milwaukee famous" and the distilling industry came up with "The whiskey without a headache"; "Every Swallow makes a Friend"; "The Whiskies of our Daddies"; "We Sold Your Grandfather. Now we want to sell you." But without doubt the most arresting headline of the early years of this century was "A Bottle of Whiskey Free!" which appeared in 1906 for—hold your breath —"Our 15-year Old Jno. E. Fitzgerald Rye or Bourbon Whiskey."

The funniest blunder in the old liquor ads occurred when the make-up man for *Puck,* the humorous weekly, locked up an advertisement for a Peoria whiskey just above "Dr. Leslie E. Keeley's Treatment for Drunkenness." The topical theme which gave the most mileage in its day was the Spanish-American War, that "splendid little war," also jovially referred to as "the war against the Dons." Cincinnati offered a cigar called "Manila Dew" and "Dewey's Old Manila Whiskey"; while the poet laureate of the Greenbriar Distilling Company wrote of the old-fashioned sour mash distilled at the Blowing Spring in Nelson County:

> Tis said that Dewey favors it
> And "Uncle Sam" does say
> That without it at Manila
> We would not have won the day.
> Our victories on land and sea
> Are grand, and 't will inspire
> The boys to greater efforts
> If you give them "Old Greenbriar."

In the expansionist mood of the times, *Bonfort's Wine and Liquor Circular* prophesied an epoch of whiskey imperialism. American bonds would follow the flag; or maybe lead it. The Hawaiian Islands have sampled it, said *Bonfort's,* under "the arm of affection, protection and possession" and there was no reason under the sun why bourbon should not soon be the national drink of Cuba. Just before U.S. involvement in World War I, Colonel Taylor expressed his views, at advertising rates, on a prudent defense policy: "Fortify the Canal Zone with Old Taylor."

Against the background of our own time in which health or medical claims are not permitted, it is interesting to read what the Duffy Malt Whiskey Co. of Rochester, New York, said of their product:

"Entirely Free from Fusil oil . . . a Deadly Poison. Positive sure cure for Malaria, Pulmonary Complaints, Indigestion, Nervous and all Wasting Diseases. . . . The recognized Antidote for Cholera . . . found on the sideboards of the best families . . . in the physician's dispensing room . . . A Beverage and Medicine Combined." For six dollars the Duffy people were prepared to send anywhere east of the Rocky Mountains, express prepaid in plain wrapper, "thus avoiding all opportunity for comment," six quart bottles and a free recipe for curing "consumption" which involved a combination of Duffy's and raw beefsteak. Together they gave nature "the upper hand in the conflict."

In fact, the promoters of Duffy's Pure Malt Whiskey went even further. An advertisement in the *New York Herald* declared that if the Hon. Calvin S. Brice, an estimable gentleman who had died recently from the effects of a cold, had used Duffy's his life would have been spared. Observers outside the Duffy circle often referred to the remedy scoffingly as a "booze medicine" because of its health pitch and the finding of three chemists employed by New York state who analyzed the liquid. They reported that Duffy's was just cheap whiskey with a little cane sugar added. Vincent Starrett, well-known author, journalist and book columnist for the *Chicago Tribune Magazine of Books,* has preserved a curious story about Duffy's that went the rounds of country newspaper offices long years ago. In Paris, during the French Revolution, "an aristocratic head had just fallen into the basket, and the executioner was about to proceed to the next victim, when he noted that the lips . . . were . . . trying to speak. . . . He snatched the head from the basket and held it close to his ear . . . the message came clearly: 'I could keep this up all day if I had a good drink of Duffy's Malt Whisky.' " Starrett concludes, "They don't write any better 'ads' than that today."

As the movement for compulsory prohibition spread, drying

up more and more states, the liquor companies turned to mail-order selling. Since interstate commerce was under federal juris-diction, the dry states could not prevent the shipment of whiskey which entered their territory from "wet" cities. Persistent efforts were made by the dry forces to close this gap. They were finally successful when the Webb-Kenyon Interstate Liquor Act was passed over President Taft's veto in 1913, the greatest coup which the Anti-Saloon League had pulled off up to that time. The Act forbade interstate shipment of liquor into states where the sale was illegal. The drys clinched their victory in 1917 when the United States Supreme Court upheld the Act's constitution-ality. The world of lawful liquor was shrinking fast. Denizens of Broadway could still follow their customary itinerary—cocktails at the Knickerbocker Hotel Bar, a floor show at the Palais Royal or Healey's. They could catch the midnight frolics at a "roof," make the rounds of Rector's, Churchill's or Reisenweber's, with breakfast at Ciro's. But their pleasures were doomed. The farmer mentality was in the ascendant. It is a sign of the times that by 1918 Sears, Roebuck & Co. were advertising home distilling out-fits in their big "wish book."

Georgia, the Carolinas and a number of other states made it a penal offense to publish an advertisement for whiskey in their territories. But because the U.S. controlled the postal service, for a generation the man in the gray uniform handed out the whiskey ads, such as one circular marked "Occupant," circulated from Jacksonville, Florida, which offered a box of cigars, a quart of whiskey and a revolver for $3.48. The Shawhan 10-year-old bourbon people sold four quarts by mail for eighty cents each, and would send as lagniappe a corkscrew, a shot glass or a bottle of "old peach." Hayner Whiskey, distilled in Troy, Ohio, came with a special tamper-proof closure so that one could keep his loved ones out of his whiskey bottle.

One whiskey advertiser tied a chinaware premium to his prod-uct. The Board of Temperance, Prohibition and Public Morals of the Methodist Episcopal Church waved the advertisement in front of the House Post Office Committee as evidence that the traffickers in liquor were pursuing the women, too. A startling proposition in the way of a premium was that made by Liebenthal Brothers & Co. of Cleveland, Ohio. They sold blended whiskey at ten dollars a case and gave a *sofa* with every case. The seller always pointed out that he shipped in unmarked packages: "It's nobody's business but yours and ours," one firm asserted.

Whiskey was also distributed by door-to-door canvassers. Houses which followed this pattern of selling were always on the lookout for "a good man in your territory to accept sole agency." All he had to do, as one concern put it, was to "take orders" for Woodland Sour Mash, the whiskey that was served on Wabash Railroad Dining Cars and used in the Pennsylvania State Insane Asylum at South Mountain. In addition to a fifty cent commission, the peddler received an "Agent's Complete Outfit" which included the following equipment: a corkscrew, jigger glass, order blanks, advertising flyers, some miniature bottles and a quart of Woodland. As a further inducement to effort, there was a bonus system of premium merchandise, scaled according to the gallonage sold and ranging imaginatively from a .38 caliber double-action revolver to a derby hat, a Columbia Gramophone, and on up to an all-wool suit in a big check pattern. No peddling license was needed, the Woodland people pointed out, and since delivery was C.O.D., "You violate no law" when selling in a dry town.

A colorful figure of the whiskey world was the commercial traveler on tour. As early as 1869, salesmen were out on "the road." In that year a drummer for a wholesale liquor merchant in Paducah was making a regular trip to West Tennessee where he collected a considerable sum of money and decamped for parts unknown. The replacement was Isaac Wolfe Bernheim who, with his brother Bernard, later started his own firm, Bernheim Brothers. The two brothers traveled over the entire South and much of the West and Northwest in the 1880's, branched out into manufacturing and created the I. W. Harper brand, made up of the initials of Isaac Wolfe and the last name of one of their top salesmen. I. W. died at age ninety-three, a philanthropist and leading citizen, who gave Louisville a hospital wing, assorted statuary and a collection of oil paintings. He is remembered for his high business principles and good bourbon.

But not all whiskey salesmen were gentlemen. One trick in the day of bulk whiskey was to slip a nail into the barrel of a competitor, while calling on a bar or tavern. Whiskey cannot tolerate

iron, and turns a repulsive black in its presence. Another stunt
was the comparative test. The drummer would pour out his own
liquor first. Then he diverted the customer with chatter so that
the drink stood for a while. Like the champagne agent, the whiskey traveler was blessed with the gift of gab. While the whiskey
stood in the glass, the drummer drummed. He pointed out the
long-lasting bead, the delightful color. If sales were small in the
territory he bragged that his whiskey was too good. The consumers wouldn't let it get far from home. When sales were boom-
ing he declared that the label was known from coast to coast. He
talked up age as a desirable feature during periods of ample inventories of aged whiskey. At other times he dropped the subject.

Finally and quickly he poured the rival brand and invited com-
parison. His own whiskey presumably won the test. Why? Because the higher alcohols, the undesirable aldehydes, evaporate
first. In days gone by, distillers sometimes left the bung out of
the barrel to get rid of the "pig tracks." To this practice the
government now says a firm no. Extra evaporation would mean
a loss in the tax.

Whiskey drummers were generous spenders. Treating in a bar
was a way of winning customers for their goods and presumably
the loyalty of the proprietor. Old Roy Bean, in his "Jersey Lily"
saloon at Langtry, Texas, had a dodge for collecting for more
drinks than he had actually served. He would line up his old
empties on the bar and insist upon payment based on the bottle
count. One salesman complained about a bottle that did not look
to him as though it had been freshly emptied.

"It does look fairly dry," Judge Bean admitted, "but it's the
way of drinkin' that some of the boys has . . . they not only
drink the bottle dry but they sop it out."

Here are two tales about escapades of wayward knights of the
grip whose "line" was whiskey. Before Kansas went dry and long
before Carry Nation, of hatchet fame, smashed the bar of the
Carey Hotel in Wichita, six indignant young women zeroed in
on the saloon operated by Bradley & Hildreth in Mound City,
Kansas, armed with axes and hatchets, just as Jim Tomlinson,
the first customer, was taking his early morning phlegm-cutter.
Miss Sarah Wattles stood on the bar and made a clean sweep
of the glassware while a whiskey "commercial" from Leaven-

worth stopped to watch the fun. His wagon, standing out in front, was equipped with barrels and faucets so that spirits could be drawn off for his customers. While he looked at what was happening to the unfortunate Messrs. Bradley & Hildreth, one of the ladies quietly stepped around his wagon and opened all the spigots. Someone called the salesman's attention to the fact that he had his troubles, too. Approaching Miss Wattles, he shouted, "I never did strike a woman, but by God I can."

At that moment Amelia Botkin stepped up with her ax and offered to split his head open. A small town in Kansas has always been a poor place for threatening a woman. The drummer had scarcely escaped from Miss Botkin's ire when he found a rope around his neck while chivalrous townsmen rushed plans for a hanging in the rear of the saloon. Better judgment prevailed and he was released and ordered to make his tracks. One horse fell dead before he was ten minutes out of town. He made it into Fort Scott riding bareback.

Whiskey sales promotion saw what is perhaps its finest hour in a story which hails from Vermont. The Daughters of the American Revolution had gathered at the Pavilion Hotel in Montpelier to commemorate the visit of the Marquis de La Fayette to Montpelier in 1825. An historical marker was to be dedicated, with appropriate oratory. A whiskey salesman observed the preparations with interest, got a bright idea which he quietly executed during the lunch hour. That afternoon the people gathered around the flag-draped tablet. The band played. The audience clapped. The speaker outdid himself in the felicity of his remarks. Pointing to the hidden tablet he rose to his climax:

"When the American flag is lifted, you will see words to be read by generations unborn."

The flag was whisked upward and a large placard appeared. On it was lettered:

"Wilson's Whiskey—That's All."

Chapter 15

BUT–WHAT *IS* WHISKEY?

A KENTUCKY distiller of the old school, Colonel Attila
Bird, central figure in Irvin S. Cobb's novel, *Red Likker,*
nourished his prejudices about his colleagues in the liquor business on such disparaging phrases as the "Whiskey Trust crowd,"
the "Dutch crowd" in Cincinnati, the "Rectifying crowd" in
Louisville. For them he expressed a sweeping contempt, as dealers in bogus wares.

The old Colonel also recognized the "Canada crowd" and the
"Rye crowds" of Pennsylvania and Maryland. Below the Kentucky state line dwelt the "Tennessee crowd." For these latter
groupings Colonel Bird felt a degree of tolerance. They were
competitors entitled to respect and to be endured with patience
and philosophy. The Colonel conceded that they sold "more or
less authentic goods." Importers didn't count, since they neither
distilled nor simulated bourbon. The Colonel also wrote, signed
and financed a pamphlet in which he collected Bible references
such as the Psalmist's recipe for gladdening the heart of man and
other instances proving to his satisfaction that the Scriptures
commend the use of alcoholic beverages.

The fictional Colonel Bird may well have been suggested by
the real-life George Garvin Brown whose flower-cutting of references favorable to wine and strong drink was mentioned earlier.
The real Brown and the imaginary Bird saw eye to eye on the

subject of What is whiskey? To both, whiskey was aged Kentucky sour mash, the goods which the government held for the bonded period and which then moved at proof to the buyer, exactly as it was made and matured on the original distillery premises.

The question, What is whiskey? is deceptively simple. Actually, no one knows what whiskey is. Its nature partakes of mystery. Arbitrary definitions have been adopted, therefore, to explain and define whiskey. Discussion of the subject has usually been carried on in the heated atmosphere of clashing economic interests. When the bonding period for American whiskey was raised from one to three years some antagonism was evident between the Kentucky interests and the compounders of what was called "domestic" bourbon. With the extension of bonding to eight years and the passage of the bottling act the tension increased as the prestige of the green stamp with the consumer became evident. The agitation for a national food and drug law, and the struggle over what the provisions of such a law should be as they applied to whiskey, set off a lively "Whiskey War" fought by Kentucky colonels, survivors of the old Whiskey Trust, lobbyists and lawyers holed up at the Raleigh and Willard hotels in Washington, congressmen and senators responding to various political and economic influences and agricultural chemists who conducted enlightening demonstrations with beakers, graduates and vari-colored liquids in the committee rooms of Congress and in at least one instance, even at the White House.

The pressure which built up for what was popularly called a "pure food law" was a part of the wave of social reform which produced the Emancipation Proclamation, the Interstate Commerce Commission, the Sherman Anti-Trust Act, prison reform, the Women's Rights agitation and the resurgence of temperance sentiment. The first food and drug bill was introduced into Congress in 1879. By 1902 one hundred and ninety variants on the idea had been dropped into the legislative hopper. None had ever come to a vote. At each session of Congress the bills were quietly shelved, especially in the Senate. *Life,* the magazine of fun and satire, commented:

"Who is that shabby-looking, patched-up individual trying to get on the floor of the House?" asks the Legislative Enactment of the Appropriation Schedule.

"What?" answers the Appropriation Schedule. "Oh, that's old Pure Food bill. When he first came here he looked pretty good, but now he has been knocked around and changed so much that his former friends don't know him at all. In a minute you'll see him thrown out bodily again."

Every senator had his angle. To Senators George F. Hoar and Henry Cabot Lodge of Massachusetts, it was the sacred codfish, then salted with boric acid. Eugene Hale and William P. Frye of Maine were not interested in a consumer measure whose central provision related to adulteration and misbranding—not as long as the humble but abundant Maine herring could be profitably packed as "Imported French sardines" in boxes with fancy labels in French, to give the goods a Gallic air. Similar considerations weighed heavily with other Big Business senators, such as John Keen of New Jersey, a state whose preserving and canning factories relied upon benzoate of soda, and Joseph Foraker of Ohio, whose home city of Cincinnati, long-time center of rectifying and whiskey-selling, wore, in the words of one study, "a rakish garland."

So the question of how "Ohio red head" would be treated under the new law got tangled up with such unappetizing subjects as the canned peas that looked garden-fresh because of a process known as "copper-greening," with pork and beans that contained formaldehyde, with veal masquerading as potted chicken, with coal-tar jellies and olive oil made from cotton seed. The ordinary man of 1900 found himself living in a big, new world of butterine and mapleine and Old Bourbon which, as we shall see, was sometimes not only very, very young, but wasn't even of grain origin.

Between 1903 and 1906 a determined effort was made to get a pure food law on the books. In essence, the bill was a labeling act.

"Tell the truth on the label," Dr. Harvey W. Wiley, Chief of the Bureau of Chemistry, U.S. Department of Agriculture, urged, "and let the consumer judge for himself."

So far as whiskey was concerned, the key issue was how rectified spirits were to be described. It was proposed that any article listed in the *Pharmacopoeia of the United States* was adulterated if it differed from the standard set in that august and erudite work listing drugs and medicines and describing their properties, preparation and use. The *Pharmacopoeia* defined whiskey. In the Eighth Revision, then in effect, it said that whiskey was an alcoholic liquid obtained by the distillation of the mash of fermented grain—Indian corn or rye, wheat, barley or their mixtures. Whiskey was an amber-colored liquid having a distinctive odor and taste, and a slightly acid reaction. Whiskey should have a specific gravity ranging between 0.945 and 0.924, an alcoholic strength by volume of 44 per cent to 55 per cent, only traces of fusel oil, and an absence of added sugar, glycerine or aromatic substances. And whiskey was at least four years old.

Was blended whiskey, then, which amounted to from 75 per cent to 90 per cent of all alcoholic spirits being drunk at the time, and usually sold well under proof, a spurious article? The National Wholesale Liquor Dealers' Association, who were in fact the manufacturers of most of the compound liquors sold in the United States, sensed a general bias among the friends of the food bill against their branch of the distilled spirits industry. This served to deepen the antagonism they already felt toward the pure food legislation.

One prong of the argument was, who's pure? At the time when the pure food agitation was picking up speed, straight bourbons often claimed purity as their distinctive feature. Old Judge was advertised as "The Original Pure Food Pot Still Whiskey." McKenna, mashed in small tubs and boiled in the old pot over open fires, was "pure and straight." Kentucky Dew was "The standard of Purity" and sour mash advertisers illustrated their advertisements with maidens fair in virginal white to push the idea. The blenders scouted the idea of aged whiskeys being "pure." They had a horrid word for such distillates—"fusel oil whiskeys." It was their own basic ingredient, neutral grain spirits, they insisted, which had every right in history, in logic and in chemistry, to be called the purest of all.

The Bottled-in-Bond law, second only to the Holy Bible in the reverence it enjoyed in bourbon distilling circles, was dragged into the affray by the rectifying interests. The law meant only, according to Warwick Massey Hough, counsel for the rectifying industry, "that at the time the tax is paid on that article the privilege is given of adding enough water to reduce it to proof, which is one hundred, and transferring it from the barrels to the bottle and putting the receipt for the tax over the neck of the bottle." You know where the whiskey came from and how old it is; but you don't know, Hough speculated, whether the whiskey is fit to drink. Fusel oil did produce hangover and headache, he pointed out—also a sense of falling. Two drachms would kill a rabbit in two hours. One-half an ounce would dispatch the rabbit in fifteen minutes. An ounce would do him in in four minutes.

J. Swagar Sherley, a Kentucky Representative sympathetic to the blending interests along "Whiskey Row" in Louisville, bridled when a fellow member remarked upon the purity of bonded whiskey.

"If one of the pages will bring me the bottle of Overholt Whiskey on the table there," Sherley requested, "I can state to the House what the green stamp does say. It carries some six things to the knowledge of the purchaser. It carries the knowledge that a certain distiller manufactured it. It carries the knowledge that the distillery is located in a certain internal-revenue district. It carries the knowledge that the whiskey was made at a certain time, that it was bottled at a certain time, that it is a certain proof, that the tax of $1.10 was paid on it, that nothing has been added after distillation but water, and that is all it does guarantee. Whiskey . . . quality depends largely upon the quality of the grain, the quality of the yeast, the cleanliness of the mash tubs, etc., and the proper distillation. There is not one line in the internal-revenue law that looks to an inspection of the grain to see whether it is a pure grain or a musty grain; not a line which looks to see whether the culture of the yeast be a proper culture, or whether it contains bacteria which are harmful. There is not a line to say that when the whiskey is distilled it is properly distilled, so as to get rid of the first run or the last run over, which contain the worst elements in whiskey."

The bourbon distillers strongly supported the pure food bill. They had no objections to the proposed labeling feature which provided that compounded alcoholic beverages should be required to place the words "imitation whiskey" on their packages while only the aged product was entitled to use without qualification the term "whiskey." If this proposal became law it would put the blenders under a serious disadvantage. Since much of the controversy turned upon the word "pure," and in a sense grain alcohol was purer than a distillate containing the flavor elements of whiskey, the bourbon branch of the industry dropped the word "pure," substituting another familiar in today's usuage— "straight" whiskey.

The bourbon distillers benefited from the scientific views of Harvey W. Wiley and his flair for dramatic presentation. Distinguished chemist, author of learned monographs on sugar, especially the syrup and sugar produced industrially by the hydrolysis of cornstarch, expert on adulteration, a man of quick wit, loaded with professional honors, Wiley also confessed to a personal preference for well-aged bourbon whiskey over the mixed goods. Dr. Wiley was almost a great man. But he was conspiratorial and something of an extremist. Real whiskey, he believed, could not be made by the blender's art. The laboratory could not tell the difference, he admitted, but he insisted that the tongue could. He did not contend that straight or bonded whiskey was more wholesome than rectified or that the whiskey compounds were unhealthful. But he could not rid himself of the feeling that when the purchaser called for "whiskey" and got blended goods he had been cheated. The rectifier, he said, "makes it in an hour or so, perhaps, and very often, I am sorry to say, puts on the bottle '12 years old.' "

As the leading personality in the fight, Dr. Wiley achieved the uncommon distinction of acquiring almost as many enemies as did Theodore Roosevelt himself. Wiley told in the hearing room of the House Committee on Interstate and Foreign Commerce how he had visited a rectifying plant in New Orleans where he saw a man barreling "Pure Bourbon Whiskey" which had just been made that morning. Then Dr. Wiley went into what the newspapers called his "tipple talk," which his appreciative audience found much more absorbing than his discourse on whole grain flour. Before the eyes of the congressmen the Doctor produced "fourteen-year-old" bourbon. Tumblers full of the resultant fluid were circulated among members of the committee. Mostly they shied away. Several sniffed and sipped. They said the beverage made them think of streets paved with asphalt.

Dr. Wiley went out of his way, however, in his remarks, to characterize such blends as Wilson and Hunter as "very pleasant," and continued:

"I will tell you the trouble in this country. Nobody knows anything about straight whiskey: and when a man asks another man what he likes, he finds that he likes what he is drinking . . . the blended article . . . [but it] is like one of those beautiful painted forms that the milliner puts up and puts a gown on compared with a real girl." (Laughter.)

"Your illustration appeals to us," remarked John Jacob Esch (Republican, Wisconsin).

"Drink straight whiskey and always add a little water to it," was the parting advice of the Professor as he concluded his testimony.

Among those who testified for the straight bourbon view of whiskey was Colonel Edmund H. Taylor, Jr., who commented so graphically upon the operations of blending, which he identified with adulteration, that one committee member inquired: "Is that what they are doing when you go into a liquor house and you see a nigger with a rubber tube and a bucket, pouring things from one place into another?" Another witness was the rising young Kentucky Representative, Owsley (Augustus O.) Stanley. Known as the "young Cicero of Fleming County," Stanley started out on his political career with a library consisting of a farmers' almanac and the *Revised Statutes of the Commonwealth of Kentucky*. The future U.S. Senator and governor of Kentucky was already able to deliver, in the words of an admirer, "a good line of verbal carnage." Holding aloft a quart of alcohol, Representative Stanley declared:

"It will eat the intestines out of a coyote. It will make a howling dervish out of an anchorite. It will make a rabbit spit in a bulldog's face . . . and when it gets into a man it is pure hell."

In rebuttal, the St. Louis attorney for the other side delivered a frightening lecture upon how fusel oil affected the vasomotor nerves and attacked "certain parts of the brain." And now, Hough complained bitterly, this so-called "straight" whiskey, this Johnny-come-lately, wants to "put on airs," and appropriate the ancient and honorable name of whiskey which had meant *rectified* whiskey from time out of mind. The public, he said, far from being deceived, preferred the milder, more palatable beverage which the blenders provided. But the pea in his shoe was the matter of whiskey color.

Mr. Hough: "All whiskey, you of course know, which has any color at all, is artificially colored. . . ."

Senator McCumber: "But not for the purpose of deceiving."

Mr. Hough: "I will not undertake to say what the interest of these people may be."

Major W. H. Thomas of Louisville, a whiskey merchant and large holder of aged whiskeys, including Old Jordan Bourbon, referred in his testimony to "the honest distiller" who "makes his whiskey in the old-fashioned honest way . . . and there is no hog wallow, as he calls it. . . ."

Mr. Hough: "I said hogwash, not hog wallow."

Major Thomas: "Hog wallow. . . . Hough is a nice fellow . . . but the people behind him want to destroy the old-fashioned, honest way of making whiskey. . . ."

The Major got in a shrewd lick that creamed them. He said of Hough "he drinks the kind of whiskey of which he has just spoken. Since I have been here he has been trying to make arrangements to buy some from me for his own use and that of his friends, and he shall have it."

Mr. Hough: "Thank you."

Major Thomas: "He knows what is good."

The food and drug bill would perhaps have passed Congress two years sooner than it did had it not been for this brouhaha between the straight whiskey men and the rectifiers. Some supporters of the legislation thought that Wiley should not have insisted, as he did, upon including whiskey in the law. But he was convinced that the bill should set up principles applicable to all products. The temperance forces might have opposed the law if Congress, as Oscar E. Anderson, Jr., has suggested in his book, *The Health of a Nation—Harvey W. Wiley and the Fight for Pure Food* (1958), had legislated against "all the evils in food and drugs except those pertaining to whiskey."

In his annual message to Congress, December 5, 1905, President Theodore Roosevelt asked for a law to regulate interstate commerce in misbranded and adulterated foods, drinks and drugs. The bill was introduced again. Pressure from the American Medical Association, women's clubs and other consumer groups, the graphic exposé of conditions in the Chicago packing houses which

occurred just at that time, and Roosevelt's skillful use of a damn-
ing report of an official commission which investigated the stockyards, finally forced a favorable vote in the Senate and later in the
House on the food and drug bill. The meat problem was actually
an unrelated matter. But an angry public was in no mood to make
fine distinctions. All of the consumer items, including whiskey,
went into the human stomach, tapped the family wage earner's
pocketbook. Roosevelt signed the bill into law on June 30, 1906.
The effective date was January 1, 1907.

Enforcement of the law was placed in the hands of Dr. Wiley.
Then the real fight began. Most manufacturers adjusted their
operations to the law and found themselves in a better position
because of it. But there were die-hards like the sugar and molasses
refiners, fruit driers, patent medicine magnates and the whiskey
rectifiers who were not ready to give up. Under the 1906 Act the
secretaries of the Treasury, Agriculture, and Commerce and
Labor were charged with drawing up rules and regulations for
carrying out the intent of Congress. This included collecting samples of foods and drugs, conducting examinations and making
analyses. That is to say, Dr. Wiley could bring charges that a
product was an imitation, deceptively branded, tampered with
or short in weight. The rectifiers of alcohol could choose between
three unpalatable alternatives. They were required to print "compound whiskey," "imitation whiskey" or "blended whiskey" on
their labels. The language of the statute did not set standards.
The issue had to be fought out in the courts.

The first case under the law involved seizure of fifty barrels of
"bourbon" which a Louisiana distiller had made out of a cheap
grade of New Orleans molasses commonly known as "black-
strap." The case was tried in Baltimore because that was where
the federal agents caught up with the hooch. A barrel of the
alleged bourbon stood on one end of the counsel table while Dr.
Joseph P. Remington, dean of the Philadelphia College of Pharmacy, author of a classic work on pharmacy and editor of the
Pharmacopoeia of the United States, told the jury that *spiritus
frumenti* was Latin for spirit of the grain and what the *Pharmacopoeia* said in defining whiskey.

The jury also heard Dr. Wiley, several whiskey dealers, and
George May, manager of the Maryland Club, who testified with

astonishment that he had never heard of old bourbon being derived from cane spirit, water, sulphuric acid, sulphate of am-
monia and yeast. Most of the testimony was pretty dry, except for
one bright moment when an examiner asked a Dr. Thomas E.
Hollander if he had any practical knowledge of whiskey. The
Doctor's reply brought down the house:

"In answer to this I might say that I have lived in Kentucky
all my life."

The judge accepted that as a responsive answer to the question.
Some witnesses insisted that bourbon had to come from Kentucky. Others weren't sure that it had to be of any particular geographical origin. But all agreed that a distillate of molasses was
not bourbon. The court ordered that the fifty barrels of prettily
named "Rose of New Orleans Bourbon" should go down the
drain and admonished the Louisiana Distillery Company to obey
the food law and sin no more.

Dr. Wiley was determined to beat the blenders. At one time
he stopped Canadian Club, which was not labeled as a blend, at
the U.S. ports of entry. On another memorable occasion, the old
food fighter carted his apparatus to the White House. There he
set up an impromptu laboratory on the Cabinet Room conference
table and made whiskey before the eyes of the President. On a
wintry day in March, 1909, William Howard Taft took office as
President. The liquor industry petitioned for a rehearing on the
"imitation whiskey" issue. Taft ordered Solicitor General Lloyd
W. Bowers to determine once again the meaning of the word
"whiskey." After taking testimony which was spread over 2,365
pages, the Solicitor General ruled that blends were not known in
the language of the consumer as genuine whiskey. No one was
satisfied. The issue went back to Taft. He decided that all potable
liquor distilled from grain had been known for a hundred years
as whiskey. Therefore, both blends and straights were whiskey
within the meaning of the Food and Drug Act, with the use of
qualifying descriptive phrases such as "Bourbon—aged in the
wood," or "Blended Whiskey" or whatever statement indicated
properly the process of manufacture. Thus standards were established based upon the methods of manufacture then current. The
Taft decision, spelled out in more detail and phrased in more precise language, is substantially in effect today.

Colonel Edmund H. Taylor, Jr., one of the legendary figures connected
with the history of bourbon whiskey.

MAKING HOME COMFORTABLE FOR HIM. YOUNG WIFE—"There, that ought to keep John home at nights. I will get the butler to fill the room with stale tobacco-smoke, and my husband will then have all the comforts of the modern barroom."

Convinced that President Taft had given in his decision more than the blenders ever hoped to get, Dr. Wiley became discontented, ran into administrative difficulties and resigned from government service in sorrow and bitterness. Noted in his salad days for his bonhomie and good humor, in his seventies Dr. Wiley became more and more dubious about the role of alcohol in modern society, enjoyed less frequently his occasional drink of "pure" whiskey. With the approach of World War I, when the question of prohibiting the manufacture of beverage alcohol assumed the guise of a food conservation measure, Dr. Wiley became convinced that all whiskey was bad. He died in 1930, an uncompromising Prohibitionist.

Chapter 16

WHISKEY FUN
AND FOLKLORE

"LEGENDS are the salad dressing of history," wrote the late Gene Fowler, who became the occasion for quite a few legends himself in his newspaper career.

What follows in this chapter is legend, mostly unverifiable and unlikely. Its matter consists of jesting sayings, fantastic adventures and farcical happenings involving an appreciation of whiskey or the results of drinking it. Its manner is that of the poker-faced blanket-stretchers who sat around the chunk stove in a cozy bar and created a kind of sub-literature for the sheer fun of it. Here is the style:

"One time there was a fellow that had the name of drinking too much popskull . . ."

Whiskey, good and bad, white and red and that yellow kind that comes from Tennessee, whiskey that is barrel proof, or weak or mean or mellow and soft, whiskey the comforter or whiskey in the disreputable character of John Barleycorn—whiskey trickles through American folklore and has sometimes illuminated the American imagination. Its place in popular culture is indicated in word combinations such as Whiskey Baptist, whiskey skin (a drink); in place names, hobo songs, gags, sayings, proverbs, stories which throw light on character or catch the flavor of locality.

Much whiskey lore has been preserved by itinerant printers, often natives of the Bluegrass state who felt both a personal and a patriotic attachment to bourbon. Whiskey has been the accomplice of the storyteller as he told of a hairbreadth escape, a frightening emergency or a regional folkway to be stored up in the national memory. And whiskey has been often enough at the center of the plot. Two sheepherders on a spree in Cheyenne got into a fancy bar by mistake where the drinks cost a quarter. "Maybe I didn't drink it all," one remarked reflectively next day as he remembered his effort to reduce the stocks of liquor available in the city, "but I sure put the price up." In New Orleans they don't pour cream on their grits; they anoint it with bourbon, or the town joke says they do.

When Davy Crockett, the Yaller Flower of the Forest, passed through Little Rock to join the Texians, he tossed off a horn of green whiskey at a single pull. Later he admitted that it was so hot that he didn't need to have his food cooked for two months, "the grub was cooked afore it got settled in my innards." On his famous tour of the East, the Colonel was greatly impressed with the exquisite manners associated with liquoring up. A Mr. Neil of Philadelphia offered Colonel Crockett the opportunity to take "a little Dutch courage," and what struck the frontiersman most favorably, Neil *didn't watch* while Crockett poured: "That's what I call genteel," he declared.

Before the church decided that whiskey was a serpent, Raccoon John Smith, backwoods evangelist, while the guest of a church elder, was sharing a nightcap with his host when the elder was called to the door for an extended parley. When he returned he looked around and inquired:

"Where's my drink?"

"Brother," said Raccoon John, "the Bible says you must watch as well as pray."

This anecdote has traveled, moved far in both time and space, and acquired a new cast of characters. In its earlier version Princeton-educated Doctor John McMillan, a leader of Presbyterianism in western Pennsylvania in the last decade of the eighteenth century, so influential a prelate that he was humorously known as the "Cardinal," was the leading figure. No man to pass up Old Monongahela when it was there, the Doctor stopped at

an inn to water the horses while traveling in the company of
Joseph Patterson. They called for a glass to quench their own
thirst. Reverend Patterson proposed that he ask grace and made
such a long job of it that Doctor McMillan drained his own glass
and then polished off Patterson's too. When the latter stared,
McMillan admonished him with the punch line, "Brother, you
must watch as well as pray."

Drinking has enriched the language with many vivid Americanisms. The bartender occupied "the sober side of the bar." Two
drinks are "a couple of burning sensations." If a drinker kept at
his libations he would soon "hear the owl hoot." The serious alcoholic would "wear calluses on his elbows leanin' on the bar."
Hitching a free ride on a freight train was described as "savin'
money for the bartender." In the hills of the Ozarks a man with
too much red liquor on board was "full as a corn crib" or, in a
special tribute to the law, "drunker than two judges." Arkansas
connoisseurs said "drunker than Cooter Brown." No one seems to
know now who Cooter Brown was.

In the days when the whiskey lecturers displayed their frightening pictures of the effects of alcohol on the human system, a lady
speaker was telling the temperance society of how the Cause had
been a blessing to her; "for," she said, "I slept with a rum barrel
for ten years; but now since my husband signed the pledge, I
have a man to sleep with—thank God." According to the *Springfield* (Mo.) *Advertiser,* which reported the event, "Then all the
spinsters laid their hands on their hearts, and said Amen!"

Fanciful stories involving liquor circulated as freely as red-eye
among the tellers of tall tales. "Bluenose" Brainard was a sawyer
from Nova Scotia who worked in the Wisconsin logging camps.
He explained how he dealt with the Wisconsin mosquitoes. He
shot a few, killed a lot with his ax. But still they nose-dived on him
in swarms. Finally he got a jug of lumberjack whiskey and poured
it into a washtub. The mosquitoes gathered for a jamboree and
got quite drunk. "Bluenose" nipped off their bills with a pair of
pincers. It was tedious work, snipping them one at a time. But it
worked. The attackers starved to death.

But wait a minute—the grasshoppers of Missouri topped the
Wisconsin mosquitoes for size, appetite and sheer ferocity. The
yarners around South West City in Missouri told of a man who

left his team standing while he visited a nearby stillhouse to get his jug refilled. This took time. When he returned, four big hoppers had eaten up both horses and were pitching horseshoes to see who would get the harness for dessert.

Drinking and fishing have always been known as supplementary activities, and this congenial association has produced a bumper crop of whiskey stories. Daniel Webster was "majestic in his consumption of liquor as in everything else," according to Hewson Peeke, author of a quaint volume entitled *Americana Ebrietatis* (1917). "It is said that he went fishing the day before he was to deliver his welcome to La Fayette, and got drunk. As he sat on the bank he suddenly drew from the water a large fish and in his majestic voice said, 'Welcome, illustrious stranger, to our shores.' The next day his friends, who went fishing with him, were electrified to hear him begin his speech to La Fayette with these same words. Webster was undoubtedly a hard drinker. Once called upon for an impromptu after-dinner speech when he was somewhat awash, a friend whispered "the national debt." The Senator nodded.

"Gentlemen, there is the national debt—it should be paid; yes, gentlemen, it should be paid." Then, stimulated by loud cheers, he said, "I will be hanged if it sha'n't be!" He took out his wallet. "I will pay it myself! How much is it?"

More recent and perhaps even harder to believe is the experience of the angler who spilled a gallon of whiskey on the ground. Digging in the same spot for worms the next day, he found plenty and they seemed to be unusually spry. Baiting his hook with a fine specimen, the fisherman immediately hauled out of the water a four-pound bass. What was curious about his catch, though, was that the worm had wrapped himself around the bass's tail.

Sam Grant, a Texas cowman, told a whiskey-laced narrative of harrowing danger and extreme privation on a cattle drive to Kansas, during which he existed for seventeen days without anything stronger to drink than root tea. Grant admitted that the experience "would have been death to a man with less nerve."

The outfit had started out all right from Fort Worth with plenty of provisions, one canteen of water and a twenty-five gallon keg of whiskey, which was a "tolerably liberal proportion of whiskey to the amount of water! But, you see, we could get water from the creeks and branches as we went along; but whiskey was not to be found on the plains." When Grant went into some timber, there was a sudden Indian attack. To his horror, he saw from a distance how the Indians killed his companions and tore into the whiskey—four dollars a gallon at Fort Worth—until the earth was soggy and the Indians dead drunk.

"The blood of my butchered companions, and the four-dollar whiskey on the ground," Grant said afterwards, "cried aloud for vengeance. You should have tasted that liquor—not a bead on it that was not as big as a baseball, and not a headache in a cord of it." Was it, one wonders now, Old Green River, the whiskey advertised as "without a headache"? At any rate, Grant scalped all the braves as they lay there holding on to the grass, escaped on a stolen horse, and was picked up by soldiers after seventeen days. During that time his crazed imagination, as he described it, returned to the dreadful night of the massacre and the old bourbon dribbling from the spigot. And he even fancied that he heard the barman at a Dodge City whiskey-den asking courteously, "What will you gents take?"

The American folk heroes who appear larger than life liked their liquor. Certainly in Paul Bunyan's day the logger who didn't take his dram was known as "The Preacher" as soon as the bunkhouse inmates had sized him up. Whiskey Jack, the famed raftsman, was seven feet tall and never left the scene of a celebration until the last bottle was killed. One day when Whiskey Jack tied up at Richland City, Wisconsin, near the tavern, he found that he had no money. He took a bundle of lath to the proprietor and found that he could exchange it for drinks. "Put it outside the back door," the saloonist said. Jack exited through the rear, picked up the bundle and handed it to a member of his crew, who entered by the front entrance and made the same deal with the bartender. Thus the torch was passed. After the crew departed the innkeeper went out to inspect the stock of lath for which he had bartered his liquor and found—one bundle!

Mike Fink, marksman, barroom fighter and king of the keelboatmen, belongs in the frontier pantheon beside Davy Crockett, the gamecock of the Tennessee canebrakes, Sam Houston, a god in Texas, and Daniel Boone, whose formal schooling ended when he mixed an emetic with his teacher's whiskey. Fink, a figure both in authentic history and folklore, is supposed to have refused his mother's milk as a babe in favor of old rye. By the time he was fifteen he was winning shooting matches for beef animals with side bets of a quart of whiskey. If that wasn't adequate for his guests, Fink would announce, "We'll liquor up at the grocery." Legend has it that Mike could put away a gallon of bourbon in twenty-four hours without getting the staggers, hoisting the jug one-handed fashion, gracefully curving his arm while he drank with relish. Refreshed, he could go on to shoot a tin cup filled with whiskey off the top of a willing comrade's head at seventy yards.

Details changed and the distances varied in the many accounts which have come down describing Fink's exploit of "shooting the whiskey cup." Some boon companion would place the brimming cup on his own head. Mike Fink stood at thirty, sixty, a hundred paces and put a bullet through the top of the chalice with such finesse that it splashed out only a few drops of the red liquor. The act was ceremonial, a ritual, a pledge of trust and affection. Mike Fink lived three lives on three frontiers, the first as a Pennsylvania borderer, then in the Kentucky region and finally on the Yellowstone River as a fur trader. There, while enjoying his specialty, he aimed too low and shot a friend in the forehead. For this carelessness or treachery, or because, as an old steamboat pilot on the Missouri told it, he "had corned too heavy," Fink was killed in revenge for the shot he missed. Mike Fink's memorial today consists of some fifty accounts of his life and good times, embroidered with eleven differing versions of his violent end— and the PWA murals in Ohio river town post offices.

The house is still standing, according to the *North Carolina Guide,* where the favorite convivial apothegm in American drinking annals originated, expressing the refreshing idea that it is time to set 'em up again. There are several variants of the story, all loaded with circumstantial detail; but the most artful teller of the tale was Major James Calvin Hemphill, a South Carolinian and editor of the *Charleston News and Courier.* His recital of the momentous incident goes as follows:

"A great many years ago the Governor of North Carolina received a friendly visit from the Governor of South Carolina. After a real North Carolina dinner of bacon and yams, the two governors lit pipes and sat in the shade of the back veranda with a demijohn of real North Carolina corn whiskey, copper distilled, within easy reach.

"There was nothing stuck up about these Governors. They sot and smoked and sot and smoked, every once in a while taking a mutual pull at the demijohn with the aid of a gourd which they used as a democratic goblet. The conversation between the two governors was on the subject of turpentine and rice, the staples of their respective states, and the further they got in the subject the lower down they got in the jug, and the lower down they got into the jug, the dryer the Governor of South Carolina got, who was a square drinker and a warm man, with about a million pores to every square inch of his hide, which enabled him to hist in a likely share of corn juice or other beverage and keep his carcass at the same time well ventilated and generally always ready for more, while the Governor of North Carolina was a more moderate drinker, and was mighty sure to strike bottom at about the twelfth drink, like as if nature had measured him by the gourdful.

"Well, they sot and smoked and argued, and the Governor of North Carolina was as hospitable as any real Southern gentleman could be, for he ladled out the whiskey in the most lavish manner, being particular to give his distinguished guest three drinks to one, and gauging his own dose with great care, for fear if he didn't he might lose the thread of his argument and the demijohn might run dry before the Governor of South Carolina should be ready to dust out for him, in which case it would be like he had not properly observed the laws of hospitality, which would have been a self-inflicted thorn in his side for years to come, and no amount of apology could ease his mind or enable him to feel warranted in showing his countenance to his fellow-men, especially in his home district, where for generations it had been a main point with every gentleman to keep his visitor well supplied with creature comforts, and to hand him a good gourdful as a stirrup cup when about to take his departure for the bosom of his family.

"Singular to relate, the cautiousness manifested by the Governor of North Carolina was of no avail, for at one and the same moment, the jug went dry and the Governor of North Carolina, much to his subsequent mortification when he learned the fact afterwards, dropped off into a quiet sleep, while the Governor of

South Carolina continued to keep on with his argument holding the empty gourd in his hand in close contagiousness to the demijohn and wondering at the apparent absent-mindedness of his hitherto attentive host, to whom, after a minute and a half of painful silence, he made use of but one remark:

" 'Governor, don't you think it's a long time between drinks?' "

"The remark being overheard by George, the body servant of the Governor of North Carolina, who knowing there was something wrong, took to the woods, where he remained in seclusion three days, but the Governor of South Carolina, receiving no reply from the Governor of North Carolina, mounted his horse and rode sadly homeward with an irrepressible feeling at his heart that there was coming to be hollowness in friendship and that human nature was in danger of drifting into a condition of chaotic mockery."

Major Hemphill did not identify the governors involved. Other sources have named them as Edward B. Dudley of North Carolina who addressed the celebrated question to Pierce Mason Butler of South Carolina while they were being entertained at the home of Mrs. Ann ("Nancy") Jones, whose clapboard residence still stands on U.S. route 70-A in eastern North Carolina. It was Miss Nancy's hospitality, according to this account, which had temporarily run out of fuel. Another attribution has it that Governor John Motley Morehead of *North* Carolina addressed Governor J. H. Hammond of South Carolina on the subject of the empty demijohn. Major Hemphill declared that this story could not possibly be true. Gesturing proudly, he explained:

"It was *not* the Governor of South Carolina who forgot his duties as host, but his illustrious contemporary. Everyone knows that a South Carolina man, to say nothing of the Governor, would never get in a condition to forget the rules of Southern hospitality."

The honor of having originated the most famous remark regarding saloon credit known to American folklore is claimed for both Chicago and Cincinnati. The story goes like this in the Cincinnati version:

"Is Casey good for a drink?" the bartender of an Irish place on Central Avenue called up the dumbwaiter to the boss who lived above.

Boss: "Has he had it?"

Mike: "He has."

Boss: "He is."

The publican could do little else than endorse the transaction inasmuch as Casey had "buried the slug where the cat couldn't get it." Chicago newspapermen, who wrote much of their daily prose in James McGarry's back room, always insisted that it was their philosopher, McGarry, who uttered those poignant words of resignation, "He is."

The horse who entered a bar and joined his rider in a snort of boiled corn fills an entire chapter in the mythology of the old West. The story appears first in an early California newspaper when one of the Argonauts rode his steed into a San Francisco saloon as a gesture of abandon and camaraderie. Some time later three or four playful cowpunchers rode their horses into a New Mexico deadfall where an overdressed commercial traveler from the East wearing ankle blankets—spats—happened to be standing at the bar. Being jostled by a horse, the knight of the sample case complained to the management; to which the bartender replied:

"What the hell y'u doin' in here afoot, anyhow?"

Texans who didn't understand city ordinances took pleasure in riding their horses into San Antonio saloons and engaging in target practice at the lamps, but all this disappeared by the mid-1880's and even the Mexicans, according to a contemporary chronicle, "spend saints' days and Sabbath evenings like Christian gentlemen, in the back-rooms of the saloons," while the Americans who were running for county offices joined the religious processions and yelled "Hurrah for Our Lady of Guadaloupe!" or whatever saint was on duty that day.

The place names of the United States provide an obbligato to our cultural history. They memorialize the nations and peoples who came here and left their mark on America, the gentlemen and the national heroes, the middling men and the little men. The "names on the land," in Professor George R. Stewart's felicitous phrase, commemorate our Indian heritage, our wars and even the efforts of Congress at name-giving. Satirists, humorists, town site promoters and the U.S. Post Office Department have all taken a hand in the game. And so have the ordinary people—with pride, with deprecation, sometimes with fun and fantasy. Strong liquor and those who have made it, sold it and used it have not been forgotten in our national nomenclature. There is a Bourbon in Illinois, Mississippi and Missouri; a Bourbon Springs in Kentucky. At Louisville the stockyards are the Bourbon Stock Yards and the city has a Bourbon Café. In Shively, Kentucky, there is a Bernheim Lane, in Bullitt County a Bernheim Forest, both honoring the creator of I. W. Harper Bourbon. And just off the Dixie Highway along the front of the Stitzel-Weller Distillery property at Shively runs Fitzgerald Road, named for the master distiller, John E. Fitzgerald, whose name is also perpetuated in Old Fitzgerald.

Across the Ohio River on the Indiana side, near Jeffersonville, there is a channel known as "Whiskey Gut." Philadelphia once had a Drinkers' Alley, Baltimore a Whiskey Alley and a Bottle Alley, too. There is a Brandy, Virginia, a Brandywine village in both Pennsylvania and Maryland. Delaware and Pennsylvania share a Brandywine Creek, whose name is also attached to a battle of 1777 in the Revolutionary War. Brandywine, a word of Dutch origin, literally means *burnt wine;* that is, a spirit distilled from grapes or fruits. In early America the term *brandy* was often used loosely to mean native whiskey.

When Chicago was earning its reputation as "the Gomorrah of the West" the Mickey Finn cocktail—a potion to which knockout drops had been added—was created on Whiskey Row. There was once a Whiskey Point, describing a promontory jutting out into the Hudson River just north of Kingston, New York. The same name was also used for a location near Pittsburgh where the murky Monongahela rolls below the site of an old stillhouse.

Among the ghost towns of Kansas there is a memory of another Whiskey Point. It was near Fort Riley, marking the spot where thirteen barrels of whiskey were spilled by the military in 1855. A little bit more is known about this Whiskey Point; this much, at least, that when Topeka was chosen to be the capital of the state, Whiskey Point was in the running. It received two votes. Wyoming has a Whiskey Mountain, a high, wooded ridge, where a cache of whiskey was once hidden. In both Ohio and Michigan there is a Whiskey Island, the former at the mouth of the Cuyahoga River at Cleveland where the rum-runners of the 1920's used to put in with their cargoes from Canada; the latter part of the Beaver Archipelago at the entrance to Mackinac Straits. Motorists still like to visit a small community some fifty miles northwest of Detroit called Hell because they can then send home a picture postcard bought from Al Dewey at the Ranch Grill saying "I've been to Hell"; or, "Don't tell me to go to Hell—I am there now." You can see the possibilities. Hell has been Hell for over a hundred years, so named, it is said, because "It was hell watchin' those men climbin' up the hill from the still."

Yes, a view card can be postmarked "Hell." Only outgoing mail is handled from Hell, a postal substation of Pinckney, open for five months during the summer tourist season. In the Yukon, 250 air miles north of Dawson, a bleak hamlet has honored the name of a famous bourbon which has brought a touch of amenity to life north of the Arctic Circle. The little community—no more than a wide place in the tundra—is called Old Crow. [Pop. 200]. Alberta has a Whiskey Gap, where Canadian whisky once flowed from the still without the blessing of the exciseman. Wyoming has one, too, about which this story is told:

Company A of the Eleventh Ohio Cavalry under Major O'Farrell was doing escort duty, conducting emigrants and the stock, wagons and merchandise of a stage line through a gap in the mountains. Shortly after going into camp one night south of the Sweetwater, the Major made some observations among the men which led him to believe someone was selling whiskey. Every wagon was searched. In the last wagon a detail under a lieutenant found the whiskey barrel. They rolled it out, knocked in the head and emptied it—right into the camp water supply. The soldiers rushed forward with cups, canteens, buckets and their camp kettles to save the liquor. Some even stomped their boot-heels into the ground, caught some whiskey in the depression and drank it lying down. The soldiery called the spot Whiskey Gap and it remains that today.

An old-timer in Wisconsin named Hank Lawrence, having been liquoring up at a country saloon, lost a jug of whiskey when he tried to make his horse cross a stream on a footbridge. And so the stream became Whiskey Creek. The old Wisconsin Central Railroad, now merged into the Soo Line, was long known in brokerage offices under the nickname of "Whiskey," but scholars have not yet established whether this was because of the phoneme "Wisc." or, more probably, to honor the beverage which never seems to be far from the thoughts of members of the New York Stock Exchange.

Nevada has a Whiskey Flat, and so has California, where the Big Blue mine once boomed and clanked. There are two Whiskey Creeks in Oregon, in addition to a Whiskey Run and a Whiskey-town. Early Californians revealed a luxuriant fancy in devising such names as Cut Throat Bar, Whiskey Slide, Murderers' Bar. Among such creations, Whiskey Creek hardly counted. It referred to a prosaic matter of fact. There someone had sold whiskey or set up a still. Most western "bar" names probably refer to sand bars in gold-bearing streams. But Whiskey Bar and Delirium Tremens clearly honor some lively episode connected with the consumption of ardent spirits. The alcoholic tradition in place-naming persists even today in San Francisco, "the city that was never a small town," where the gripmen on the cable cars call out facetiously "Paul Jones" for Jones Street and "Old Taylor" at the corner of Taylor Street. The deep-seated distrust of able-bodied alcoholic beverages in the one-street villages also shows up in U.S. place names; for the gazetteers record hamlets known as Temperance, Temperance Hall and two Temperancevilles.

In the plant world there is Whiskey Cherry—the common name for *Prunus serotina*—and the Whiskey Plant, a cactus growing along the Rio Grande. The juice of the root, the Indians learned, produces a powerful intoxicating effect. Whiskey has been used with affection in the naming of animals. The reader will recall how Captain John Fries named his faithful dog Whiskey during the troubles over the alcohol tax in western Pennsylvania. The literary cowboy from Matagorda, Charles A. Siringo, who called himself "an old stove up cow puncher," recounted in his fine autobiography how he had a mighty tough pony, Whiskey-peet. In a dusty little town on the Canadian River, so insignificant that the stock in the only store consisted of half a dozen boxes of soda crackers and three barrels of whiskey, Siringo sampled the spirits too liberally and fell down dead drunk under the feet of his Whiskey-peet; and his stomach was "filled with scorpions, wild cats and lizards." For that misdemeanor and the shame of it, Siringo swore off. He kept his oath, too, except for once—the time when he received the glorious news of Cleveland's election.

And that is how it was. From local tradition, poignant experience, humorous indiscretion, slang and folksay, the merry myths of the liars' syndicates across our land—from these and similar sources one may catch a glimpse not available in formal historical writings of the part whiskey has played in the American experience. As the proprietor of McMakin's Hotel in Jackson, Mississippi, used to call out in a loud voice, after announcing the day's bill of fare, "Gentlemen, don't neglect my liquors. *Gentlemen, we are a great people.*"

Chapter 17

THE SWINGING DOOR

SCARCELY a man is now alive who has bellied up to the mahogany in an old-fashioned corner saloon and said to Mike or Otto, "the usual."

For more than fifty years over half of the states have been without saloons. Indeed, half of the total geography of the United States was legally dried up as long as seventy years ago. Since few women, other than painted Jezebels, ever saw the inside of a pre-World War I saloon, only a handful of grizzled male survivors remain who can remember the gilt beer sign at the corner, the swinging door screen, the mouth-watering free lunch; or who can recall the sheer intellectual pleasure of discussing with Gus, the bartender, the progress of the labor movement, the baseball situation, women's fashions, President Taft's definition of whiskey, or the finer points of the Shakespeare-Bacon controversy.

In the complex set of circumstances which produced constitutional Prohibition, the saloon died and its traditions and legends died with it. For the idea of the saloon became so intertwined and associated with evil, the very word so soiled and damaged, that after Repeal new and mellifluous euphemisms had to be invented to describe any premises devoted to the consumption of alcoholic solace by the drink. Thus we have ye olde inn, all quainted up, taprooms, the cocktail lounge paneled often in exotic woods, atmospheric taverns, cafés, the piano-bar and chromium-plated lounge bars. But the modern drinkerie, done up in red leather and fluorescent lighting, is no longer recognizable as the plain citizen's club, refuge or palladium of liberty. The décor has changed and there are strangers present. They scent the air with Nuit de Noël. "Gone forever," Don Marquis, the humorist-philosopher and creator of The Old Soak, mourned, as he thought of the old-time saloon; and soon after he died.

Perhaps only now, with time running on and passion spent, is it possible to stroll back to the brass rail days and recapture without rancor the manners and protocol, the etiquette and atmosphere of the pre-Prohibition American bar. The picture is not all black or all white, but rather a nocturne in gray, the color range extending from the dives of San Francisco and the barrel houses of Chicago's Levee, to the decorous neighborhood *Bierstube* of Milwaukee which had a European flavor and entertained poppa, momma and the kids—with a highchair for Junior.

Successive waves of Irish and German immigration brought to our shores a population of accustomed drinkers, untouched by the moral arguments of U.S. preachers and reformers, who expanded the market for liquors, and staffed the bars with the mustached gents who pulled the beer faucets, polished the whiskey glasses and kept alive the memory of the homeland.

"The names over the saloons, beer gardens and low groggeries are mostly foreign," wrote Daniel Dorchester, D.D., in the 1880's, although such business names over the swinging door as "The Fred" and "Ed & Frank's" and "The Democratic Headquarters of the Eighteenth Ward" scarcely supported such a sweeping generalization. A vein of American nativism undoubtedly colored and stimulated the temperance movement. Increasingly, there were overtones of religion and politics. The saloon men were at least nominal members of the Roman Catholic Church. The political alignment is expressed in the remark, "I never said all Democrats were saloonkeepers. What I said was all saloonkeepers are Democrats."

The interior of the nineteenth-century saloon was dimly lighted. The bar ran lengthwise down the left side as one entered, heavily hand-carved, done in oak, mahogany, cherry or hollywood. Often a screen divided the bar from a space where bottled liquors were sold. The floor was covered with sawdust to absorb the foam and the drip. The lower end of salooning was conducted in an institution known as the "barrel house." The barrel house handled hard stuff only. Along the wall were lined up 50-gallon barrels of whiskey lying in racks on the floor, with a second tier on top of the first. Each had a spigot. Bulk sales were made direct from the barrel to the customer who purchased by the quart or the gallon. Drinks were dispensed directly from the barrel to the glass over a plain, unvarnished plank. Barrel houses specialized in rectified whiskey, flavored with a little bourbon and a squirt of glycerine to take the scratch out of the alcohol.

At the other end of the spectrum were the fancy places. They all gloried in having "the longest bar in the world"; for example, in Erickson's saloon in Portland, Oregon, the bar once measured 684 feet and there was a $5,000 pipe organ and a ladies' orchestra, prudently surrounded by an electrically charged railing. If the license fee was low, the bars offered more comforts, because the competition was keener. If the license fee was high, the saloon had a plainer character because there were fewer publicans and plenty of customers. A one-armed bandit stood in a corner, or perhaps the John L. Sullivan Athletic Punching Machine. "How hard," it asked, "Can You Hit at the Great John L.?"

The bartender was an important feature of saloon life. He was a craftsman, even an artist, a philosopher, encyclopedia of sporting information, a belles-lettrist and a great humanitarian, always ready to throw out the lifeline. The barmen used oil to slick down their hair, wore their lodge emblems on a jacket of white, or once white, duck. A glittering rock sparkled on the ring finger and another stone was screwed into the middle of a stiff-bosomed shirt. In the Irish places, a slighting reference to the Black and Tan would often produce a drink on the house. It was a matter of professional pride with the bartenders to be able to run up on order some one hundred and fifty cocktails, rickeys, fizzes, cobblers, punches and divers "cups." But the staples were beer and red liquor. Mostly the job consisted of turning the beer taps or reaching for the bottle of bar whiskey and setting out a glass of water as a chaser. Only the effete touched the water. The ordinary joints served two kinds of whiskey which were called for as rye or bourbon. The liquors were stored in barrels in the cellar, brought upstairs in jugs to be decanted into bar bottles. If a rube came in, the mixologist might slam down what was known as the "cops' bottle"; i.e., the cheapest cut whiskey in the house.

The patrons poured their own. If the customer was a gentleman he took about an ounce and a half. It was unwritten etiquette that the dram never approached the rim. If it did, the bartender threw the purchaser a hard look, or a gentle, tired inquiry, "Will you need a towel, too?" The implication was that the customer might be planning to take a bath in his bourbon. In general, the duties involved in keeping bar were to see that the walking board behind the bar was always dry, use a chamois cloth on the woodwork, shine the brass, keep the cash straight, relieve the opposite watch promptly and say to argumentative drinkers, "Yes, sir, ain't it th' truth?" Professionally, the barkeep avoided all clashes over religion and shied away from associating himself with proposals involving the emasculation of Congressmen and the burning of Washington. But here is a curious thing. A cup-bearer in a Memphis or East St. Louis ginmill may not have had the literary polish of his colleagues in south Boston or New York's old Ninth Ward. But he invariably stood up for Shakespeare when the revisionists got around to the question of whether Bacon wrote the plays. This should be investigated further by the professorate. The only clue which can be suggested here is that Shakespeare was known to be a good customer of the Mermaid Tavern. The drinking habits of Bacon remain obscure.

A good bartender did not drink while on duty. If urged, he would say, "But I will take a mild cigar." This ultra-Colorado is known in the history of whiskeyana as "the saloon cigar." At the end of the day, it went back into the box and the barman took credit for it on the cash register. If pushed hard to take something by a very special friend, the bartender would draw what was known as a "snit" of beer in a private glass he kept on the work board under the bar. It was about the size of an eyecup. The knowledgeable bartender filled it with foam and could put down a hundred if necessary and still not know that he had received a message. The customer paid each time for a full glass.

Behind the bar was the "mantel"; also the back-bar mirror, decorated with mottoes, some serious, such as "Don't Ask for Credit"; some in lighter vein, "If you spit on the floor at home, spit on the floor here: We want you to feel at home." Bartenders often bought up temperance pledge cards at an agreed price of from five to ten free drinks and displayed them as trophies. The central section of the mantel was a kind of high altar of shining glassware. Out on the flanks lay a bung-starter, assorted lemons, bottles of muscatel, port, catawba, and that sovereign remedy, rock and rye. No one called for these esoteric articles, but they were mentioned in the retail license—"wines and liquors," it said—and, as George Ade once remarked, they gave an air of elegance to a business venture "terribly short on social standing."

Various snappy placards decorated the walls of the saloon, such as "If Drinking Interferes with Your Business, Cut Out Business." Harry Hill, who ran an orderly whiskey mill on West Houston Street in New York City, stated his rules of behavior poetically: "If you wish to here remain / Do not talk loudly or profane." A sign in a Helena, Montana, saloon admonished the customers: DON'T FORGET TO WRITE TO DEAR OLD MOTHER. SHE IS THINKING OF YOU. WE FURNISH PAPER AND ENVELOPES FREE, AND HAVE THE BEST WHISKEY IN TOWN.

A favorite wall decoration consisted of a facsimile copy of a document popularly known as Lincoln's tavern license. The license was issued to the Lincoln-Berry store and consisted of a tavern license and a bond for good behavior, which was defined as not selling whiskey to Negroes, Indians or children. The signature said "Lincoln" but the handwriting was Berry's. It has never been established that the store sold liquor by the drink during the time that Lincoln was connected with the venture in New Salem, Illinois.

Pictorial advertisements supplied by brewers, distillers and rectifying houses lent a vivacity to the saloon interior. The subject matter was patriotic, classical and allegorical, pugilistic or aphrodisiac. Some were quite elaborate, such as the big color lithograph of Cassily Adams' gory but fascinating "Custer's Last Fight" which was handed out for years by the Anheuser-Busch people to advertise their Budweiser Beer. The subject of the painting is an imaginary re-creation of the disaster which befell General George A. Custer's detachment of the U.S. Seventh Cavalry in 1876 on the Little Big Horn. It was necessarily imaginary since the only survivor was a horse. The picture tells a powerful, melodramatic, nightmarish story. Indeed, the event was all of that. Intended to be taken as history, the picture is better appreciated as American myth-making. Saloon statisticians assert that there have been more casualties as a result of barroom arguments over the picture touching, for example, on the question of whether Sitting Bull attacked because Custer and his command were drunk the night before, than resulted from the massacre itself.

There was a large and appreciative audience of art lovers for scenes in which elegant but somewhat overweight sirens shaped like bass viols by some accident or inadvertence displayed an expanse of leg. Outright indecent pictures were not common. But the patrons' artistic sensibilities were frequently stimulated by examples of easel art which combined pleasingly the spicy with the allegedly classical, such as "Venus in the Bath," or "Diana Surprised." These pictures and others of their genre were known collectively as a school, "Saturday Night."

In Clyde Brion Davis' middle-western novel, *Jeremy Bell*, the author has two small-town boys venture into a saloon for the first time. They gaze with astonishment at the picture over the bar, a luscious confection in pink and white. One asks the other if he has ever seen anything like that before.

"Nope," was the reply. "Not since I was weaned."

Detroiters who were "live ones" and collected pictures of opera stars in tights enclosed with Duke's Cameo cigarettes and Sweet Caporals, could find a similar portrayal of the "perfectly formed female" by dropping in at Churchill's Saloon on Woodward Avenue. There hung the original of a large and explicit oil painting of a nude beauty, "La Venera Bruna," or "The Auburn Venus," as it was popularly called, the work of Julius Rolshoven. The picture may still be appraised by connoisseurs who are members or guests of the Detroit Athletic Club, where they will find it in the taproom adjoining the grill.

The notorious psychopathic lady, Mrs. Carry Nation, of hatchet and "spilling party" fame, who, ironically enough, was a product of Kentucky, exercised her destructive talents on saloon art as well as bottles. When the old busybody advanced upon the long, curved bar in the basement of the Hotel Carey in Wichita, the most elegant joint in all Kansas, the enormous oil painting by John Noble, "Cleopatra at the Bath," which delineated the Serpent of the Nile disporting herself with her maids and eunuchs, was slashed and riddled by the implacable Carry. For good measure, she also broke the mirror which "cost fifteen hunnert dollars," according to bartender Parker. In Chicago, Mrs. Nation ordered a nude female statue to be covered with a Mother Hubbard and a poke bonnet. The old agitator's last battle with the artistic side of salooning occurred in Butte, the tough Montana copper camp, where she denounced the pictures on the walls of the Windsor dance hall. But she lost the verdict in a hair-pulling to May Malloy, who gave her a mouse and kicked her out into Galena Street.

"She doesn't want me in there," observed Carry in the understatement of the century.

While the hicksters tramped through Longacre Square looking for a $1.25 table d'hôte on the Great White Way, newspapermen with steady work, fight promoters, and New York's boulevardiers repaired to the southeast corner of Broadway and Forty-second Street to the Knickerbocker Hotel where Maxfield Parrish's "Old King Cole" hung over the Flemish Oak bar. Prohibition proved to be too much for the bar, known to its regulars as "The Forty-Second Street Country Club." When the doors closed in 1920 the painting moved to the Racquet and Tennis Club. There it found a safe sanctuary and looked down upon private libations during the arid years. It is now the chief decorative feature of the "King Cole Bar" of the St. Regis Hotel.

The bar of the old Waldorf on 34th Street in New York was decorated with elks' heads, massive if not always inspired statuary and a picture, "The Ballet Dancer," whose lingerie and legs were the occasion of much scrutiny and comment. The bourbon set out at the Waldorf was the best pre-war stuff, the tables furnished with a carafe so that each patron could water to taste. Regulars included Tom Platt, the New York state political boss; General Nelson A. Miles; Admiral "Fighting Bob" Evans; "Marse Henry" Watterson, the Louisville publisher and editor; Richard Harding Davis, the journalist; assorted Philadelphia Drexels, members of the *New York Herald* staff who were in funds, and 263 persons named Jones who stepped up to the rectangular bar often enough to be noticed and identified.

When handsome Edward S. Stokes shot Colonel Jim Fisk for the love of a luscious lady of the theater, Josie Mansfield, he spent a brief sojourn at Sing Sing prison, the short length of his stay being commensurate with the triffling offense of removing the notorious Fisk from the earthly scene. Emerging from Sing Sing in 1877, Stokes bought a controlling interest in the sightly Hoffman House, then a famous New York rendezvous, and purchased the breath-taking Bouguereau masterpiece, "Nymphs and Satyr"—four ripe maidens prancing around a reluctant faun. The frolicsome dryads were installed on the wall opposite the bar. There the picture remained until Stokes' death in 1901.

The Hoffman House Bouguereau was reputed to have cost Ed Stokes $10,000; indeed, it was part of the barroom art *mystique* that whiskey-mill oils *always* cost that sum. In this historic spot seventeen drink dispensers stood watch at a bar seventy-five feet long. P. T. Barnum, James Gordon Bennett, celebrities from the world of the stage, Grover Cleveland and other Democratic sages gathered under the picture. John W. Gates, promoter and speculator; Chauncey W. Depew, railroad president, wit and U.S. Senator; and William Randolph Hearst also dropped in. William F. ("Buffalo Bill") Cody, no enemy of the red essence of Kentucky, in accepting an invitation to liquor, invariably said, "Sir, you speak the language of my tribe," and soon, under Bouguereau's fleshly bacchantes, was telling once again the tale of his duel with Yellow Hand.

A picturesque habitué was Congressman John Mills Allen, of Tupelo, Lee County, Mississippi, who called himself "Private John Allen" because he said he found the South so overrun with officers of field rank that he concluded he was the only private in the armies of the Confederacy who had survived the War. On one occasion, just to accommodate a whiskey drummer,

Private John called loudly for Old Green River which he declared in stentorian voice was his favorite bourbon.

"I am very sorry, sir," said the bartender apologetically. "We
haven't such a whiskey . . . But we have ——"

"What, suh?" bellowed Allen. "Do you mean to tell me, suh,
that you haven't any of that famous soul-inspirin' liquah; the joy
of every American father, the pride of every American mother,
and for which American children cry?"

The bartender was sorry.

"Well, by Gawd," exclaimed Private Allen, "you haven't got
Old Green Rivah! Suh, I refuse to drink in such a low-down
place. Come on, fellahs!" And he led his auditors out of the
Hoffman House. The next day his commercial crony, a Major,
sold seventy-five cases to the Hoffman House management.

There were, of course, other decorative motifs than scantily
clad ladies. John L. Sullivan in fierce fighting pose was useful
for covering water stains on the side wall. One Chicago saloon
was ornamented with human skulls, ropes used by suicides, and
various blunt instruments which had been collected by resourceful newspapermen at the scenes of homicides. At Mike Torio's,
on New York's Newspaper Row, there was a blackboard where
staff artists of the then-numerous daily newspapers drew their
own pictures. They were mostly unfavorable sketches of Hearst
executives, accompanied on one occasion, when a great editor
was about to receive an honorary degree from some institution
of higher learning, by scurrilous verses, including the line: "He
suffered paresis while writing his thesis."

A copy of Paolo Veronese's "Wedding at Cana, in Galilee"
hung in the Waldorf-Astoria bar for those in whom a glass of
proof whiskey inspired a mood of religious contemplation. In
sharp contrast, the Buckhorn Saloon in San Antonio was garnished with a collection of antlers, rattlesnake skins and a too-
clever parrot which announced to all comers in a parody of the
sing-song of the litany, until finally shot for blasphemy, "Ora pro
nobis (pray for us)—gad-dam it!" The only other bird of possibly equal precocity which traveled in similar social circles was
the pet of Carrie Watson. Carrie operated an elegant brown-
stone parlor house in Chicago where, the proprietess said, joy
"reigned unrefined." The feathered Pandarus occupied a cage

near the front door and was trained to say, "Carrie Watson. Come in, gentlemen."

New Orleans has been frequently credited with the invention of the saloon free lunch. At the City Exchange Bar early in the last century the house set out Louisiana gumbo, barbecued meats and varied oyster dishes. A challenger from the far West advances the claim that this distinction should go to San Francisco where the hard-rock miners learned early the technique of approaching the lunch counter under the suspicious eye of the bartender with the easy air of a man of the world, while avoiding the required purchase of at least a schooner.

There has been much sentimental and ethnocentric writing in praise of the free lunch provided in one place or another. Certainly the bar of the Palace Hotel in San Francisco or the Waldorf-Astoria were places of gastronomic marvels. Mr. William C. Smith, the rare bookman of Cincinnati, remembers fondly the ordinary German places in the West End. They provided ham which was "not carved with a safety razor but was thick enough to provide a job for your molars . . . a treat for the gods, anybody's gods."

A customer who bought two seidels at the bar of any good *Stube* in Wisconsin, such as "Unser Fritz" Genske's in Madison, where they talked of the football greats of the University of Wisconsin, and sang *Auf Wiedersehen,* could make out very well on the soup, bologna, onions, pickles, *Sardellen,* wurst and rye bread. Yet the free lunch was not philanthropic and it wasn't always dainty. The whole layout—soiled tablecloth, the bowl of baked beans, the forks standing in the glass of water as a gesture toward sanitation, the peppery hot franks, were there because salty food provokes a thirst. There was a code about diving into the victuals. Lunchers were supposed to give the house some trade first. In the cheap places where the bartenders wore tattoos and could bend a horseshoe with their bare hands, it was dangerous to sashay up to the crackers and cheese without doing some business across the way first.

The standard spirits were rye whiskey in the eastern United States and bourbon in the South and West. At Barth McGrath's drink emporium, for instance, in Cheyenne, Wyoming, there was a bottle of Old Overholt bonded rye on the back bar. No one ever asked for it. But it gave the house an aristocratic tone. Cocktails were known but generally avoided. Some had a temporary vogue. The theater, of course, inspired "The Merry Widow." "McKinley's Delight" pleased the Grand Old Party. "The Cornell" complimented an institution of higher learning located on the shore of Cayuga's waters. "September Morn" was a Clover Club in which Bacardi Rum replaced the gin. The Spanish-American War was commemorated in "Hobson's Kiss," presumably without the consent or co-operation of Richmond Pearson Hobson, Spanish-American War hero, who later became a Congressman from Alabama, an organizer of the Alcohol Education Association and a sensational success as an anti-whiskey lecturer. Colonel James E. Pepper introduced to the Eastern seaboard the Old-Fashioned cocktail which he had known at the Pendennis Club in Louisville. A succulent confection of the 1890's was the Baby Titty—equal parts of anisette, crème yvette, whipped cream, topped with a red cherry.

But the serious drinker, the man of wide experience who naturally headed left as he entered a saloon which he had not visited before, scorned the novelties. "The veterans," said the late James Leslie Marshall in his closely observed study of saloon life, *Swinging Doors* (1949), "stuck to straight Bourbon and rye." Both were believed to be effective in warding off effeminacy and to act beneficially upon the stomach as a preservative and polishing agent. Mixed drinks were not held in high regard in the sawdust places. For instance, at Tom Moran's saloon on Randolph Street in Chicago, the barman would serve seltzer, to be taken with lemon juice, if it was necessary as a therapeutic measure. But Moran's catered to a sophisticated clientele whose interest was confined to the better grades of corn squeezings, properly aged. Those who had the temerity to call for a Gin Daisy were politely requested to leave quietly. The price of a drink of whiskey in the bars of the nation provided Finley Peter Dunne's Mr. Dooley with one of his philosophic observations upon permanence and change. Mr. Dooley regarded whiskey as a standard of value far superior to gold or silver. He described it to his friend Hennessy as "somethin' ye can exchange f'r food an' other luxuries," and meditated upon its extraordinary stability: "Whiskey stands firm an' strong, unchangeable as th' skies . . . at fifteen, or two f'r a quarther."

It should not be supposed that the saloon atmosphere was given over wholly to the conviviality of dull lowbrows. There was, of course, lavatory humor and the stories about the Traveling Salesman and the Farmer's Daughter. In general, things were called by their right, or at least their vernacular names. But often the atmosphere was unabashedly sentimental. Traditions were honored, holidays observed, the dead eulogized. The mantle of charity was draped. Plans for the social betterment of man were warmly approved, provided they did not involve sumptuary legislation. Mr. Leon Karpel, now a well-known administrator in the public library field, recalls vividly that when he was a Western Union messenger boy, the place to head for with a sheaf of telegraph blanks on Mother's Day was any Brooklyn saloon.

Treating was an ancient ceremonial custom of barroom camaraderie—disapproved of by Governor Winthrop, legislated against in the Massachusetts Bay Colony in 1639, dialectically destroyed to the author's satisfaction in 1687 when Increase Mather published his *A Testimony Against several Prophane and Superstitious Customs Now Practised by some in New-England*. But incorrigible revelers persisted in raising the social glass to Liberty, to the Grand Old Flag, or, jocularly, to the Hardware Trade—"Although they profess honesty, they sell iron and steel for a living."

Sometimes there was lawing about the issue of treating. In *City of Tacoma v. Keisel,* a legal struggle which occurred when Tacoma passed an ordinance prohibiting treating, with penalties assessed against the saloon, appellant argued in vain that treating is an act of hospitality which has always been exercised by a free people. The Supreme Court of Washington rejected the argument, ruling that regulation of all aspects of alcoholic consumption comes under the police power and is not an inherent right of United States citizenship. However, men persisted in quaffing one more round when Junior made a grade of one hundred in geography, or when Myrtle graduated from high school. If, guiltily, a patron lingered too long, he could ease his distress by suggesting one last tribute in absentia "To the wife, the best little housekeeper in the world."

Robert Burns was the favorite barroom poet—"a man's a man

for a' that." The line-up along the bar liked, too, to hear the
recitation of "Shamus O'Brien" in the "Mike" places, and were
always ready to raise a cheer for free Ireland. In "Bock Beer
Days in St. Louis" Lucille Kohler has written a delightful
memoir of the German saloon atmosphere as she recounts how
bock beer time came one Easter in her childhood at Herman
Klein's proper and *behaglich*—cozy—saloon. On Easter Mon-
day, after the girls brought home the foaming bucket from Herr
Klein's, they went to a play—even more exciting than a concert
at Liederkranz Hall, or the times when Herman Klein himself
led the singing of *Ja, Das Ist Ein Schnitzelbank*. The play was
about Little Eva. It was very educational, for it had much to do
with the Civil War which Lucille and her sister knew had been
won by brave General Carl Schurz.

The choral work encountered in the saloon usually emphasized
a repertoire of songs about mother—"Just a little band from my
dear old mother's hand"; or weepers about poor working girls
being tempted and falling:

> Just tell them that you saw me
> And they will know the rest.

Close harmony quartets tore the lining out of "I've been floating
down that old Green River," and butchered "Sweet Adeline"
long before the latter song moved up socially to the locker rooms
of the country clubs. The saloon songsters also belted out various
anti-drinking songs with especial gusto, like "The Drunkard's
Doom," and "Oh, Mr. Bartender, Has Father Been Here?";
or, in San Francisco, "What Was Your Name in the States?"
And sometimes, when he wasn't splashing out the drinks or
pushed by the bucket trade, the barkeep down by the beer cooler
joined in, helping to bring out the color, harmony and dynamics
of the ballad, hitting the minor notes hard, and holding the high
ones.

The crowd at the bar represented an egalitarian society. From
the Old Ship Saloon in Eastport, Maine, to the Fountain in
San Francisco, men in work clothes, with dinner pails on their
arms and mourning bands under their finger nails, could meet as
equals with an editor, the postmaster or a member of the state
assembly. Urban life had cut off the working man from other

emotional outlets which were previously available. But the expenditure of as little as five cents in a barroom put a man in a social temper.

Saloons were ready to provide their customers with a wide variety of services—a bath, a cigar, a card game, a fund of the latest jokes as well as a shot of sour mash whiskey. The saloon was the place where the stranger could check his grip. In a country which has never provided public comfort stations, the saloon substituted for that facility, also. It was the place to find a pool table, a gramophone, a "Hand Kinetoscope" for viewing a midway dance, the Corbett fight or a picture of an express train going sixty miles an hour. There were free forms for scoring baseball games and racing meetings, and a weekly drawing for a gold watch or a bicycle. On fight nights, the news of "the mill" came in by special wire.

There was, in short, a need for certain practical services and for social expression, a personal feeling of belonging to an in-group, for warmth and companionship. The saloon met those needs, with no time limit, because the clock over the bar bore a fly-blown sign which said "This clock is always out of order." Social critics of the saloon system devoted little thought to the contribution it made or the development of substitutes. Perhaps that is why Alvin Hulteen, of Evanston, Illinois, when sentenced to attend Salvation Army services for three successive Sundays or go to jail, chose jail; or why a patient in St. Ann's Hospital in Butte, Montana, leaped from a second-story window in the dead of winter and made his way to the geniality of a Main Street barrel house, clad only in his nightshirt, and did a "ghost dance" in front of the bar.

The personality of the proprietor was important. It helped to boom business if he was a philosopher, a comic, an alderman, or a man of the people who had been in the public eye: such as Steve Brodie, who did or didn't jump from the Brooklyn Bridge on July 2, 1886, and parlayed his notoriety into a popular pot-house on the Bowery with a picture of himself over the entrance. Retired fighters moved easily, almost inevitably, into salooning; Jack Kilrain, Tom Sharkey, "Gentleman Jim" Corbett (so-called because when he was a bar customer he always left a tip), Joe Walcott and Kid McCoy. John L. Sullivan, high up in saloon hagiology, tried over and over again to be a boniface. But he wasn't cut out for it. Himself a man who got up in the morning with the feeling that he was spitting cotton, John L. could go through several pints before he felt even a little bit wet, and he was so expansive by nature that he was always inviting his paying guests to promenade up to the bar and have one on the house. Sullivan wore out several partners and finally landed in bankruptcy court, his liabilities including a personal liquor bill for $2,658.

A saloonkeeper could under the right circumstances be a woman, such as "Mother" Heiser in Milwaukee, who entertained brewers, lithographers and members of the press in her bar, known informally as "The Reichstag." Long before "Texas" Guinan was greeting her patrons in the New York of the 1920's with "Hello, Suckers," Martin Heinegebubler, proprietor of a pouring spot on South State Street in Chicago, was capitalizing on the principle that Americans enjoy and will pay for getting a belt in the teeth. Heinegebubler's place had the usual long mahogany bar, chairs and tables along the wall, back bar mirrors and a stairway to the second floor where there was allegedly a museum of natural wonders. In one corner stood two slot machines. One promised a peep at a show entitled "Fire in the Harem." Another choice was "Fun at Vassar." The second machine vended Sen Sen.

The first drink which was set out for a new visitor went down without incident. But the second dribbled over his shirt front. If he sat down, the chair collapsed. "Fun at Vassar" squirted water in his eye. Mounting the stairs to view the educational exhibit, the gull found himself on a ramp that dropped him into the cellar. The washroom facilities were wired so as to apply the principle of the induction coil to the fixtures. Despite all this, or on account of it, this odd-ball joint prospered from the time of the World's Columbian Exposition in 1893 to the end of the century.

Perhaps George F. Busse, who ran a respectable family resort in the Hyde Park section of Chicago, sums up the type. Busse rose to the position of saloonkeeper from being a commercial traveler for a piano house. He had a certain amount of background, being the son of the heaviest man in Chicago

(350 lbs.). Busse was a college man—Bryant & Stratton's Business College—and a "society man." This, in the vocabulary of the Liquor Dealers' Protective Association of Illinois, meant that Busse was affiliated with the Odd Fellows, Knights of Pythias, Independent Order of Foresters, Royal Arcanum, Second Regiment Band and the Englewood Commandery of the Mystic Shrine of the Masonic Order.

The grand opening of a new saloon in any American city was a jovial and stylized occasion. There was a formal parade. Great Percheron horses in a four or six hitch drew a beer dray followed by a brass band composed of players named Johann Sebastian Schwartz. Aldermen Kowalski and Costello were in the line of march as well as thirsty citizens in mufti. The bartenders took their places with a clean jacket and a geranium wrapped in silver foil in their lapels, a white four-in-hand at the neck, hair well pomaded with Lucky Tiger and carefully roached up in front. Gambrinus, in overalls and a flannel shirt, rolled in the kegs of mahogany-colored beer and exchanged facetious greetings with the throng of well-wishers. The brewer's sales promotion man was on hand, a hail fellow well met, who stood treat, passed out cigars, arranged for the license at city hall, went bail for good customers and fixed the cops.

In the present century, the automobile, the movies, the quickened pace of life and political corruption, associated with what was termed the "liquor traffic," all signaled changes which weakened the position of the saloon. At the same time, the competition for the trade of the stand-up drinker grew sharper. This scramble brought further abuses. Much of the responsibility for this deterioration rested upon the brewing industry. After the 1870's, breweries multiplied faster than customers. Rough price wars and forced consolidations followed. In the next decade the squeeze tightened. British financiers turned from their traditional investments in oriental bonds and African mining ventures and bought up some eighty American breweries. The retail outlets came to be the creatures of the brewers. They owned the corner locations, arranged for the bar's license, took a chattel mortgage on the fixtures, hired the bondsman and saw the judge when there was trouble. Thus developed what was known as the "tied house," with the supplier occupying a monopolistic position at the beer taps. Pushed by promissory notes, mortgages, the need for ever greater volume, the saloonkeeper could only keep his head above water by breaking the law.

The liquor dealers threw open the doors and threw the key away, as the saying went, purchased votes, stuffed ballot boxes, sold drinks to minors and hopeless winos—served anyone and everyone who could lay down the price. On those rare occasions when a saloonkeeper was hauled off in the patrol wagon, an alderman appeared in police court.

"Your honor, I've known this boy for years," he said. "He's a good boy an' works hard and takes care of his ole mother." Since the alderman had helped to place the magistrate on the bench, the "boy" was quickly released.

During San Francisco's infamous era of graft in the early 1900's, the city provided a classical instance of systematic, organized corruption. Abraham Ruef, the political boss, acted as "attorney" for the liquor dealers' association, a euphemism for furnishing protection. Ruef owned a piece of a wholesale liquor house. The red light saloons had to stock Ruef's whiskey because the police could review their licenses every three months. Behind Ruef stood "the push"—a police commissioner who supplied the saloon cigar, the fire commissioner who sold the taprooms their beer.

A spectacular instance of the virtuosity of the saloonists in law evasion occurred in New York state in the 1890's in connection with what came to be known as the "Raines Law sandwich."

This was a subject of great interest to drinking men and the cause of much merriment. The law, named after an upstate statesman from Canandaigua, was intended to stop the sale of all liquor on Sunday, except when served with food in a hotel having at least ten bedrooms. So the New York City dispensers of alcoholic drinks promptly acquired what was generally regarded as an indestructible sandwich which everyone except visitors from Meriden knew was not to be disturbed. Once in a while some yokel picked up a Raines Law sandwich and tried to eat it, and everybody had a good laugh. There is a legend that at least one back room fracas ended tragically when a man snatched up a venerable Raines Law sandwich and brained his adversary with it in one blow.

Worse was to follow. With ten microscopic bedrooms upstairs added to the rent, and no legitimate hotel business, the
saloons became houses of assignation and a new class of
hangers-on appeared on the premises, characterized by George
Ade as "chalk-white ladies who wore their sailor hats down
over their eyes." The landlord, the licensing authorities, the
brewer and the distiller, the bonding company and the patrolman,
the girls who had reached the end of the line, the working man,
were all caught up in a social syndrome. The most effective
strategy against the whole liquor industry became the attack on
its vulnerable distribution system, expressed in the war cry, "The
Saloon Must Go." The issue of compulsory Prohibition was
fought out politically. Every saloon, observed the *Liquor Men's
Advocate* with satisfaction, averaged eighty customers, "and
these eighty customers have eighty votes." When a constitutional amendment banishing liquor came up one time in Michigan, more votes were cast against the proposal in Gogebic
County than the total number of registered voters in the county.

Hinky Dink Kenna, astute saloonkeeper and political power
in Chicago, once summarized the political realities in the Ninth
Precinct in a sentence: "There are fourteen saloons, twelve lodg-
ing houses, nine five-cent restaurants, four opium joints and six
livery stables in the Bloody Ninth, and if any Republicans got
in they're colonizers to be bought at fifty cents a throw."

Prohibition was a struggle between the rural voters and the
rising power of the cities. It was fundamentalist religion react-
ing to immigration and the flourishing Roman Catholic com-
munion. It was middle-class American morality and the traditional folkways aligned against a fast-changing technology. It was
the Ku Klux Klan and the lodges and the vocal women. The
determining factors were war hysteria and the superb political
maneuvering of the corps of Grand Cyclops who headed the
Anti-Saloon League. The League dealt only in sharp blacks and
whites and did not always stick to the truth. Every man who
took a drink was an "inebriate." His children, if any, could only
be mental defectives. Any homicide was a "Whiskey murder." If
a misguided youth out on the town took a swing at a police officer, it appeared in the papers as WHISKEY REIGN OF TERROR.
By the 17th of January, 1920, liquor was an outlaw. The next

Know all men by these presents:

We, William F. Berry, Abraham Lincoln and John Bowling Green, are held and firmly bound unto the County Commissioners of Sangamon County in the full sum of three hundred dollars, to which payment well and truly to be made we bind ourselves, our heirs, executors and administrators firmly by these presents, sealed with our seal and dated this 6th day of March. A. D. 1833. Now the condition of this obligation is such that, whereas the said Berry and Lincoln has obtained a license from the County Commissioner. Court to keep a tavern in the Town of New Salem to continue one year. Now if the said Berry and Lincoln shall be of good behavior and observe all the laws of this State relative to tavern-keepers, then this obligation to be void or otherwise remain in full force.

ABRAHAM LINCOLN. [Seal]
WILLIAM F. BERRY, [Seal]
BOWLING GREEN. [Seal]

A. Lincoln

Courtesy of Blumhaven Library and Gallery

The Bond portion of the liquor license issued to the Lincoln-Berry store at New Salem, Illinois. It was signed by W. F. Berry for Lincoln.

The bar at the fashionable Hoffman House in New York. Seated in the foreground, left to right, are Nat Goodwin, the actor; M. L. Hilson, a cigar manufacturer; Edwin Booth. Behind Booth, against the wall, is David B. Hill, Governor of New York, 1885–1891. Denman Thompson, playwright and actor, stands under Bouguereau's "Nymphs and Satyr." After the third drink, the nymphs were said to do a reverse.

day the "alky" cookers were steaming and a man did feloniously and unlawfully take a swig of cologne spirits behind the storm doors of the New York Public Library.

Whiskey, even good whiskey, as dispensed via doctors' prescriptions, remained reasonably abundant. But the environment and flavor of the old-time men's bar, the niceties of communal drinking, were swallowed up in the raucous, coeducational speakeasy. Only south of the border did the American saloon, with Mexican trimmings, live on—in Tiajuana, Nogales, Juarez, Laredo and Matamoras. There, during the dreary years of Prohibition, the familiar figure of the bartender stood before an array of bottles bearing famous labels and expertly poured a rainbow of multi-hued liquids from shaker to shaker to glass.

When the end came, Don Marquis agreed for once with the Hearst thinker, Arthur Brisbane. Brisbane had predicted that Prohibition would pass, but the saloon would never return. Being a man of religious feeling, Marquis hoped to enter the New Jerusalem. With death approaching he expressed the wish that in the hereafter he might be permitted to run a barroom along the old lines.

"Kit Marlowe will be there," he said, "and Kit Morley, too, and Shakespeare and John L. Sullivan and Frank O'Malley, and Benjamin De Casseres, and Benvenuto Cellini. There will be a good deal of Talk. And if they make me let women in, I'll take my saloon to hell. If they invade those precincts, I suppose I'll have to move to Hoboken.

"P.S. There will be a Back Room."

A few vestiges of the old saloon *joie de vivre* have persisted into our latter days. Diamond Dan O'Rourke's Bowery pub reopened after Repeal in lower Manhattan with the old fixtures intact, including Diamond Dan's oil portrait of Jim Jeffries. The saloon fell before the wreckers in 1962, a good year for builders, a bad one for nostalgia. The end is in sight also for that bit of Ireland on New York's Third Avenue, presided over by the Dublin wit, Mr. James A. Glennon. His building, too, is coming down soon. Mr. Glennon's personal view of life, based upon wide observation, is expressed in a motto on the wall behind the bar: "It's better to be Rich and Healthy than to be Poor and Sick." On the mantel behind the bar beside a card announcing a raffle for the Irish Carmelite Fathers appears a photograph of Elizabeth II, the Queen of England, wearing all her decorations and the royal diadem.

The Queen has a black eye.

Chapter 18

THE ZENITH
OF MAN'S PLEASURE

"THERE is nothing like a drink of bourbon to tone up a
person," according to "Pappy" Van Winkle. As a sage of
the industry and the Grand Old Man behind Old Fitzgerald
sour mash, whose business life-span includes both the modern
industry and the memory of the old days before Prohibition, Mr.
Van Winkle may possibly lack complete objectivity when he
discusses this topic.

Yet his personal experience only serves to enhance the reputation of his favorite solace which Sir William Osler called, referring to whiskey generally, "the milk of old age." For 'way
back when he was only eighty-six, Mr. Van Winkle contracted
pneumonia and had to spend some time in the Kentucky Baptist
Hospital. Worried visitors found "Pappy" with his evening highball in one hand and a cigar in the other. The doctors were afraid
to rile him.

Mr. Van Winkle's views are echoed by John E. Ryan, one
of the surviving "Blizzard Men of '88" who was still able to
shovel the snow out of his driveway this past winter without
difficulty. "How do I live?" he exclaimed while viewing slides
of the great blizzard at the Statler Hilton Hotel in New York.
"Well, I believe in eating good food and drinking good whiskey."

There have been an embarrassing number of these octogenarians whose experience controverts the cirrhosis-of-the-liver theories sponsored by the advocates of restrictive legislation. Venerable John Wagner, once the oldest man in Buffalo, who reached the age of one hundred and four, was saluted by Mark Twain for his temperate habits. Twain said of the old gentleman that he "never tasted a drop of liquor in his life . . . unless you count whiskey." Captain Jack Haines, in St. Louis, who reached one hundred and ten, despite the St. Louis climate, once said out of his lifetime of experience, "Keep good company, preserve a good conscience, be happily married and never drink any but good whiskey."

The colorful Kentucky congressman, state governor and later minister to Mexico, Robert Letcher, once wrote to his friend, Orlando Brown, then Commissioner of Indian Affairs, that he was forwarding some Old Crow to him. "That's all you need to make you well—you have been deprived of your 'native victuals,' and that creates a Rebellion in your abdominal regions— Old Crow will put down the insurrection." On another occasion, Letcher wrote: "Your Old Crow starts for Washington tomorrow— Now don't make yourself a d—d fool, and deal out the 'Red Cretur' to fellows who don't know the difference between that and 'Red Head.' "

These letters were written during the summer of 1849. They are of considerable historical interest, for they demonstrate that Dr. Crow's elixir was known on the national scene, and that it had acquired the authentic ruddy color of bourbon which had matured on wood.

In the age of plush and red-and-gold magnificence after the Civil War, bourbon began to acquire the aura it now enjoys. When Prince Henry of Prussia visited the United States, the Pennsylvania Railroad introduced him to Pepper Whiskey and Old Crow. Civil War generals, leading political personalities, judges, bon vivants, gun runners in the Caribbean, millionaires from the latest gold strikes, all toasted fortune and destiny in full-bodied bourbon. "Hail to the San Franciscan," a visiting reporter once wrote, "whose cool climate both fosters a desire for liquor, and enables him to carry it!" And even today the artistic life of San Francisco is enriched by the unforgettable music-making of a light-hearted group of instrumentalists who took their name from a whiskey label—the Guckenheimer Sour Kraut Band.

Old Jim Gore, at his Chapin & Gore Café in Chicago, played host to William McKinley; the first Carter Harrison, martyred mayor of Chicago who fell before Prendergast's bullets; George Pullman; and the ubiquitous Colonel Cody, likely to be found wherever there were good listeners and good bourbon. While the city was burning in 1871, Jim Gore rolled eighty barrels of prime bourbon out into Lake Michigan. Recovered a few days later they were, Gore announced proudly, "fine as silk." He bottled his liquid poetry and sold it as "Lake Whiskey." Chicago loved Jim Gore Whiskey, a label no one in Kentucky ever heard of, and was willing to pay the then stiff price of $32 a case for it.

The arts flourished under Gore's genial eye. Theodore Wust sketched and caricatured the patrons as they sipped and talked. The walls were adorned with his quick studies of stage celebrities like Joseph Jefferson, DeWolf Hopper, William H. Crane and other Jim Gore regulars. Most illustrious of Gore's guests was Mark Twain, who loved the good things of this world, including whiskey. When Mrs. Rutherword B. Hayes reigned in the White House as "Lemonade Lucy," so-called because she banished alcoholic beverages from the executive mansion, Twain announced that he was not willing to contribute his famous signature to a volume of autographs honoring "the nation's matron" for her stand. Mr. Twain explained that he was abstaining from abstinence. "When others drink, I like to help," the author drawled at a dinner given in his honor. "I have lived a severely moral life. But it would be a mistake for other people to try that. . . ."

William Marion Reedy, editor of the lively St. Louis monthly magazine, *Reedy's Mirror,* himself a two-bottle man, once led a group of newspapermen on a literary pilgrimage to pay homage to Mark Twain. The idea was to place a plaque on a house where the writer had lived, if they could find it. "This is it," said Reedy confidently, indicating a dwelling standing next to an inviting-looking oasis. "No two-fisted writer would want to live anywhere except next door to a saloon."

When Mark Twain was in England he put up at the Savage Club on the Thames Embankment, a famous gathering-place of congenial spirits from the arts and upper Bohemia. The American author remarked at one of the Saturday evening dinners that he loved London but missed the joys of Kentucky bourbon. Without his knowledge his fellow-members imported a half-dozen cases and presented them to Clemens as a testimonial of admiration and affection and some of them even gallantly switched from Scotch to share Twain's pleasure in the beaded product of his native culture. Then came an urgent call for Mark to return to America. There were two cases of bourbon left.

"I will be back very soon," Mr. Clemens said. "Save them for me. Let no one touch them while I am gone."

But Mark Twain never returned. According to one account, there is to this day some of this bourbon lying in the cellar of the Savage Club. The late Malcolm Bingay of the Detroit *Free Press,* who knew the Savage Club before World War II, said that he personally went down into the sub-basement of the Club building and saw there two cases of whiskey, wrapped in heavy oil-cloth. The package was labeled "Property of Samuel L. Clemens (Mark Twain)." Bingay mentioned to his host that the humorist had been dead for quite a long time.

"That makes no difference," came the reply. "He told us to keep them here until he came back."

There is no way now of verifying this sentimental and whimsical story. The Savage Club was destroyed in the bombing of London. But the Honorable Secretary of the Savage, now located at 1 Carleton House Terrace, has commented:

"It was the sort of happy jest that Brother Savages might put over. As to the presence of bottles of Bourbon in our cellars with Mark Twain's name on them, this I fear must be regarded as a kind of legend, for I cannot imagine our Brother Savages leaving bottles of whisky in our cellars merely as historic relics."

Today men still gather at the traditional "children's hour" to enjoy fellowship, common feeling and the generous juices of old bourbon. Edward Ball, who has built up the $27,000,000 Florida interests of the Alfred Irénée du Pont estate to a $300,000,000 pot, likes to relax at the end of the working day with friends, business associates and Old Forester. Eugene R.

Black, who has recently stepped down from the presidency of the International Bank for Reconstruction and Development and is, according to James Reston of *The New York Times,* "the greatest natural wizard to come out of Georgia since Ty Cobb," possesses a connoisseur's appreciation of the four B's—baseball, bridge, bourbon and Balzac.

Yet a grave injustice would be done if the inference were allowed to stand that the enjoyment of a good bourbon is in some way confined to those who man the levers of power in the world of great affairs or to those who are socially well-placed, like Dave Falk. Some years ago when he lived at the Fairmount Hotel in San Francisco, Falk noticed that the level was falling in a bottle of fine old bourbon. He made a tiny cross on the label where the ruddy spirit stood in the flask. The next evening he found a note from the chambermaid. "Please don't put a pencil mark on the bottle," she wrote, "because I don't want to put water in such good bourbon."

The open bottle in the inner sanctum of the Speaker of the House of Representatives has been effective from time immemorial in smoothing the way of legislation. This tactic was practiced by Nicholas Longworth, later improved upon by John Nance ("Cactus Jack") Garner. When Alben W. Barkley was majority leader in the Senate and "Cactus Jack" was Vice President and the presiding officer of the Senate, Barkley would stop in Garner's office with other senators after working hours. Barkley, once a prohibitionist, although a Kentuckian, mellowed and grew tolerant in his later years, and remembered how Garner "would invite the group to 'strike a blow for liberty,' as he called the well-known bourbon-and-branch-water ritual." Barkley, a great raconteur, compared a good story to a fine Kentucky whiskey . . . "if you don't use it too much, it will never hurt anyone."

The political uses of setting out the glassware, and letting ripe spirits embrace the ice cubes, were brought to a peak of artistic perfection by the late "Mr. Sam" Rayburn. During the many years when Rayburn was Speaker, it was his custom to assemble a small group of House elders in a loose social and informal gathering which met at a hideaway on the floor below the House chamber in the late afternoon. There legislative and political situations were canvassed over drafts of bourbon and Scotch and the mood of the House was assessed. The regulars included Representatives Carl Albert of Oklahoma, Hale Boggs of Louisiana, Richard Bolling of Missouri, Homer Thornberry of Texas and a couple of fortunate newspapermen. It may be significant that under the Speakership of Mr. Sam's successor, John W. McCormack, the legislative machine has not functioned as smoothly as formerly. McCormack has attempted to carry on the hallowed custom of his distinguished predecessors. But the present Speaker is personally a teetotaler. You know how it is when the host sets it out but doesn't pour a couple of fingers for himself. There is an atmosphere of inquiry and a certain constraint. It was steadily maintained by the late Bernard De Voto, historian and sensitive appreciator of our American attitudes and institutions, that bourbon whiskey, taken without ice by American statesmen and patriots, quickened the political processes. The doubts and shadows dispersed. Men of good will were able to resolve their disputes and find the middle way.

From the historic days of Henry Clay and Daniel Webster to the present time there has been an intimate association between sour mash whiskey and the art of governing. "Whiskey," said Napoleon Achille Murat, son of the King of Naples, who married a great-niece of George Washington, was "the best part of the American government." There is no sign that this relationship is on the decline. Washington drinks more bonded whiskey per capita than Kentucky itself, about seven times as much liquor as is required to satisfy the legal thirst of Alabama. The dwellers along the Potomac with a taste for the unusual even furnish their bars and game rooms with ice buckets, service bars, chairs, sofas and game tables made from used bourbon barrels.

Under Chief Justice John Marshall the Supreme Court developed a rule that its members would take a drink only in rainy weather. But with so many subtle legal minds at hand, it was easy to interpret the rule to mean wherever it rained within the Court's jurisdiction. And it was further assumed that there was always some rain falling somewhere in the continental United States or its outlying territories. Most Presidents of the United States have taken a drink when they felt like it, and some of them have felt like it with considerable regularity. George Washington was temperate according to the standards of his time. But he was by no means a total abstainer. Jefferson was a punch and Madeira man. Madison, Monroe and John Quincy Adams all served wine in the White House. Tyler, a below-average President, but always the Virginia gentleman, kept a sideboard garnished with decanters of ardent spirits. Tradition says that Buchanan, "Old Buck," kept the best whiskey of any President up to his time. Grover Cleveland took a flask of Old Jordan with him on his jaunts to the Adirondacks, as did Benjamin Harrison when he visited the eastern shore of Maryland.

Mrs. Alice Longworth has recorded what she saw upstairs in the White House during the Harding administration—"bottles containing every imaginable brand of whiskey." Harry Truman as President liked his bourbon along with poker, piano music and the study of history. The presence of hard liquor at White House functions has been publicized frequently in the press lately and has been the subject of a resolution by the Baptist General Convention of Texas which has called President Kennedy's attention to the message of Proverbs 20:1: "Wine is a mocker, strong drink is riotous; and whosoever reeleth thereby is not wise." The present administration gives every indication, however, of associating itself with the George Garvin Brown rather than the Baptist view of this passage; that it refers only to excessive use. President Kennedy may yet do for the old colonial liquor, rum, what he has done for the rocking chair. He is reported to have a personal preference for the rum-based daiquiri cocktail.

Meanwhile the Baptists, the old-line Methodist dry crusaders, the United Texas Drys, the alcohol-free youth groups around the country and the Woman's Christian Temperance Union under the energetic leadership of Mrs. Fred J. Tooze, whose name rhymes with you know what, labor diligently to stir up the voters back home against the role of bourbon along the Potomac.

There is a running joke extending far back into our political history to the effect that there is a special affinity between bourbon whiskey and Democrats. But the best evidence is that a taste for the star-spangled beverage crosses all party lines. One of the earliest brand names was Sterne's Celebrated Con-

gress Bourbon. The label showed a picture of the House of
Representatives in session in the old chamber, now known as the
Hall of Statuary. Until the early nineteen hundreds there was a
saloon, or at least a very damp "hole in the wall," in either end
of the Capitol for the convenience of legislators who drank
water after pouring bourbon into it to kill the germs. Colonel
Robert G. Ingersoll, a member of the House who sat on the
Republican side, called it "liquid joy" which has spent "the
dreamy, tawny dusks of many perfect days . . . within the
happy staves of oak."

Of all the compatibles man has discovered in the world of
food and drink, none excels the harmony with which mint blends
into a silver goblet filled with ice, a dusting of sugar and several
ounces of mellow bourbon. The mint julep symbolizes the tradition of hospitality and domestic joy. Its gentle sway has produced a lore that is vast, intricate and controversial. The word
julep goes back about five hundred years. Milton wrote of

> . . . this cordial *julep* here,
> That flames and dances in his crystal bounds,
> With spirits of balm and fragrant syrups mix'd.

The diarist, Pepys, proceeded on June 22, 1660, "Thence to
my Lord's and had the great walk to Brigham's, who gave me a
case of good julep." But the julep made with our fragrant, native
mint is our own American invention. The introduction of sprigs
of bruised, muddled or virginal mint probably occurred in Virginia. As early as the year the Constitution was adopted, Virginians took their eye-opener in a silver goblet at breakfast,
made with brandy or rum. The volunteers who fought the Mexicans departed for the seat of war with the aid of the julep bucket.
Hard-rock miners on the California lodes took the mint julep
with them and "saw the elephant" and other strange beasties if
they sipped too many chalices powered with three or four ounces
of 100-proof whiskey. The great Confederate raider, General
John H. Morgan, lifted the frosted glass in the Richmond café
called Congress Hall.

Johnnie Solon, gifted weaver of symphonic compositions in
alcohol, who came to the Waldorf Bar soon after the Spanish-
American War and stayed to help close it up in 1920, made a

specialty of the mint julep as an ornamental and ceremonial drink for great occasions. It took Solon thirty minutes to erect the edifice of a julep, the rim of the glass icy with polar cold, the frost a good half inch thick, the commingling of scents and flavors said to have "combined the perfumes of Araby with the nectar of Olympus."

But it is not with Richmond or New York or the high Sierras that this great ritualistic drink is peculiarly associated. The mint julep belongs to Kentucky and to bourbon. In the Bluegrass state it is as sacred as Derby Day or the memory of Henry Clay. When the shadows of afternoon begin to lengthen and there is a pause in the day's affairs, from deep within the interior of the house comes the musical tinkle of cracked ice and glassware. Shaky old grandpa settles himself in the shady corner of the veranda while George builds the mint julep and with a final flourish thrusts into the beaten coin cup a few sprigs of the dark-green, pointed leaves which the Colonel's little granddaughter gathered on the sheltered side of the old springhouse. If grandpa uses the recipe of the Pendennis Club in Louisville, there are five or seven leaves of mint and they are *not* crushed. Other schools of thought, also backed by impressive authority, call explicitly for bruising the greenery.

Considerable heat can be generated over this question of whether to crush or not to crush. But it is as nothing compared to the distress which a Kentuckian feels when he contemplates the use of alien liquors, as he regards them, in a mint julep. This is the issue which estranges and embitters. A proper julep must be made with bourbon whiskey. Marylanders crush and they also pour in rye whiskey. Colonel Irvin S. Cobb, a man who had a cigar, a bridge and a mint julep named after him, felt constrained to say of his good friend, H. L. Mencken, the Baltimore Nestor and critic of life and manners, "Any guy who'd put rye in a mint julep and crush the leaves, would put scorpions in a baby's bed."

Variants on the basic mint julep have been reported from West Virginia and deep in Mississippi. But Kentuckians, who were awarding silver julep cups as prizes at county fairs as long ago as 1816, scoff at the pretensions of usurpers. As Lawrence S. Thompson, who is a scholar and a Kentucky gentleman, puts it, "Pretenders and upstarts . . . even remote Louisiana . . .

knavish Georgians . . . have attempted to produce 'the very dream of drinks' from corn whiskey sweetened with molasses . . .'' and he goes on to assert flatly, "There is but one bona fide mint julep . . . [it is] indigenous to the Bluegrass."

The most lyric tribute ever penned by the encomiasts of the mint julep comes from the files of the *Lexington Herald*. A *jeu d'esprit* of the Lexington attorney, Judge Soule Smith (1848–1904), Smith's recipe and panegyric is one of the great set pieces of southern eloquence, wit and humor. It goes like this:

"Then comes the zenith of man's pleasure. Then comes the julep—the mint julep. Who has not tasted one has lived in vain. The honey of Hymettus brought no such solace to the soul; the nectar of the Gods is tame beside it. It is the very dream of drinks, the vision of sweet quaffings. The Bourbon and the mint are lovers. In the same land they live, on the same food are fostered. The mint dips its infant leaf into the same stream that makes the Bourbon what it is. The corn grows in the level lands through which small streams meander. By the brookside the mint grows. As the little wavelets pass, they glide up to kiss the feet of the growing mint, the mint bends to salute them. Gracious and kind it is, living only for the sake of others. The crushing of it only makes its sweetness more apparent. Like a woman's heart, it gives its sweetest aroma when bruised. Among the first to greet the spring, it comes. Beside the gurgling brooks that make music in the pastures it lives and thrives. When the Blue Grass begins to shoot its gentle sprays toward the sun, mint comes, and its sweetest soul drinks at the crystal brook. It is virgin then. But soon it must be married to Old Bourbon. His great heart, his warmth of temperament, and that affinity which no one understands, demand the wedding. How shall it be? Take from the cold spring some water, pure as angels are; mix with it sugar till it seems like oil. Then take a glass and crush your mint within it with a spoon—crush it around the borders of the glass and leave no place untouched. Then throw the mint away—it is a sacrifice. Fill with cracked ice the glass; pour in the quantity of Bourbon which you want. It trickles slowly through the ice. Let it have time to cool, then pour your sugared water over it. No spoon is needed, no stirring is allowed—just let it stand a moment. Then around the brim place sprigs of mint, so that the one who drinks may find a taste and odor at one draught.

"When it is made, sip it slowly. August suns are shining, the breath of the south wind is upon you. It is fragrant, cold and sweet—it is seductive. No maiden's kiss is tenderer or more refreshing; no maiden's touch could be more passionate. Sip it and dream—you cannot dream amiss. Sip it and dream, it is a dream itself. No other land can give so sweet a solace for your cares, no other liquor soothes you so in melancholy days. Sip it and say there is no solace for the soul, no tonic for the body like Old Bourbon."

A variation upon this reverent and poetic approach to the mint julep was suggested by "Marse Henry" Watterson: "Pluck the mint gently from its bed, just as the dew of the evening is about to form upon it. Select the choicer sprigs only, but do not rinse them. Prepare the simple syrup and measure out a half-tumbler of whiskey. Pour the whiskey into a well-frosted silver cup, *throw the other ingredients away and drink the whiskey.*"

Whatever the recipe, he who sips wisely, takes his time to appreciate the minutiae of flavor and meditate upon the meaning of life and the lovely mysteries of the corn-spirit, of the char and the oak barrel, will find by the time he can see the sugar in the bottom of the glass that there is a balm in Gilead.

Chapter 19

BOURBON: FROM 1920 TO THE DAY BEFORE YESTERDAY

AT PRECISELY 12:01 A.M. on Saturday, January 17, 1920, any beverage containing one half of one per cent of alcohol or more was outlawed in the United States, as the Eighteenth Amendment to the Constitution and the act for its enforcement went into effect. The latter measure, known as the Volstead Act, named after Representative Andrew J. Volstead of Minnesota, the devoted "dry" who introduced the bill into the House, provided drastic penalties for making or selling liquor.

The administration of the law was placed under the Bureau of Internal Revenue. Enforcement machinery was incomplete when Prohibition Eve arrived, but national prohibition officials declared that no difficulty was expected. Although millions of dollars' worth of liquor left New York and other U.S. ports during the last weeks before constitutional Prohibition, National Prohibition Commissioner John F. Kramer reported that 60,-000,000 gallons remained in government warehouses. He asked Congress in January for 2,500 watchmen to guard the liquid treasure during the period when it was contemplated that legal withdrawals would gradually reduce the supply. By 1925, according to official estimates, the country would be bone-dry. William Jennings Bryan told 600 festive drys at his sixtieth birthday celebration, "The liquor issue is as dead as slavery."

The dry crusade had advanced swiftly in 1917 in an atmosphere of war psychology. On August 9, 1917, Congress passed the Lever Food and Fuel Control Act to prohibit the use of foodstuffs in the manufacture of spirits. The climactic event came on December 18, 1917. On that day Congress adopted a resolution to submit to the states a constitutional amendment prohibiting the manufacture, sale or transportation of intoxicating beverages. The states were given seven years for a three-quarters majority to ratify. They performed the task in thirteen months. And so the Secretary of State proclaimed the Eighteenth Amendment as a part of the organic law of the United States, effective January 16, 1920.

But the momentum of prohibition sentiment was too great for a delay while the states deliberated. And so Congress in September, 1918, approved a bill for "wartime" Prohibition. There is an element of irony in the fact that this "war" measure took effect about seven months after the shooting had stopped, at midnight, June 30, 1919. Most of the big places in New York played it safe and closed down their bars. The more adventurous saloons served whiskey under the euphemism "special brand ginger ale." It was still lawful, until the end of the first minute of the 17th of January in 1920, to possess and carry a bottle of whiskey, to take a drink in a public place and to treat a friend. That night, white clouds of snow swirled downward to soften the lights of Broadway, driving chilly crowds to shelter under marquees and into subway kiosks. Overhead the advertising spectaculars flashed and winked. The chewing gum twins jumped and twinkled, the kitten played with the ball of thread. A little Eskimo boy cracked his electric whip as his huskies mushed along to advertise ginger ale, a commodity soon to enjoy an extraordinary demand as a smoother for the raw edges of bootlegger hooch. The subways that evening were filled with package pilgrims carrying their own wet goods, taxis with men and women in formal evening dress, all headed toward the Gay White Way with suitcases, parcels and cretonne knitting bags that clinked.

"There will not be any violations to speak of," insisted Colonel

Dan C. Porter, Supervisor of the Internal Revenue Bureau. But there were other observers who, noting a certain professional languor on the part of the New York City police force, and that the Internal Revenue Bureau had only 800 employees in New York City, of whom 700 were stenographers, were not so sure. The Park Row places, which in their time had dispensed more *spiritus frumenti* to more men than any similar footage of real estate in the western hemisphere, picked up new hope when they heard that a foot patrolman who asked his lieutenant to clarify the law, was advised, "Polish your shield and trust in God."

Oscar of the Waldorf said that the evening would be a hummer. Hotels were flooded with thousands of reservations by diners who, the managements said, would be permitted to consume their own liquor. The Hotel Majestic, for instance, operated a special "flask" checkroom in connection with a dinner dance that lasted until 6 A.M. Sleighs were in attendance if patrons wished to cool off with a turn in Central Park. At Healy's Golden Glades, there was a special entertainment called "The Execution of Bacchus." Maxim's issued notices edged with mourning, inviting the public to the funeral of John Barleycorn. The party didn't start until a half hour before midnight, which gave the mourners exactly thirty-one minutes for a strictly legal celebration.

To newspapermen, touring the entertainment district, it seemed that if everyone who publicly emptied a couple of highball glasses in midtown Manhattan between midnight and dawn on January 17, 1920, received a $500 fine for the first one and $1,000 for the second, there would be enough money collected to retire two or three issues of Liberty Bonds. The mood of the city, and indeed of the whole country, excepting Connecticut and Rhode Island, which never did ratify the Amendment, was strangely fatalistic about the extraordinary sumptuary legislation which had been adopted. Thus the most controversial social experiment of the 1920's, which ran its course for thirteen stormy years, was launched on its licit and illicit way.

During Prohibition times, when bourbon was merely a fond memory of days gone beyond recall, it was a common occurrence for dusty pilgrims to visit the cemetery at Versailles, Kentucky, to pay homage to the creator of Old Crow. Wistful tourists

Courtesy of Historical Society of Montana

A companionable moment along the mahogany at Taft's Holdup Saloon, Red Lodge, Montana, in 1900.

Barrels aging in a modern warehouse. White whiskey takes on the authentic sour mash individuality in stout, charred oak barrels.

clamored to be routed past the old sites of famous distilleries, then choked with jimson weeds. The tumble-down premises became objects of veneration and romantic interest like the storied castles on the Rhine. This was hallowed ground, where once flowed Old Jordan, Indian Hill and Sunnybrook, these the ruins where Mellwood slumbered. Happy Hollow was a shambles. Cedar Brook? Just a memory. The Chickencock distillery was a seed company. Rolling Fork was the site of a stockyards. All that was left as physical evidence of the existence of a once-famous bourbon distilled by John A. Headley and C. Y. Peck near Lexington was some brick incorporated into the walls of the clubhouse of the Picadome Golf Club.

After the Twenty-first Amendment repealed the Eighteenth, a new distilling industry took shape. The post-Repeal industry moved toward bigger plants, larger aggregations of capital, centralized management and wider distribution. The smaller distilleries for the most part found that they could not finance the making, the waiting period and the costs of advertising and distribution. So they joined up with the corporate giants, especially if their bargaining position was strong because they were warehousing a substantial block of aged whiskey, and the small family distiller found the capital gains tax less unpalatable than the income tax. The problem of how to raise the money to pay the inheritance rates where an estate was in the illiquid form of a family corporation persuaded many owners of prestige whiskey trademarks to become willing sellers.

In this way such old firms as Labrot & Graham, Buffalo Springs and McKenna were absorbed by the large companies who distilled, blended, distributed, marketed by-products, acquired timberlands, bought in cooperage companies, balanced their line with California wines and imported liqueurs, and diversified into chemicals and biologicals. These socially desirable activities might well serve to blunt the attack of the Prohibitionists if they should rise again behind a Frances E. Willard or a new Messiah like the late Bishop James Cannon, Jr., the powerhouse of the Anti-Saloon League.

At midnight on April 7, 1933, legal wines and beer returned to the United States. Near the end of the year, on December 5th, at 5:32 P.M., the repeal of the Eighteenth Amendment was proclaimed. Bourbon was back, in theory at least; although by that time there wasn't much genuine bourbon to be had. The federal government took a series of steps to eliminate the abuses of the pre-1920 period. A "bottle law" placed rigid restrictions on the sale or re-use of whiskey bottles. As a result, public confidence rose as to the quality of goods offered by the legal industry. The Federal Alcohol Administration Act which became law in 1936 banned the sale of liquor in bulk to the wholesale and retail trade, modernized and harmonized the law, pruning out obsolete provisions reaching back as far as 1875. Enforcement authority was vested in the Federal Alcohol Control Administration, later reorganized into the Alcohol and Tobacco Tax Division of the Bureau of Internal Revenue.

The law set forth the most precise classification of liquors attempted since the definitions set up by President Taft in 1909. Neutral spirits were defined as a distillate made from any material at or above 190 proof. Grain neutral spirits were distilled from any grain. If the proof was under 190 and the mash made from grain, the distillate was plain whiskey. Straight bourbon was, and still is, a whiskey distilled at not exceeding 160 proof from a fermented mash of not less than fifty-one per cent of corn. In distilling practice, it is usually from sixty to seventy-five per cent corn. The remainder of the mash is rye and barley malt. If eighty per cent or more of the mash is corn, the distillate is corn whiskey.

Straight bourbon whiskey must be aged in new, charred oak barrels for two years or more. The provisions covering bottling in bond remain as described in Chapter 9, except that the bonding period has recently been extended to twenty years. Similarly precise definitions cover rye whiskey, corn whiskey, the various types of blended whiskeys, gin, brandies and rum, cordials, Canadian, Scotch and Irish whiskies and the use of geographical designations; also vodka.

Straight bourbons are lighter now than they were before Prohibition and are generally sold at 90 or 86 proof. How does whiskey quality compare with that of the whiskeys in the old days? Many industry leaders assert that today's whiskey is better because there is complete technical control of the process from raw grain to the man-made weather in the modern warehouse.

Yet there is a dispute about this. "Old Fitzgerald sleeps better with the windows open," declares Mr. Van Winkle. And Colonel Frank B. Thompson, Chairman of the Board of Glenmore Distilleries, Inc., who has the faith of a dedicated missionary in the virtues of his bonded Old Kentucky Tavern and Yellowstone Kentucky Straight Bourbon, agrees that whiskey should rest in "open rick" warehouses and "breathe in the barrel" without artificial temperature controls.

The issue here is science vs. art, chemistry vs. knowhow. Certainly in the days before 1917 even the best brands lacked stability. Yeasts were difficult to control, whereas now a pure culture is easily maintained. Generally speaking, the industry has put its money on bacteriological methods, backed up with thermostats and gauges as against the "green thumb" approach. But the exceptions to this view should be marked. They have done well, too. Although most consumers of bourbon know little enough about how whiskey is made, many show a pronounced preference for the product of craftsmanship and experience as against chemistry and instrumentation. There is an undeniable charm about the conception of the little old still up among the laurel bushes with the associated ideas of family recipes, secret processes, small production and distinctive taste. It is the dream of a Garden of Eden, equipped with a set of stills. Nostalgia can even include packaging. There is a legal corn whiskey, sold regionally in the southeastern states, called Georgia Moon. It is guaranteed to be less than thirty days old and comes in a squat fruit jar, the kind in which Georgians customarily purchase their moonshine. This inspired venture into applied psychology is the idea of a gifted young woman from south Georgia who got her start selling cemetery lots by playing Dixieland jazz, and closed her radio program with the assurance, "My sponsor will be the last man to let you down."

Since distillers are jealous of the character of their product and variations from the standard might jeopardize an equity built up over many long years, they often display reluctance to abandon traditional methods of manufacture. Indeed, quaintness can be sold quite effectively. For in trade as in manners, customs or the arts, cults spring up or can be nourished, which place a high valuation upon the rare, the esoteric or the folksy. A sign hangs over the door of the distillery where Old Fitzgerald is made: "No Chemists Allowed." After warning off the men of science, the sign adds, "This is a distillery—not a whiskey factory." The makers of Ezra Brooks, a Kentucky straight whiskey, proudly announce that they operate the *smallest* distillery in the state. They are down-to-earth folks, too, and drop their g's when they talk up their "sippin' whiskey," of which "there just ain't enuf to go around."

Reagor Motlow, head of the distillery which makes the distinctive Tennessee whiskey, Jack Daniel's, declares:

"Why, Uncle Jess here [the Motlow practical distiller] never read a chemistry text in his life, but after fifty-four years of stillin' whiskey you can't fool his eye, his nose, or his tongue."

And Uncle Jess' face crinkles up with something like a leathery blush as he protests, "Why, Lord a' mercy, I don't know nothin' about diastase and such things as Reagor talks about."

The cost of a bottle of whiskey bears some relation to the cost of manufacture, but not very much. Advertising, mark-ups on manufacture, wholesale and retail prices and taxes account for most of the final price; especially the tax item. The federal excise tax remains where it has been since the Korean War at $10.50 per proof gallon. Alcoholic beverages are also subject to numerous state taxes, the most important of which are gallonage taxes ranging from seventy-five cents to $3.50 a gallon. On a "fifth" of a gallon of 86.8 proof whiskey over half, or about fifty-five per cent of the cost at retail, represents taxes.

Do people stop drinking when the price goes up? The experience is—not that one can notice. They shift to a lower-priced label or drink untaxed liquor, the " 'shine" often sold at gas stations, "after-hours clubs" and nip joints specializing in illegal "corn." The ease of illicit distillation and small bulk of the product in relation to value continue to give moonshining a significant role. It has been estimated that fifty million gallons a year of spirits are trickling from stills located in old warehouses, coal bins, harbor barges or swamps. The product moves in gasoline cans, oil drums or pop bottles by trailer truck, airplane, or, as has actually happened, in a passenger car registered in the name of the agent who was chasing it.

Some distillers in the legitimate industry, recognizing the con-

sumer's problem—that he doesn't know the definitions the industry works under—have tried to bring wisdom and enlightenment
to the purchasers of liquor by promoting the back labels on their
bottles which carry mandatory descriptions designed to convey
solid information about the contents. But informative labeling
has made little headway with the sentimental and romantic customers. Traditionally, they prefer to buy on atmosphere and
trade names and have, on the whole, shown a fanatical if not
particularly well-informed loyalty to their favorites.

Whiskey advertising operates under both government restrictions and voluntary limitations adopted by the industry. Just as
distillers strive for uniformity in their products, they seem also
to have the same aim in their advertising, relying upon prestige-
building symbols indicating social approval, plus claims of product "differences." Since there are 800-odd U.S. brands of whiskey, these often miniaturized differences create a dilemma for
the consumer who would like to be knowledgeable about his
drinking but was born, alas, with run-of-the-mill taste buds. The
industry is entitled to a measure of sympathy for the sameness
of its advertising because of the complexity of the laws governing
what can be introduced into an advertisement. The advertiser of
a whiskey which sells nationally must prepare twenty-seven different versions of the same announcement. In thirteen states the
price of the whiskey cannot be mentioned. Kansas permits no
reference to Father's Day. Pictures of women are *verboten* in
seven states. A social setting involving drinks is off the reservation in eight states. It is a violation of the law in West Virginia
if a man's hand is shown in contact with a glass or bottle. The
official guide to the laws governing the advertising of spiked beverages runs to 592 pages. And new pages are being added all the
time.

Not only advertising, but the whole mechanism involved in the
purchase of a bottle or a drink is surrounded with involved regulations. Although the result is often one of confusion and contradiction, the aim is to prevent the return of old abuses, such as
the defiance of closing hours celebrated in this episode:

"Aren't you open rather late?" a newcomer once asked Luke
Short, pistol-quick gambler and part owner of the notorious Long
Branch Saloon in Dodge City, Kansas. It was then four o'clock

in the morning.

"It *is* rather late for night before last," the tolerant Texan conceded, "but it is just the shank of the evening for tonight."

Some states prohibit moving displays. A dealer brightened up his counter with some balloons. When a state investigator opened the door, the balloons fluttered. The retailer got a summons for having a moving display. Drinks can't be served in the state of Washington on Arbor Day. Women can't approach a bar in Connecticut and it is unlawful to sell whiskey to persons posted as "drinkers" by the board of selectmen. In Massachusetts, possibly because of the vivid memory there of the Boston Massacre in 1770, liquor cannot be sold by the drink during a riot. An Indian can't belt off a few in Minnesota unless he is "civilized," a definition which could call for some very close reasoning. Utah bartenders are prohibited from serving anyone living with an Indian woman. And so on.

With social drinking acceptable in more sectors of our society than ever before, nearly one-third of the members of the Methodist Church now see no harm in taking an occasional refresher. Even the farm youth of Iowa follow urban drinking patterns when they move to the city; and as for the women—at Hyannis, Massachusetts, near the Kennedy enclave, the girls promenade along Main Street wearing tight-fitting black jerseys emblazoned "U.S.A. Olympic Drinking Team." And recently a young Chicago secretary, Miss Virginia Wantroba, challenged the constitutionality of an Illinois law that raised the minimum legal drinking age from eighteen to twenty-one years because, Virginia said, the law interfered with her constitutional liberties and if it was enforced she would suffer "irreparable injury." This is a significant phenomenon, the Woman's Crusade, so to speak, in reverse.

With more women sipping, the feminine influence is a large factor in a trend toward milder whiskeys. All drinkers oxidize alcohol at the same rate. But some drinkers are more petite than others. Also, weight-conscious women get fewer calories at the lower proof. The less potent whiskeys are growing so fast in popularity that even many of the famous-name bonds are now available in "companion items" at 86 proof, but of course without the green stamp.

Despite the more tolerant attitudes toward drinking, the abuse of liquor is definitely not acceptable. The burden of life's sorrow may be cast upon the Lord, or consolation may be sought in a bottle. There is social sanction for the one, but not the other. A gentleman is expected to enter and to leave a tavern in good condition, and to tailor his use of alcohol in private gatherings to his personal capacity and a sense of situation.

When one reviews how continuously the act of drinking is portrayed in art, in either romantic or "tough" novels, on the stage, in magazines and all forms of mass communications as an intimate part of the life enjoyed by the rich and the powerful, and how the elite classes, such as members of Congress or the American Booksellers Association, are constantly photographed with a well-filled glass in hand—in view of all the evidence that leaders in our national life find spirits pleasant to consume, it is remarkable that we drink as little as we do. A good many people including, one suspects, those who have had access to the statistics of the American Dental Association, would argue that whiskey today is doing considerably less damage than the lolli-pop. Per capita liquor consumption stands at 1.3 gallons. This is somewhat less than people were drinking after Repeal, sub-stantially less than the intake in speakeasy days, a mere drop on the tongue compared with the nearly 4.8 gallons per head which Americans were consuming a hundred years ago.

Along with the trend to lower proofs, observers note a shift from blended whiskeys to straight bourbons which have chalked up a thumping 400 per cent increase in the last dozen years. Both have their embattled partisans for their performance as a re-laxer, agreeable aperitif before dining or festive adjunct to trade conventions, college reunions and other tribal rites. Although some of the biggest firms, such as Seagrams-Distillers Co. and Hiram Walker, Inc., are still known for their dedicated attach-ment to blended whiskeys, and while others, such as National Distillers and Schenley Distillers Co., emphasize their position as "straight whiskey" houses, actually all the larger factors in the industry today have diversified. All offer bonds, straight bour-bons in several price brackets, a variety of blended American whiskeys, "white" liquors like gin and vodka and a varied line of imports. Their aim is a full line that covers the market, just as Ford Motor Company and General Motors build cars to meet all the categories of the automotive field.

Men might be more saintly if the alembic had never been invented, although the point cannot be established on the evidence accumulated up to the present time. Furthermore, only a few men seek sainthood. Most of mankind do find that a glass and a pause at the end of the day paves the way to common thoughts and feelings. A man, sipping, sees himself and his environment in a more bearable light. Holding a tumbler in which the soul can shimmer, he finds that he can carry on his task while appreciating on the fleshly level the special qualities of a Hiram Walker, a Glenmore or a Wathen distillation whose influence is to make him more honest, more humane and kinder in his outlook upon his fellow men.

Would you like to have a barrel of prime bourbon of your very own, as your grandfather probably did? You can, if you like. It is possible for the consumer to purchase a barrel from a broker who deals in bulk whiskeys. But you can't take your friends, business associates or your mother-in-law down to the cellar and let them gaze upon the oak barrel or let them sniff the aroma of your golden elixir as it slowly evaporates. The United States government requires that whiskey for consumers be bottled. You can devise any label, though, which pleases your fancy—Old Stock Exchange, Cannonball Special, Confederate Raider, Old Gerald—anything you like, provided that the whiskey has passed through the normal trade channels, wholesale and retail, and you have paid their respective mark-ups.

Beady old bourbon, which takes age so gracefully, has recently been accorded recognition as one of the world's small number of authentic spirits, unique to the United States. The Fédération Internationale de Vins et Spiriteaux, composed of the wine and spirits makers of fourteen nations in Europe, have granted bourbon the same standing and protection accorded Scotch whisky and cognac; that is, the name can be properly applied only to U.S.-made liquor meeting the definitions in force here. Bourbon is the *fine champagne cognac* of the western hemisphere. They are even drinking it, with happy unbelief, in Scotland. Bourbon has helped to shape American life and society. It has been a father of American agriculture, a pillar of the early church. It did in the Indians, comforted a continent. With a genius native to our climate and suited to the temperament of our people, bourbon has survived the vicissitudes of Prohibition and Repeal. I give you, then, the Great Spirit of America, worthy companion in their hours of leisure of a nation of honorable men and gracious women.

CHRONOLOGY

1640 First spirits distilled from grain, on Staten Island, New York, by William Kieft, Director-General of New Netherland.

1657 Earliest American reference to rum, in the records of the Massachusetts General Court.

1698 Applejack was being distilled in Monmouth County, New Jersey.

1733 The Molasses Act imposed by England upon the American colonies; a prohibitive duty intended to restrict the importation of rum, molasses and sugar from the non-British West Indies. Largely ignored by the American colonists.

1750 The New England rum trade reached its fullest development.

1764 The Sugar Act extended the Molasses Act forbidding the importation of rum and spirits from foreign sources; one of the causes of the American Revolution.

1770 The first distillery for producing spirits from American grain in the West; erected at Pittsburgh.

1775 Daniel Boone blazed a trail to Kentucky. First corn patches planted in what is now the bourbon whiskey region of Kentucky.

1783 Evan Williams was distilling corn whiskey at Louisville, Kentucky.

1785 Bourbon County organized by the Virginia Legislature.

1785–87 First settlers from Maryland arrived in what is now the state of Kentucky and set up distilling apparatus.

1789 The Reverend Elijah Craig, a Baptist minister, was making whiskey from corn near Georgetown, in what is now Scott County, Kentucky.

ca. 1790 Jacob Spears and others erected the first distillery in Bourbon

County.

1791   The United States government imposed an excise tax on the do-
        mestic manufacture of spirits. Violent opposition in North Carolina,
        Virginia, Kentucky and especially western Pennsylvania.

1792   Kentucky admitted into the Union.

1793   Last Indian foray into Kentucky.

1794   Militia from four states marched to western Pennsylvania and sup-
        pressed the "Whisky Rebellion."

1802   The tax on distilled spirits repealed.

1808   The United States banned the further importation of slaves from
        Africa; consequent decline of the rum industry.

1811   Kentucky had 2,000 distilleries.

1814   The excise tax on domestic liquor revived to help finance the War
        of 1812.

1817   U.S. excise tax on domestic liquors repealed.

1830   Temperance sentiment on the rise in the U.S.; liquor ration abolished
        in the U.S. Army.

1846   First appearance in print of the word "bourbon" as applied to
        whiskey (known to the author of this book).

1848   First appearance of the word "bourbon" on the label of a bottle
        (known to the author).

1862   The ration of spirits ("grog") abolished by the U.S. Navy. Internal
        Revenue Bureau established to collect taxes on liquor and other com-
        modities to help defray costs of the Civil War. Whiskey tax was
        twenty cents a proof gallon.

1864   Tax on liquor increased to $1.50 a proof gallon.

1865   Tax increased to $2 a proof gallon.

1868   Federal tax reduced to fifty cents to meet problems of widespread
        illegal distillation. Bonding period of one year set up. General
        Ulysses S. Grant elected President of the United States.

1869   Prohibition Party organized. Operations of a "Whiskey Ring" to
        defraud the government of the excise tax became a matter of general
        knowledge.

1872   Excise tax on whiskey raised to seventy cents a gallon. Grant elected
        for his second term as President.

1874   Woman's Christian Temperance Union organized.

1875   Government action was successful in breaking up the "Whiskey
        Ring"; tax increased to ninety cents a gallon.

1878   Period for which whiskey could be held in bond without payment
        of the tax extended to three years.

1881–82 Overproduction of whiskey; pools formed to limit output and
        control prices.

1887   The "Whiskey Trust"—the Distillers' and Cattle Feeders' Trust—
        organized to replace the pools.

1890   The Sherman Anti-Trust Act passed to regulate large industrial
        combinations controlling oil, whiskey, sugar, beef, etc., in interstate
        commerce. The Distillers' and Cattle Feeders' Trust successfully
        prosecuted under the Sherman Act.

1894   Bonding period for whiskey extended to eight years. Tax increased
        to $1.10.

1895   Anti-Saloon League, militant dry organization, established.

1897   The Bottled-in-Bond Act signed into law by President Grover
        Cleveland.

1903   Michael Joseph Owens invented the automatic bottle-making ma-
        chine.

1906   The first federal Food and Drug Act brought whiskey labels under
        regulation on January 1, 1907, and touched off a "whiskey war"
        over the definition of whiskey.

1909   President William Howard Taft issued a legal decision defining
        whiskey types.

1913   Prohibition forces obtained passage of the Webb-Kenyon Interstate
        Liquor Act which prohibited the shipment of liquor into states where
        local law made the sale illegal.

1914   All wines and malt beverages prohibited within the jurisdiction of
        the U.S. Navy.

1917   The Lever Food and Fuel Act ended legal distilling in the U.S.
        Excise tax on existing stocks of beverage whiskey raised to $3.20
        a gallon. The Eighteenth Amendment submitted to the states; rati-
        fication by thirty-six states required.

1918   Armistice with Germany signed, November 11.

1919   "Wartime" Prohibition, a stop-gap law while the states were voting
        on constitutional Prohibition, became effective June 30. Nebraska,
        the thirty-sixth state, ratified the Eighteenth Amendment, to take
        effect in January, 1920. Congress passed, over a presidential veto,
        the Volstead Act which set up legal machinery to enforce Prohibi-
        tion. Spirits withdrawn for beverage use taxed at $6.40 a gallon.

1920   The United States was legally dry on January 17.

1922   The Liquor Concentration Act designated certain warehouses where
        stocks of aged whiskey were impounded and released under a permit
        system.

1924   National Distillers Products Corporation organized.

1929   The manufacture of whiskey for medicinal purposes resumed.

1933   With the adoption of the Twenty-first Amendment, Prohibition
        came to an end at 5:32 P.M. December 5th.

1933 Schenley Distillers Corporation organized.

1934 The liquor gallonage tax levied at $2.

1936 Federal Alcohol Administration Act established Standards of Identity for all the various whiskey types on the market.

1938 Excise tax increased to $2.25 a gallon. '

1940 Distilled spirits taxed at $3 a gallon.

1941 Tax increased to $4 a gallon. Distilling industry totally converted to war production.

1942 Tax increased to $6 per gallon.

1944 Tax increased to $9 a gallon.

1945 Production of beverage alcohol resumed.

1951 Federal excise raised to $10.50 a gallon.

1958 Bonding period extended to twenty years.

1960 Distillers and vinters of Europe grant bourbon whiskey which meets U.S. government regulations the same international recognition and protection extended to the Scotch whisky of Scotland and the cognac of France.

GLOSSARY

Age, Aging—The period of storage, after distillation and before bottling; the mellowing, maturing and developing of a distinctive character while a whiskey is "on wood."

Alcohol, *or* ethyl alcohol—The intoxicating principle in distilled liquors, a colorless, volatile, inflammable liquid represented by the chemical symbol C_2H_5OH.

Aldehyde—A colorless, volatile liquid found in alcohol.

Alembic—An early type of still.

Back Label, *or* "government label"—It appears on the back of a bottle giving alcoholic content, net contents, percentages of neutral spirits and whiskey, name of the commodity from which they are distilled and the state where the whiskey is manufactured.

Bead—Bubbles which form at the surface of the liquor around the rim of the glass, associated with fully mature, heavy-bodied whiskeys.

Beer, *or* distiller's beer, *also known as* Fermented Wort—An alcoholic mixture made by fermenting finely ground grain, which is then distilled.

Blend—The mixture of various percentages of straight whiskeys; or of straight whiskeys with neutral spirits. Under present law, a blended whiskey must contain at least twenty per cent by volume of 100-proof straight whiskey. The resulting mixture must proof at not less than eighty.

Blended Bourbon whiskey—Must be at least fifty-one per cent by volume straight bourbon whiskey; the rest grain neutral spirits.

Blended Canadian whisky—A mixture of whiskies distilled in Canada, all two or more years old.

BLENDED CORN WHISKEY—Whiskey and grain neutral spirits, at least fifty-one per cent straight corn whiskey.

BLENDED RYE WHISKEY—Grain neutral spirits mixed with at least fifty-one per cent straight rye whiskey.

BLENDED SCOTCH WHISKY—A blend of malt and grain whiskies distilled in Scotland by the pot still method and aged for at least three years in uncharred oak barrels or used sherry casks.

BLENDED STRAIGHT WHISKEYS—Composed of straight whiskeys—no spirits added.

BLIND TIGER—Old slang term for a place where liquor is sold illegally.

BONDED BOURBON—A straight bourbon whiskey which meets the requirements of the Bottled-in-Bond Act. *See* Bottled-in-Bond. The same definition applies to bonded rye whiskey, with rye substituted as the dominant grain.

BONDED WAREHOUSE—A warehouse under federal government supervision for the storage of spirits.

BOTTLED-IN-BOND—A "bond" is a whiskey entitled to the grain designation, aged in barrels in a government warehouse for at least four years, bottled at 100 proof and sealed with the U.S. government green strip stamp. It must be the product of a single distillery, made during a single season and year.

BOURBON WHISKEY—A whiskey distilled at 160 proof or lower from a fermented mash with corn not less than fifty-one per cent of the grain used. All bourbon must be stored in charred new oak cooperage.

BRANDY—A distillation of a fermented mash of fruit or fruit juice, taken from the still at less than 190 proof, bottled at 80 proof or higher.

CHAR—The result of burning the interior of whiskey barrels used for aging spirits. The char gives whiskey its ruddy color and contributes to the process of ripening.

CONGENERS—Volatile secondary products, members of the amyl branch of the alcohol family. Potentially toxic, they are modified by aging and give an old whiskey its most admired qualities.

CORN WHISKEY—A spirit distilled at 160 proof or lower from a mash containing at least eighty per cent corn, stored in uncharred or reused charred oak barrels.

DOUBLER—A pot still used for redistilling singlings, or low wines.

EXCISE TAX—A tax computed either on the alcoholic content or on the basis of a wine gallon of a domestic liquor.

FERMENTATION—The conversion of sugar into alcohol prior to distillation.

FIRST SHOT, *or* FORESHOT—The first portion of spirit that vaporizes when the still begins to work. The term is applied to both the production of low and high wines.

FUSEL OIL—An oily liquid found with ethyl alcohol after distillation.

GRAIN NEUTRAL SPIRITS—A grain mash distilled at very high proof, over 190, to produce a product that is almost odorless, tasteless and colorless.

HEADS AND TAILS—The condensate obtained at the beginning and the end of a run, containing undesirable amounts of the congeneric substances.

HIGH WINES—The finished spirit produced when low wines are redistilled.

LOW WINES—A spirit low in alcoholic content resulting from the first distillation of the still beer; the first run. Also known as singlings.

MALT—Dried, sprouted grain, usually barley, introduced into a slurry with the ground-up grain to turn starch into fermentable sugar.

MASH—The starchy material which is subjected to the action of water, heat, stirring and fermentation to prepare it for the still.

MESCAL—An alcoholic beverage made from pulque, the fermented juice of the Mexican century plant.

MOONSHINE—Distilled spirits on which the tax has not been paid or federal regulations observed as to materials and sanitation.

NEUTRAL SPIRITS—A distillate run at or above 190 proof and obtained from molasses, grain or the redistillation of whiskey, brandy or rum. Used for blending with straight whiskey and making gin, vodka, cordials and liqueurs.

OUTAGE—Loss during the aging period due to evaporation and soakage.

POT STILL—A vessel shaped like a kettle with a tapering neck connected to a condensing coil in which the alcohol is liquefied and collected.

PROOF—A statement of alcoholic strength. The proof number is twice the percentage of alcohol by volume. Example: a whiskey marked 100 proof contains fifty per cent alcohol. The remainder is water.

PROOF GALLON—A wine gallon at 100 proof or its alcoholic equivalent. *See* Wine Gallon.

RECTIFIED SPIRITS—Whiskey which has been redistilled at high proof to strip out the whiskey flavor elements; or whiskey flavoring agents and alcohol mixed together to produce a homogeneous blend.

RUM—A beverage distilled from molasses or other cane products or by-products and bottled at not less than 80 proof.

RYE WHISKEY, *see* BOURBON WHISKEY—The difference is that rye must make up not less than fifty-one per cent of the mash.

SCOTCH WHISKY—*See* BLENDED SCOTCH WHISKY.

SINGLINGS—*See* LOW WINES.

SOUR MASH—Bourbon whiskey made by using in the fermentors part of the spent beer from a previous day's run, along with fresh yeast, to start a new batch of mash.

SPENT BEER—The distiller's beer after the alcohol has been removed; also called slop or stillage. Formerly used wet to feed stock, now dried and marketed as cattle feed.

STANDARDS OF IDENTITY—Specifications describing whiskey types established by federal law under the Federal Alcohol Administration Act of 1936.

STRAIGHT BOURBON WHISKEY—*See* BOURBON WHISKEY.

STRAIGHT WHISKEY—A whiskey distilled at not more than 160 proof from a grain mash; aged for a minimum of two years.

STRIP STAMP—An internal revenue stamp over the neck and cap of a bottle of spirits indicating that the federal excise tax has been paid.

TEQUILA—A liquor distilled from the juice of the century plant.

TIED HOUSE—A retail outlet controlled by a brewer or distiller or liquor wholesaler for the purpose of eliminating competition. (Illegal under present law.)

WAREHOUSE RECEIPT—A negotiable financial instrument against which specific barrels of spirits stored in a government warehouse are pledged as collateral.

WHEAT WHISKEY—*See* BOURBON WHISKEY—But wheat must make up not less than fifty-one per cent of the fermented mash.

WHISKEY—Federal regulations define whiskey as an alcoholic distillate made from a fermented mash of grain, distilled at less than 190 proof, withdrawn from the cistern room at not more than 110 proof and not less than 80 proof and bottled at 80 proof or higher.

WINE GALLON—A measure of liquid volume, not of alcoholic content. It is the standard United States gallon, 128 fluid ounces or 231 cubic inches.

WORM—A water-cooled coil of pipe in which the hot alcoholic vapor from the still is condensed.

CHAPTER NOTES

The author has desired to make available adequate bibliographical information while, at the same time, avoiding the distractions of a text decorated with superior numbers and footnote references. The method adopted has been, first, occasionally to cite in the flow of the narrative especially important or interesting sources. But for the most part, the authorities consulted have been gathered into the chapter notes. The first citation of each title gives full information. Subsequent appearances follow a shortened form. To conserve space, some of the more unwieldy titles of government publications and others in the prolix style of the early nineteenth century have not been given in full. But there is enough detail to identify the source. Occasionally the notes introduce new material. But I have tried to resist the temptation to start a new book in the closing pages of this one.

Foreword

The quotation from Professor Morris Bishop appears in a symposium, "Outstanding Books, 1931–1961," *The American Scholar.* 1961 30(4): 600. On bourbon as America's distinctive spirit: J. Stoddard Johnston, *Memorial History of Louisville from its First Settlement to . . . 1896.* 2v. Chicago: 1896, chapter XIX; Paul White, "Red Likker," *The Courier-Journal* (Louisville, Kentucky), May 3, 1953; Poppy Cannon, "The True American Spirit," *House Beautiful,* December, 1955. Colonel Taylor's declaration appears in a collection of clippings, *Newspaper Scrapbook, 1903–1919,* in the library of National Distillers Products Corporation. The place of our native whiskey in general American history is indicated by Alfred J.

Liebmann, "Early American Spirits," *Autograph Collectors' Journal.* 1951
3(3) ; and *ibid.* 1951 3(4) ; also Robert W. Hill, "The Liebmann Collection of American Historical Documents," *Bulletin of The New York Public Library,* July, 1954. Alcoholic beverages as a source of revenue are
studied by Tun Yuan Hu, *The Liquor Tax in the United States, 1791–
1947; a history of the internal revenue taxes imposed on distilled spirits.*
New York: 1950.

The prominent citizen who sneaked into the bar: observed by George
Ade, in *The Old-Time Saloon, Not Wet—Not Dry—Just History.* New
York: 1931; 158. The pronunciation of "bourbon" is discussed in Luther
Huston, "Bourbon on the Potomac," *The New York Times Sunday Magazine,* December 15, 1946, and may be caught orally in even the most super-
ficial contact with any authentic Kentuckian. The affectionate tribute to
bourbon from the old paper maker appears in Frances L. S. Dugan and
Jacqueline P. Bull, *Bluegrass Craftsman, Being the Reminiscences of Ebenezer Hiram Stedman, Paper Maker, 1808–1885.* Lexington: 1959; 181.

Chapter 1

Alcohol easy to make: see George W. Hackett, "Distiller Van Winkle
Prefers Nature's Brew," *The Courier-Journal,* July 30, 1961. The use of
the word "brew" in connection with Kentucky's famous distillate is an
inexplicable error. On psychological factors and cultural patterns: Raymond
G. McCarthy and Edgar M. Douglass, *Alcohol and Social Responsibility.*
New York: 1953; 88–89, 98, 103ff.; Clarence Hodges Patrick, *Alcohol,
Culture and Society.* Durham: 1952; 3–29, *passim;* and H. F. Willkie's
pamphlet, a useful summary, *Beverage Spirits in America: A Brief History.*
New York: 1949; 7–8. The presence of small quantities of alcohol in the
normal blood stream is pointed out in Harold J. Grossman, *Grossman's
Guide to Wines, Spirits, and Beers.* New York: 1943; 174.

For drinking habits in early America, I consulted Daniel Dorchester, *The
Liquor Problem in All Ages.* New York: 1884; 124–126; Foster Rhea
Dulles, *America Learns To Play. A History of Popular Recreation, 1607–
1940.* New York: 1940; 16–27, 30, 70; Ulysses Prentiss Hedrick, *A History of Agriculture in the State of New York.* (Albany): 1933; 155–156,
224–226; John Allen Krout, *The Origins of Prohibition.* New York:
(1925); 2–3, 28–30, 34, 37, 60; Patrick, *op. cit.,* 33, *passim;* Harry
Bischoff Weiss, *The History of Applejack or Apple Brandy in New Jersey
from Colonial Times to the Present.* Trenton, N.J.: 1954: 9–10, 94;
Willkie, *op. cit.,* 13. Willkie, 15, records also the ingenuity of the colonists
in finding native materials to brew and distill. See also Michael Krafft,
The American Distiller (short title). Philadelphia: 1804; 97–100.

For the topic, liquor and mourning in New England, I am indebted to

Alice Morse Earle's chatty but not yet superseded *Customs and Fashions in Old New England.* New York: 1893, quoted in Edward R. Emerson, *Beverages, Past and Present.* 2v. New York: 1908, II, 471. Quaker customs appear in Stevenson Whitcomb Fletcher, *Pennsylvania Agriculture and Country Life, 1640–1840.* Harrisburg: 1950; 450. The folksay about apple spirit building the stone walls of New England is taken from "How Hard Do Americans Drink?", *Fortune,* March, 1953; 4.

I traced the heavy dramming in the old South through Dorchester, *op. cit.,* 139; Dulles, *op. cit.,* 30, 70, 150–151; Emerson, *op. cit.,* II, 460–462; James K. Paulding, *Letters from the South.* 2v. New York: 1817, quoted in Warren S. Tryon, ed., *A Mirror for Americans. Life and Manners in the United States 1790–1870 As Recorded by American Travelers.* 3v. Chicago: (c. 1952), II, 259. The alcoholic amenities available in Virginia are surveyed by Philip Alexander Bruce, *Social Life of Virginia in the Seventeenth Century.* Lynchburg, Virginia: 1927; 61, 151, 173, 184–185; and Louis B. Wright, *The First Gentlemen of Virginia. Intellectual Qualities of the Early Colonial Ruling Class.* San Marino, California: 1940, 89–91. The doughty old Georgian, McGehee, surfaces in H. A. Scomp, *King Alcohol in the Realm of King Cotton.* (Oxford, Georgia): 1888; 205.

The applejack material rests upon the impeccably researched and delightfully written Weiss, *op. cit.* On the sale of liquor by the drink: developed here from licenses, petitions and surety bonds in Dorchester, *op. cit.,* 125–126, and the Liebmann Collection. I am indebted for information regarding colonial inns to *The American Tavern,* Seagram-Distillers Company, n.p., n.d.; "Tabulae: a Short History of Taverns," *Kentucky Beverage Journal.* 1961 12(5):8; *King's Handbook of New York City.* Boston: (1892); 198.

Of rum: I used Krout, *op. cit.,* 36–37, 50, 60, 99; McCarthy and Douglass, *op. cit.,* 10ff.; Weiss, *op. cit., passim;* Willkie, *op. cit.,* 12–15. An authoritative work relating rum to the slave trade is William B. Weeden, *Economic and Social History of New England, 1620–1789.* 2v. Boston: 1890, I, 416; II, 459–462, 472, 502, 641, 756. British restrictions on the colonial rum trade are conveniently summarized in Fred Albert Shannon, *Economic History of the People of the United States.* New York: 1934; 28–29, 44–45, 556. The report of the Spanish commander at St. Louis was printed in Lawrence Kinnard, *Spain in the Mississippi Valley, 1765–1794.* 3v. Washington: 1949; I, 346, quoted in John Francis McDermott, *Research Opportunities in American Cultural History.* (Lexington: c. 1961); 20.

Rum as a therapeutic agent is wittily discussed in "Spring Medicines," *Druggists Circular and Chemical Gazette,* May, 1906; I also used Albert M. Hirschfeld, *The Standard Handbook on Wines and Liquors.* New

York: 1907, 46, *passim*. The eighteenth-century slang was compiled by Mason Locke (Parson) Weems in "The Drunkard's Looking Glass," a pamphlet reprinted in *Three Discourses*, with an introduction by Emily E. F. Skeel. New York: 1929; 60. Fletcher, *op. cit.*, describes the Pennsylvania ethnic groups and the popularity of whiskey *circa* 1790; 51–56, 212, 451. The distiller quoted is Harrison Hall, *The Distiller*. Second Edition. Philadelphia: 1818; 13.

Chapter 2

The most comprehensive treatment by a modern scholar of the protest against taxing whiskey is Leland D. Baldwin, *Whiskey Rebels; the Story of a Frontier Uprising*. (Pittsburgh): 1939. I acknowledge a general indebtedness to Baldwin in this chapter. For a less sympathetic point of view, cf. J. B. McMaster, *A History of the People of the United States from the Revolution to the Civil War*. 8v. New York: 1883–1913; v2., 42–43, 189–203. I have examined contemporary material relating to the Whiskey Insurrection in the Liebmann Collection. *Pennsylvania Archives*, Second Series, IV, Harrisburg: 1876, is devoted to "Papers Relating to What is Known as the Whiskey Insurrection in Western Pennsylvania, 1794." A generally useful work is J. J. Lawlor, ed., *Cyclopaedia of Political Science, Political Economy and of the Political History of the United States*. 3v. Chicago: 1881–84; articles on "Distilled Spirits," I, 809–815; "Internal Revenue of the United States," II, 573–574; and "Whiskey Insurrection," III, 1108–1111. Extracts from the letterbooks of Isaac Craig, General Wayne's deputy quartermaster, give an eyewitness account in Richard C. Knopf, ed., "Personal Notes on the 'Whiskey Rebels,'" *Historical and Philosophical Society of Ohio Bulletin*. 12(4). William Findley defended his own role in *History of the Insurrection in the Four Counties of Pennsylvania in the Year 1796*. Philadelphia: 1796. I have also used an account written while participants were still living, James Carnahan, "The Pennsylvania Insurrection of 1794, Commonly called the 'Whiskey Insurrection,'" *Proceedings of the New Jersey Historical Society*, VI, 1851–1853.

Writings in local history, each of which added some element of corroborative detail, are: George D. Albert, ed., *History of the County of Westmoreland, Pennsylvania*. Philadelphia: 1882; Neville B. Craig, *The History of Pittsburgh*. Pittsburgh: 1857 (Reissued, Pittsburgh: 1917); Alfred Creigh, *History of Washington County*. Harrisburg, Pa.: 1871; and Erasmus Wilson, ed., *Standard History of Pittsburgh, Pennsylvania*. Chicago: 1898. Also useful were these articles in Allen Johnson and Dumas Malone, eds., *Dictionary of American Biography*. 22v. New York: 1928–44 and Supplements I and II: "H. H. Brackenridge" by Claude M. Newlin, "William Findley" by Eva Anne Madden, "Albert Gallatin" by David S.

Muzzey, "Alexander Hamilton" by Allan Nevins, "Meriwether Lewis" by Louise Phelps Kellogg and "Daniel Morgan" by Daniel C. Haskell.

One recaptures the atmosphere and incident of the westward march of the militia in personal narratives, such as David Ford, *Journal of an Expedition Made in the Autumn of 1794, with a Detachment of New Jersey Troops into Western Pennsylvania, to aid in Suppressing the "Whiskey Rebellion."* N.p.; n.d.; and "Journal of Major Wm. Gould during an Expedition into Pennsylvania," *Proceedings of the New Jersey Historical Society. 1848–49.* 3:173–178. Hamilton's ms. letter, August 3, 1791, is in The South Caroliniana Library, University of South Carolina.

For the impact on Kentucky: I used Thomas D. Clark, *History of Kentucky.* New York: 1937; 139ff., 249; Lewis Collins, *Historical Sketches of Kentucky.* (Maysville, Ky.): 1847; 38–51; Alvin F. Harlow, *Weep No More, My Lady.* New York: (1942); Willard Rouse Jillson, *Early Kentucky Distillers, 1783–1800.* Louisville, Kentucky: 1940, 14–29. References to the wild night in Lexington appear in Harlow, *op. cit.,* and "Amber Forever," *The Wooden Barrel,* April, 1959.

Charles Cist, *Cincinnati in 1859* (Cincinnati: 1859) describes the Scotch-Irish whiskey-makers as men whose grandfathers were out in the '45 with the Pretender, emigrated to Ireland after the battle of Culloden. Attitudes in the East and West toward the excise tax and related issues are studied in Margaret Woodbury, "Public Opinion in Philadelphia, 1789–1801," *Smith College Studies in History.* 1919 5(1, 2); and Shannon, *op. cit.,* 333–335. My paragraph about Meriwether Lewis is based upon John Bakeless, *Lewis and Clark.* New York: 1947; 59–60. Samuel Hodgson's regret over the slight blood-letting is quoted from *Historical and Philosophical Society Bull., loc. cit.* The remark of Freneau—"that rascal Freneau," George Washington once called him—is from Philip M. Freneau, *Letters on Various Interesting and Important Subjects.* New York: 1943. (Facsimile reproduction of the Philadelphia 1799 edition.)

Chapter 3

Arrival of the farmer-distillers in Kentucky: I drew upon data appearing in Harlow, *op. cit.,* 360; Jillson, *op. cit.,* xi, 41, *passim;* Arthur K. Moore, *The Frontier Mind: A Cultural Analysis.* (Lexington, Ky.: 1957), 3–26, 60, 71–79. Ready-Money Jack appears briefly in "John D. Shane's Interview with Pioneer John Hedge, Bourbon County," *Filson Historical Quarterly.* 1940 14(3). The scoffing remark of the Yankee, Thatcher, may be located in *The Autograph Collectors' Journal, loc. cit.* Final settlement of the tax issue in Kentucky is chronicled in Jillson, *op. cit.,* 6–46.

Difficulties in raising wheat: discussed in J. D. B. De Bow, *The Industrial Resources of the Southern and Western States.* 3v. New Orleans:

1852; I, 403–404. There are many testimonies to the abundance of corn, among them Lewis Collins, *op. cit.*, 273, 429; Richard Collins, *History of Kentucky*. 2v. Covington, Kentucky: 1878; II, 70, 468, 552, 559, 564, 602, 605–606; Millard Dee Grubbs, *The Four Keys to Kentucky*. Louisville, Ky. (c. 1949); 268; and a typescript *History of the Development of Whiskey*, n.p.; n.d.; in the library of the *Courier-Journal*. The tall tales of the Indians about Kentucky corn are quoted in Moore, *op. cit.*, 18.

Regional patterns of whiskey preferences are explained in Roy Evans, *The Whiskey Salesman's Handbook*. Duluth, Minnesota: (c. 1953); 110, *passim*. The drinking situation in Illinois: Marshall Smelser, "Material Customs in the Territory of Illinois," *Journal of the Illinois State Historical Society*. 1936 29(1). Willkie, *op. cit.*, 22, tells the story of how Kentucky "white" whiskey was collected and forwarded. It should be remembered, as Johnston, *op. cit.*, 268, points out, that before the Civil War bourbon whiskey was not aged. The manner in which some of the rough edges were knocked off Kansas moonshine is recalled in a letter to the author from John W. Ripley, March 17, 1961. Ohio newspapers of *ca*. 1800 reflect the flourishing trade in "proof whiskey," barrels, give statistics of freight movement, price quotations at Natchez; see Charles Cist, *Cincinnati in 1841*. Cincinnati: 1841, *passim*.

Audubon as a whiskey merchant: reconstructed from information in Alexander Izsak, *Distilled Spirits Industry and Contributions to the Distilling Science*. Typescript, n.p.; *ca*. 1938; and Box File of newspaper clippings, *Distilleries*, in Kentucky Room, Louisville Free Public Library. No one knows how long blended whiskey has been colored to resemble the amber of brandy or of straight whiskey. I cite only a few references from a copious literature: Grubbs, *op. cit.*, 270; William T. Brannt, *A Practical Treatise* (short title). Philadelphia: 1904; 257–259; *Grocer's Companion*. Boston: 1883, 165; George Coes Howell, *The Case of Whiskey*. Altadena, California: 1928; 139, *passim*. According to Hall's manual, already cited, many methods for coloring whiskey were employed in the early 1800's. Hall is summarized in Warren Massey Hough's fighting tract directed against Kentucky bourbon, *The Fable of the Arab and the Beggar*, n.p.; *ca*. 1909; 22–23. Hough was an attorney who frequently represented rectifiers and blenders in the whiskey wars of the early 1900's.

The Thorpe story: I am indebted to Clifford Dowdey, *The Great Plantation*. New York: (1957); 29–45; *History of the Development of Whiskey, op. cit.*, 5; Charles McDowell, "Moonshine on the James," *Times-Dispatch* (Richmond, Va.), June 17, 1959; John Ed Pearce, "Did Old Virginny Give Birth to the Booze?", *ibid.*, July 22, 1959; "The Truth About Bourbon," *ibid.*, July 31, 1959. Fowler's reminiscence of corn whiskey that smelled like old potato bagging appears in *Skyline*. New York:

1961; 297–299. I met the old gentleman who liked "whiskey as was whiskey" in Alex. E. Sweet and J. Armoy Knox, *On a Mexican Mustang Through Texas, from the Gulf to the Rio Grande*. St. Louis and Houston: 1884; 459–460. Fowler, again, describes how Wilbert Robinson used to fete the sportswriters, 273–274.

The barefoot belles of southern Indiana and Dennis Hanks brighten the pages of William H. Townsend, *Lincoln and Liquor*, New York: 1934; 14–17. The physiological study of alcohol appeared in *The Lancet* (London), December 8, 1900.

Chapter 4

Information about the Pepper family, its distillery and trademark is drawn from a six-page typescript, Fred Pauly, *History of the 'Jas. E. Pepper' Distillery at Lexington, Kentucky, Established 1780*. Lexington: 1956; *The Bourbon Institute Fact Book*. Typescript. (New York): 1959; 21; and Harlow, *op. cit.* I found the World War I episode in Box File, *Distilleries*, Louisville Free Public Library.

Conflicting claims for distilling "firsts" are recorded in *Fact Book, op. cit.*, 26; R. Collins, *op. cit.*, II, 67; Reuben T. Durrett, *The Centenary of Kentucky*. Filson Club Publications. No. 7. Louisville, Kentucky: 1892; 79; *ibid., The Centenary of Louisville*. Filson Club Publications. No. 8. Louisville, Kentucky: 1893; 192–194; Harlow, *op. cit.*, 360; File, *Distilleries*, Louisville Free Public Library; Lawrence S. Thompson, *Kentucky Tradition*. Hamden, Connecticut: 1956; 34; and in Willkie, *op. cit.*, 19. The enthusiasm for names associated with the French monarchy is interpreted in L. Collins, *op. cit.*, Cincinnati: 1850, 192; and R. Collins, *op. cit.*, II, 66; also George R. Stewart, *Names on the Land*. Boston: 1958; 167. When Paris, seat of Bourbon County government, celebrated its sesquicentennial, among native sons honored were preachers and missionaries, members of the legislature, two painters and a sculptor; but no distillers. This is something to ponder. Source: Julia Hoge Ardery, *Paris (Hopewell) Sesquicentennial* (short title). Lexington: 1939; 36–39.

The declaration of Senator Davis may be found in *The Congressional Record*, May 22, 1862; 2288. Why the place name, Bourbon, was applied to whiskey is discussed in Ardery, *op. cit.*; and in "How Bourbon Whiskey Got its Name," *American Wine and Liquor Journal*. January, 1937; 47. The special characteristics of corn and rye are treated in *ibid.* 47. About the charred barrel: versions of its origin appear in *Fact Book, op. cit.*, 18; *The Courier-Journal & Louisville Times*. Southern Prosperity Number. March 25, 1913; and *ibid.*, May 3, 1953; Millard Cox, letters to Lee Adler, February 16 and 18, 1959; Grossman, *op. cit.*, 194–195; and typescript, *Legends About Discovery of Charred Barrels*, n.d.; n.p., made available to me by Lester R. Rodenberg.

Data for my treatment of the Reverend Elijah Craig was drawn from Clark, *op. cit.,* 243; *Mrs. W. H. Coffman Reviews Early History of Georgetown and County,* a cutting from an unidentified newspaper published in Georgetown, Kentucky, *ca.* 1921; L. Collins, *op. cit.,* 112–113, 510; R. Collins, *op. cit.;* I, 516, 696–700; Charles R. Staples, "Pioneer Kentucky Preachers and Pulpits," *The Filson Club History Quarterly.* 1935 9(3):136–157; B. O. Gaines, *History of Scott County, Kentucky,* 1904, reprinted, Georgetown, Ky: 1957; 12–13, 17–18; Alexander Izsak, letter to author, December 28, 1961; Jillson, *op. cit.,* 46; William Henry Perrin, ed., *History of Bourbon, Scott, Harrison and Nicholas Counties, Kentucky.* Chicago: 1882; 164; Robert B. Semple, *History of the Rise and Progress of the Baptists in Virginia.* Philadelphia: 1894; 24, 238, 241; and J. H. Spencer, *A History of Kentucky Baptists from 1769 to 1885* (short title). 2v.; n.p.: 1886; 12, 27–31, 87–89, 174–175.

There is also material in David Benedict, *A General History of the Baptist Denomination in America and Other Parts of the World.* 2v. Boston: 1813, II, 291–293; and in Thompson, *op. cit.,* 34. The letter of Mr. Schools appears in the *Times-Dispatch,* July 31, 1959. The old church minutes are quoted from Staples, *Filson Club, loc. cit.,* 157. For background on L. Collins I examined J. M. Gresham, compiler, *Biographical Cyclopedia of the Commonwealth of Kentucky.* Chicago: 1896; 276–277; and *The Biographical Encyclopedia of Kentucky of the Dead and Living Men of the Nineteenth Century.* Cincinnati: 1878; 402. Richard Collins appears in the same work. For a careful evaluation of Garrard and the claims of Bourbon County for originating bourbon whiskey, see Jillson, *op. cit.,* 55–57, whom I have followed. Statistics on stills appear in Dugan, *op. cit.,* 23; and Grubbs, *op. cit.,* 270.

The nature of congeners: I have abstracted from *Fact Book, op. cit.,* 45–46; Grossman, *op. cit.,* 171, *passim;* Berton Roueché, "The Shortest Way Out of Manchester," *The New Yorker,* January 16, 1960; 70–72, 77; and A. L. Liebmann and Bernice Scherl, "Change in Whisky While Maturing," *Industrial and Engineering Chemistry,* 41, March, 1949; 534. Cycling and the "red layer" are discussed in a pamphlet on modern distilling practice, *Six Steps to Quality. The Early Times Story.* Early Times Distillery Co.; n.d.; Louisville, Kentucky. For my material on traditional methods of making whiskey by hand in small batches, I drew upon: (George Wesley Atkinson), *After the Moonshiners* (short title). Wheeling, W. Va.: 1881; *Fact Book, op. cit.,* 36, 40–41; Brannt, *op. cit.,* 1885 edition, 197–198, 255, 669; Emanuel Greenberg, "Bourbon, Return of the Native," *Gentlemen's Quarterly.* 1960; 30(2):128; Izsak, *op. cit.,* 105–110; Isaac Stapleton, *Moonshiners in Arkansas* (short title). Independence, Missouri:

c. 1948; 23, *passim;* and "Old Kentucky," *The World* (New York), September 14, 1872; 2.

Simple distilling apparatus is described in Grossman, *op. cit.,* 169–171. Dr. J. W. Spanyer, Jr., Assistant Technical Director, Brown-Forman Distillers Corporation, in an interview with the author discussed technical aspects of distilling in "hand-made" days. The quotation from Mr. O'Rear appears in Jefferson Brown, "Gold in Your Glass," *Argosy,* December, 1958; 64. Krafft, *op. cit.,* 20–22, explains how they chose the location for a country still and runs through the technical processes. Cf. with methods of today—not basically different—summarized in Bretzfield, *op. cit.,* 6, 38–41. I found material on the small stillhouse in Everett Dick, *The Dixie Frontier. A Social History of the Southern Frontier from the First Transmontane Beginnings to the Civil War.* New York: 1948; 225. I have taken information on the "noble spirit" with the scorched flavor from "What You-all Should Know About Bourbon," *Liquor Store and Dispenser,* May, 1940; 20–23. The happy hogs cavort in Lilburn A. Kingsbury, "The Franklin Mill and Distillery," *Missouri Historical Review.* 1942 36(4) :467.

For the historical background of "proof" I am indebted to Grossman, *op. cit.,* 172. My statement about the difference between "sour mash" and "sweet mash" rests upon Colonel Thomas F. Brown and Dr. H. H. Schopmeyer, "The Fine Points of Rye Production," *American Wine and Liquor Journal,* September, 1935; 33, 43; Emerson, *op. cit.,* II, 477; *Fact Book, op. cit.,* 19; "Rare Jack Daniel's," *Fortune,* July, 1951; 104; and W. E. Bradley, "Kentucky Whiskey," *The Southern Magazine,* 1894 4(24) :615–627. Dr. James Crow: my paragraphs are based upon "Kentucky's James Crow To Be Honored on Old Crow's Anniversary," *The State Journal* (Frankfort, Ky.), June 15, 1960; and J. J. Dickinson, "Kentucky's Great Original Scientist Jim Crow Was the Founder of the State's Peculiar Institution," *St. Louis Republic,* October 3, 1897. This article includes the Joe Blackburn incident and names of other celebrated admirers of Crow's product.

Hough, *op. cit.,* 2, quotes the pioneer, W. F. Bond, on the character of Kentucky whiskey in the 1840's, and himself testified in 1909 before the U.S. Solicitor-general that aged whiskey was unknown before 1855. The old bourbon lover, Stedman, appears again because I cannot resist his dedication and his spelling; Dugan, *op. cit.,* 181. James Beck's gift bottle: R. Collins, I, 190 (1924 reprint of the 1874 edition), cited in letter to author from Mrs. Dorothy Thomas Cullen, Curator and Librarian, Filson Club, November 9, 1961. The Watterson letter is in the Manuscript Division, New York Public Library. An early mention of a bourbon trade name: E. B. and W. B. Coleman's advertisement: "Bourbon Whiskey. We have a large stock of Howard's and Harp's Old Bourbon—some of it over six years of age—which is unsurpassed for smoothness and richness of flavor"; quoted in Cist, *Cincinnati in 1859, op. cit.,* 371.

The preacher who equated Heaven with Kentucky appears in Timothy Flint, *Recollections of the Last Ten Years* (short title). Boston: 1826; 64. The anecdote has been in circulation ever since.

Chapter 5

The old dream of an earthly paradise is reviewed in Moore, *op. cit.,* 13–14, 18–22, 27–35, 148. The boatman to Hoffman: appears in Charles Fenno Hoffman, *A Winter in the West.* 2v. New York: 1935; II, 141, quoted in Moore, *op. cit.,* 18. The social atmosphere of old days in Kentucky is recreated with humor and affection by Thomas D. Clark., ed., in his indispensable *Bluegrass Cavalcade.* Lexington, Ky.: 1956, a skillful weaving together of contemporary material with modern commentary. Some choice examples of Kentucky boasting are preserved in Charles Cist, *The Cincinnati Miscellany, or Antiquities of the West.* 2v. Cincinnati: 1845–1846. II, 134–135. My Crockett anecdotes are drawn from *The Crockett Almanacs, Nashville Series 1835–1838,* edited by Franklin J. Meine, with a note on their humor by Harry J. Owens. Chicago: 1955. I found the Kentuckian's apologia for committing homicide in the brittle files of the old trade journal, *Bonfort's Wine and Spirit Circular,* May 18, 1898; 20. A story of similar character has two Kentucky colonels in a hot controversy over a bill with a Boston hotel clerk. One cautions the other: "Remember, John, who you are. Remember you are a Kentuckian. Pay the bill and *shoot the scoundrel!*" Source: Henry Watterson, *Compromises of Life* (short title). New York: 1906; 60.

The tribute to the proficiency of Kentuckians at a saloon free lunch counter comes from Wells Drury, *An Editor on the Comstock Lode.* Palo Alto, California: (c. 1948); 125. I found Valkyrie in Marmaduke B. Morton, *Kentuckians are Different.* Louisville: 1938; 44. I met the gentleman who made it in France as a Marshal of America in Thompson, *op. cit.,* 5. "Marse Henry's" eloquent salute to Kentucky, which suggested the title of this chapter, may be located in Bennett Henderson Young, *Kentucky Eloquence, Past and Present.* Louisville: 1907; 392.

The quotation from Hoffman may be found in Tryon, *op. cit.,* III, 561. Slavery as a contributory reason why southern orators admired classical times was pointed out by Professor Edwin A. Miles in a panel-session at the 1961 Annual Meeting of the American Historical Association, reported in *The American Historical Review.* 1962 67(3):867. Data on Kentucky elections: from Dick, *op. cit.,* 242; Harlow, *op. cit.,* 148, 370; and Henry C. Knight, writing under the pseudonymn, "Arthur Singleton, Esq.'" *Letters from the South and West.* Boston: 1824, portions quoted in Tryon, *op. cit.*, II, 266. Littell published his observations on electioneering in *Festoons of Fancy*. Louisville: 1814. Clark's *Cavalcade, op. cit.*, 186–187, makes the satire easily available. The editorial comment in *Bonfort's* was published June 10, 1887.

I obtained distilling statistics from *The American Issue*, New York Edition. 1908 4(6):6; from Clark, *History, op. cit.*, 568–569; and I am indebted to Clark, *Cavalcade*, for the quotation from Watterson. It appeared originally as a "Temperance Lecture" in the *Courier-Journal*, February 9, 1919. The imaginative profanity of the Covington butchers is noted in F. Garvin Davenport, *Ante-Bellum Kentucky. A Social History, 1800–1860*. Oxford, Ohio: 1943; 22. My paragraph on Kentucky virtuosity in the invention of place names, nicknames and insults rests upon Allan M. Trout, *Courier-Journal*, October 17, 1961; Harlow, *op. cit.*, 118–121, 424; and Thompson, *op. cit.;* 75–97; 171.

About Kentucky Colonels: I used "The Kentucky Colonel: a Study in Semantics," *American Notes and Queries*. 1947 7(4):3–8; and *ibid*. 7(7), a reply; "Only the Quart of Bourbon Remains," *Courier-Journal*, July 30, 1959; John Thompson Gray, *A Kentucky Chronicle*. New York: 1906; 203–205; Grubbs, *op. cit.*, 285; Harlow, *op. cit.*, 419; "Derby Day Calls for a Mint Julep of Kentucky Bourbon," *The New York Times*, May 5, 1962; and *ibid.*, "Decidedly Wins Kentucky Derby," May 6, 1962; Marion Porter, *Howdy Colonel*, n.p.; c. 1947; and Thompson, *op. cit.*, 70.

Chapter 6

Flower-cuttings from Mrs. Royall's *Sketches of History, Life, and Manners in the United States*. New Haven: 1826, are gathered in Tryon, *op. cit.*, from which I have extracted material: I, 52–53, 84. Dick, *op. cit.*, 292, also quotes from her *Letters from Alabama*. Washington: 1830. For alcoholic manners in Illinois, 1830–31—"them trying times"—see *Jour. Ill. State Hist. Soc., loc. cit.*, 28–30; and Nance Fern Pond, "The Memoirs of James McGrady Rutledge, 1814–1899," *ibid.*, 82–86. My Maryland material is based upon James W. Thomas, *History of Allegany County, Maryland*. Cumberland: 1923; 163, 167. Drinking habits on the frontier become vivid in F. A. Michaux, *Travels to the Westward of the Alleghany Mountains*. London: 1805; 239–240, and Charles William Janson, *The Stranger in America* (short title). London: 1807; 300, both quoted in Walter Blair, *Native American Humor*. San Francisco: (c. 1960); 29. "Slingers" and "eleveners" are explained in *ibid.*, 374.

The incident of the Louisville church rejecting distillers moved the *Courier-Journal* to raise an even more serious question, "Should Distillers Be Permitted to Go to Heaven?", quoted in *Bonfort's*, October 10, 1899; 413–414. The dialogue regarding the amount of alcohol required for a revival meeting appears in Dick, *op. cit.*, 188–189. The gold rush guide book is William B. Parsons, *The New Gold Mines of Western Kansas*. Cincinnati, Ohio: 1859; quoted in *Southwest Historical Series* (short title), ed. by Ralph P. Beiber and Le Roy R. Hafen. 12v. Glendale, California: 1931–1943; 4(168).

Mrs. Trollope's opinions appear in *Domestic Manners of the Americans*. New York: 1927; 16–17, 42, 83, 97, 101, 163, 238. For ideas interpreting American indulgence in the generous juices of our native maize I acknowledge a debt to Arthur Meier Schlesinger, Sr.'s, paper, "A Dietary Interpretation of American History," *Proceedings of the Massachusetts Historical Society,* LXVIII. October, 1944–May, 1947; 202–203, 210. For data on Illinois lawyers and temperance: I used Townsend, *op. cit.,* 44, 52, 59–61, 91–93. For lyceum lecturers I consulted David Mead, *Yankee Eloquence in the Middle West. The Ohio Lyceum 1850–1870.* East Lansing: 1951; 185–187.

The Temperance Crusade: see chapter of that name in Alice Felt Tyler, *Freedom's Ferment. Phases of American Social History to 1860.* Minneapolis: (c. 1944). The temperance novel: I used Edmund Pearson's flavorsome *Queer Books*. Garden City: 1928. Suggs' soliloquy was reprinted in Henry Watterson's anthology, *Oddities in Southern Life and Character.* Boston: 1892; 77. Tavern prices: Walter B. Stevens, "The Missouri Tavern," *The Missouri Hist. Rev.,* 1921; 15(2):262.

Per capita consumption of liquor: see *Facts About the Licensed Beverage Industry.* New York: 1960; 25; and *U.S. Department of Commerce Statistical Abstract of the United States.* Washington: 1957; 806. The rosy view of our people was expressed by the editor of a newspaper in Jefferson City, Missouri, in 1848, found its way into wider circulation in John L. Peyton, *Over the Alleghanies* (short title). London: 1869; quoted in Tryon, *op. cit.,* III, 599.

My sources on whiskey flasks: Lyman S. Goodbody, "Early American Liquor Bottles," *Arizona Beverage Journal,* December, 1951; Stanley Baron, *Brewed in America. A History of Beer and Ale in the United States.* Boston: (c. 1962); 60–61, 134; ms. of a speech, Gordon Bass, *Moulded Moments in American History;* Carl W. Drepperd, *The Primer of American Glass.* New York: 1927; 148–150; George S. and Helen McKearin, *American Glass.* New York: 1941; chapter on "Pictorial and Historical Flasks," by the same authors, *Two Hundred Years of American Blown Glass.* Garden City: 1950; 93–98; "Flasks of Fame," *True,* 1957; 38(247):68–73; Stephen Van Rensselaer, *Check List of Early American Bottles and Flasks.* New York: 1921; 5, 16, 54, 72; William S. Walbridge, *American Bottles Old and New.* Toledo: 1920; 20–37.

Chapter 7

For this chapter I have drawn upon two books of Professor Bell Irvin Wiley, *The Life of Johnny Reb. The Common Soldier of the Confederacy.* Indianapolis: 1943; and *The Life of Billy Yank. The Common Soldier of the Union.* Indianapolis: (1952). The effect of the war upon the temperance movement is developed in Will Irwin, "The American Saloon," *Collier's,* February 29, 1908; E. Merton Coulter, *The South During Reconstruction, 1865–1877.* (Baton Rouge): 1947; 336–337; Dorchester, *op. cit.,* 393; and McCarthy and Douglass, *op. cit.,* 27. Gould and his jug show up in Vance Randolph, *Who Blowed Up the Church House?* New York: 1952, xix. "Oliver Optic's" opinion about whiskey and secession is mentioned in Thompson, *op. cit.,* 36.

The U.S. Army whiskey ration was abolished by the Adjutant General's office, *General Order #72,* December 8, 1830. The fifer, C. W. Bardeen, wrote a frank account of army life, *The Little Fifer's War Diary.* Syracuse, N.Y.: 1910. The song poking fun at the German soldiers was published in *From Our War Songs North and South.* Cleveland: 1887, reprinted in Earl Schenck Miers, *Billy Yank and Johnny Reb.* Chicago: 1959; 81–82. The letters of the bootlegger are preserved in the ms. collections of The Vermont Historical Society.

General Grant's drinking habits: I have consulted F. B. Carpenter, *Six Months at the White House.* New York: 1866; 247, quoted in Townsend, *op. cit.,* 132; Louis A. Coolidge, *Ulysses S. Grant.* Boston: 1922; 33, 126; Frederic L. Paxson, "Ulysses S. Grant," *Dictionary of American Biography,* 7(493); and Walter B. Stevens, *Grant in Saint Louis.* Saint Louis: 1916; 85, 87. The news article linking Grant specifically with Old Crow was printed in *The World* (New York), August 7, 1885, "Anecdotes About Grant, Col. Stewart's Recollections of the Great Soldier."

Whiskey in the Confederate armies: I have drawn on E. Merton Coulter, *The Confederate States of America, 1861–1865.* (Baton Rouge): 1950; 437, 461–462; and Wiley, *Johnny Reb,* 43, 188–189, 223. Coulter says that some of the Confederate whiskey was so mean that one drop would fall on a cobblestone with the sound of a thunderclap. See, too, "Whiskey Making in State Started Because Farmers Had No Market for Corn," *Lexington* (Kentucky) *Herald,* February 21, 1937. On wartime Prohibition in the Confederacy: William M. Robinson, "Prohibition in the Confederacy," *American Historical Review.* 1931–1932; 37:50–58; "The Correspondence of Robert Toombs, Alexander Stephens, and Howell Cobb," *Annual Report of the American Historical Association.* 2v. Washington: 1913, II, 609; Coulter, *Confederate States,* 437, 461–462; various executive orders of state governors, Liebmann Collection, File #42;

Scomp, *op. cit.*, 540–579. Whiskey as a medicine: see George Worthington Adams, *Doctors in Blue.* New York: 1952; 13–15, *passim;* Wiley, *Johnny Reb,* 259–260.

Negroes and liquor in the ante-bellum South: *Annual Report of the American Historical Association for the Year 1903.* 2v. Washington: 1904, I, 465; Krout, *op. cit.*, 17–18; Coulter, *Reconstruction,* 336; Frederick Law Olmstead, *The Cotton Kingdom.* New York: 1953; 195. Further observations of Olmstead are reprinted in Tryon, II, 366–367, 378–379. See also Scomp, *op. cit.*, 127, 187, 575; Sinclair, *op. cit.*, 423. The Star Bourbon Whiskey label is in the Prints and Photographs Division, Library of Congress.

I found the legend of the yeast jug in Richard Dunlop, "An American Spirit," *Bon Appétit.* 1958; 2(5):10. Material relating to the G.A.R. reunion in Louisville: Newspaper clippings, *Distilleries* file, Louisville Free Public Library; Isabel McLennan McMeekin, *Louisville, the Gateway City.* New York: 1946; 173–174; Watterson, *Compromises;* vii, 313. The *Sporting Guide* was published in 1895, but the place of publication is understandably, considering that it was a whorehouse directory, omitted. The Ozark anecdote is told at length, but beautifully, by Randolph in his *Who Blowed,* 162–163.

Chapter 8

The situation of the distillers at the end of the war is summarized in *Fact Book, op. cit.*, 69–70; and Willkie, *op. cit.*, 23. A sketch of a returning Confederate veteran, Lieutenant Paul Jones, whose name is preserved in a whiskey and a dance, appears in the *Herald-Post* (Louisville, Ky.), January 1, 1936. More on the Jones family: I. E. Lambert, *The Public Accepts.* Albuquerque, N.M.: (1941).

I have chosen a few family names associated with fine bourbon whiskeys for illustrative purposes. The Monarchs: I used the *Biographical Encyclopedia of Kentucky,* 1878; 71–72; *History of Daviess County, Kentucky.* (Chicago): 1883; 477–478, 819, 870; and a helpful pamphlet, *Kentucky's Distilling Interests. By the Kentucky Distillers' Bureau Co., of Lexington, Ky. An Illustrated History Containing Sketches and Announcements of the Most Celebrated Makers and Brands in the State. World's Fair Edition.* N.p.: 1893.

Struggles over the names Monarch and Pepper are discussed in *Mida's Compendium* (short title). Chicago: 1899, 195. The two McBrayers and their successors dueled over the merits of their sour mash whiskeys: Harlow, *op. cit.*, 368; *Kentucky's Distilling Interests, op. cit.*, 95–97; *Spirits,* April, 1935; 32; and *The Wine and Spirit Bulletin,* March and April, 1892. Production figures for bourbon from 1863 to 1912 appear in the *Courier-*

Journal, March 25, 1913.

Colonel Applegate's whiskey and horse are the subject of an entertaining column, Art Williams in *Spirits.* 1960 27(10). Harlow, *op. cit.,* tells of Granville Bourbon, 45–46. The Wathens, originators of Old Grand-Dad, were important distillers for four generations. See *Spirits.* 1935 4(2): 24–27. Other historic whiskey names and dynastic marriages are listed in *Fact Book, op. cit.,* 63. The Roach family: I used *Bonfort's,* December 25, 1898; 130; *Bonfort's Wine and Spirit Trade Directory* (short title). New York: 1905; 182; *Caron's Louisville Directory.* Louisville. 1893; and a typescript, *Old Sunnybrook Plant,* National Distillers Corporation; n.p.; n.d.

The Megibben story rests on letters to the author from Miss Lucy L. Addams, Miss Katherine Megibben, letters and miscellaneous biographical material supplied by Mrs. Bessie M. Fightmaster; *Kentucky Distilling Interests, op. cit.,* 58; Perrin, *op. cit.,* 649, 664–667. Information on Cynthiana in Megibben's time is taken from R. Collins, *op. cit.,* II, 321–323.

Hope Distillery fiasco: I used R. Collins, *op. cit.,* II, 366; *Fact Book,* 54–55; Durrett, *Centenary of Louisville,* 46; William J. Stone, "The Hope Distillery Company," *Filson.* 1953; 27: 29–35; Johnston, *op. cit.,* 263; Dr. H. McMurtrie, *Sketches of Louisville.* Louisville: 1819; 127–131.

The quotation from the Bourbon County distiller appears in G. Glen Clift, ed., "War Diary of William B. Northcutt," *Register of the Kentucky Historical Society.* 1958; 56(2). Sources on the expert judges of bourbon: "Master Tasters," *Spirits,* April, 1935; 23; testimony of Major W. H. Thomas of Thomas & Son, Louisville whiskey merchants, *United States. Senate Reports. 58 Congress 2 Session Serial 4573,* "Hearings Before the Committee on Manufactures" (short title). What General Taylor's aide said: see Silas Bent McKinley and Silas Bent, *Old Rough and Ready. The Life and Times of Zachary Taylor.* New York: 1946; 181–182.

Biographical material about Colonel Taylor will be found in *Fact Book, op. cit.,* 85–87; Gresham, *op. cit.,* 392–394; E. Polk Johnson, *A History of Kentucky and Kentuckians. The Leaders and Representative Men in Commerce, Industry and Modern Activities.* 3v. Chicago-New York: 1912; File, *Distilleries,* Louisville Free Public Library; William E. Railey, *History of Woodford County.* Frankfort: 1938; *American Wine and Liquor Journal,* June, 1938; *The World, loc. cit.* Mrs. Charles P. Farnsley told me about the Colonel's disposable white lawn ties. Gerald Kirshbaum gave me background on Taylor. He didn't drink but was, like many distillers, a hedonist for others. The standing of Old Taylor is described in a pamphlet composed by its creator, entitled, *The Rule of the Regions* (short

title), Frankfort, Ky.: (1909), which also deals with distilling practice
before the 1870's.

The continuous still and other technical advances: *The Courier-Journal,*
March 25, 1913; *Fact Book, op. cit.,* 71; Izsak, *op. cit.,* 111; and an interview with Louis Rodenberg. A critical estimate of the sanitary conditions
among the small distillers is quoted in Willkie, *op. cit.,* 22. The effects of
large capital requirements and high taxes: *Fact Book, op. cit.,* 70; and
Harold Louis Wattel, *The Whisky Industry.* 2v. Typescript; n.p.; 1953,
66–76. How J. B. Thompson burlesqued the clichés of whiskey promotion: from *Kentucky Distilling Interests,* 99–100. For my explanation of
warehouse receipts: I used *Bonfort's.* 1894; 42(1); and *ibid.,* October 10,
1894; "A Way to Use Warehouse Receipts," *Business Week,* October 17,
1936; "National Distillers Products Corporation," *Fortune.* 1933; 8(5);
"Let's Get This Question of Whiskey Warehouse Receipts Straight,"
Mida's Criterion. 1934; 38(5):28–30; and conversations with Gordon
Bass and Louis Rodenberg.

Bourbon at the Chicago World's Fair, 1893: *Kentucky Distilling Interests,* 48–49; and *Spirits,* April, 1935. The renewal of temperance agitation: see Clark, *History of Kentucky,* 568; Tyler, *op. cit.,* 334. The little
girl's fantasy about the inside of her papa's stomach will be found in
Bardeen, *op. cit.,* 86.

Chapter 9

Consulted generally for this chapter: David A. Wells, "Distilled
Spirits," *Cyclopedia of Political Science,* I, 809ff.; and *ibid.,* "Taxation,"
III, 871; *History of . . . Whiskey,* Courier-Journal Library; Hu, *op. cit.;*
Shannon, *op. cit.;* Edmund W. Taylor, *A Few Notes on the Background
of the U.S. Bottled in Bond Act.* N.p.; (1938), a typescript made available
by Louis Rodenberg. Also valuable is Jeremiah W. Jenks, "The Development of the Whiskey Trust," *Political Science Quarterly.* 1889 4(2):
296–297; and Scomp, *op. cit.,* 563.

The supremacy gained by corn over rye is discussed in Izsak, *op. cit.,*
100. Megibben's tax windfall is recalled in "Monticello's Builder An Outstanding Man," *Cynthiana* (Kentucky) *Democrat,* April 13, 1961. A
reminiscence concerning successful whiskey speculators of the Civil War era
occurs in George Presbury Rowell, *Forty Years an Advertising Agent,
1865–1905.* New York: 1906; 437–438. How taxation gave liquor a new
social standing is noticed in (John Lardner), Roger Kahn, ed., *World of
John Lardner.* New York: 1961; 217; in James Leslie Marshall, *Swinging Doors.* Seattle: 1949; 245; and Shannon, *op. cit.,* 555. Hu, *op. cit.,*
gives percentage figures for U.S. revenue derived from liquor. My comment on taxation as a means of social control is indebted to ideas ex-

pressed in Cark Shoup, Roy Blough and Mabel Newcomber, *Facing the Tax Problem* (short title). New York: 1937; 197–199, 440. The famous declaration by Chief Justice John Marshall pops up almost anywhere in American historical literature since it was printed in 4 Wheaton, 316. I checked it in Alpheus Thomas Mason, *Free Government in the Making. Readings in Political Thought.* New York: 1949; 343. The intricacies of government management of distilleries may be appreciated after an examination of *United States Internal-Revenue Gaugers' Manual* (short title). Washington: 1888, *passim;* and Wattell, *op. cit.,* 34.

The revision of the law in 1868: I synthesized information collected from *Bonfort's,* October 10, 1894; 576; "Fine Bourbon and Rye Whiskies," *The Daily Graphic* (New York), January 16, 1880; 558; Hu, *op. cit.;* and Taylor's *Notes.* The case the government lost against Mallon is reported in "Whiskey and Water," *The New York Times,* December 21, 1882; 2. My sources on the bonding of whiskey: *Bonfort's.* 1894; 42(1): 23; and the *History of . . . Whiskey, op. cit.* The "Export Law" is treated in Howell, *op. cit.,* 138, *passim;* also in testimony of Major W. H. Thomas and Dr. Harvey W. Wiley in *United States. Senate Reports, op. cit.,* 53, 57–58. Regarding whiskey shrinkage in the wood: I located information in *Bonfort's, loc. cit.,* 24; Evans, *op. cit.,* 126–128; Hough, *op. cit., passim;* and Wattell, *op. cit.,* 109. The episode of Carlisle and the poker game is told by a participant, Henry Watterson, *Marse Henry: An Autobiography.* 2v. New York: (1919); 211–212.

The "outage bill": See the *Congressional Record,* April 29, 1880; 2841, 2876–2878ff. The conditions before the Bottled in Bond Act are summarized in "The Bottled in Bond Act," *American Wine and Liquor Journal,* June, 1938; 173, *passim.* Significance of the green stamp: see Bretzfield, *op. cit.,* 68; *Courier-Journal,* March 25, 1913; Grossman, *op. cit.,* 200; and Dr. Wiley's testimony in *United States. Senate Reports, op. cit.*

Chapter 10

Acknowledgment of a general obligation as to this chapter is made to (George Wesley Atkinson), *After the Moonshiners. By One of the Raiders. A Book of Thrilling, Yet Truthful Narratives.* Wheeling, W. Va.: 1881; Randolph, *Who Blowed, op. cit.;* and Stapleton, *op. cit. Kentucky's Distilling Interests, op. cit.,* 12–14, describes the manufacture of "white" woods whiskey. The remark of the representative from Memphis may be seen in the *Congressional Record., loc. cit.,* 2878. I encountered the story about distilling as a subject in the school curriculum in Joe Creason, "Raiding Party," *Courier-Journal,* November 3, 1957.

How to make brush-arbor whiskey: see H. C. Nixon, *Lower Piedmont Country.* New York: c. 1946; 123–124; and Wattel, *op. cit.,* 78–80. The litter connected with making illegal "cawn" is realistically described in David W. Maurer and Quinn Pearl, "Wanted: Branch Water," *Courier-Journal*, September 19, 1954. The description of moonshine stills is based upon personal observation. How the 'shiners got a new apparatus at the expense of the taxpayers is narrated in "Mint Juleps Add to Fame of Blue Grass," *Lexington Herald*, April 15, 1917. The reputation of "moon" as a destroyer of microorganisms is recorded in Nixon, *op. cit.*, 123. Cobb's warning: see *Red Likker*, New York: 1929, 127.

"Squirrel whiskey" is defined in the *Cong. Rec.*, December 22, 1914; 499. My paragraph on legal and illegal distilling is based upon *Eleventh Biennial Report of the Bureau of Agriculture of the State of Kentucky*. Louisville, Ky.: 1895. The molasses consumption in Sitka, Alaska, is cited from John W. Caughey, *History of the Pacific Coast*. Los Angeles: 1933; 378, *passim*. New York's cellar industry is surveyed in "Much Moonshine Made in This City," *New York Herald*, August 13, 1899; 6. Data on illegal distillation after Repeal was drawn from Hu., *op. cit.*, 101; and *Operation Moonshine . . . a Decade of Peril*. New York: 1960, publication of the Licensed Beverage Industries, Inc. The song is *Kentucky Moonshine*, c. 1940, Carl Fisher, Inc. The scheme of sweating bourbon out of used barrels is investigated in Joe Cresson, "Wring Out the Barrels," *Courier-Journal*, April 25, 1954. The colorful Gibson family broke into print in the *Courier-Journal.*, n.d., reprinted in *Bonfort's*, February 10, 1899; 334.

Moonshine whiskey trickles and gurgles through Jean Thomas' delightful *Ballad Makin'*. New York: 1939. The story ending "You ain't coming back" appears in Stapleton, *op. cit.*, 76; Homer Croy, *What Grandpa Laughed At*. New York: 1948; and many magazines, newspapers and collections. Croy calls it "immortal."

Chapter 11

The following writings were consulted so frequently in the preparation of this chapter that they may be grouped together as the underpinning of this narrative of rascals: Grayson L. Kirk, "The Whiskey Ring Fraud," *The American Mercury*. 1935 34(136); "Whiskey Ring," *Cyclopedia of Political Science, op. cit.*, III, 1112ff.; Matthew Josephson, *The Politicos. 1865–1896*. New York: 1938; H. V. Boynton, "The Whiskey Ring," *The North American Review*, October, 1876; John McDonald, *Secrets of the Great Whiskey Ring* (short title). Chicago: 1880; Lucius E. Guese, "St. Louis and the Great Whisky Ring," *Missouri Historical Rev.* 1942 36(2): 160–183; and Stevens, *op. cit., passim*.

Congress was aware of the frauds in 1867: see *Congressional Globe*.

40th Cong., 1 Sess., v38 (1867); Davis Rich Dewey, *Financial History of the United States.* New York: 1934; 569; and the chapter on the Ring in Allan Nevins, *Hamilton Fish. The Inner History of the Grant Administration.* New York: 1937; 762. The moral climate and the spoils system are discussed in William Archibald Dunning, *Reconstruction, Political and Economic. 1865–1877.* New York: 1907; 234, 246, 285. Material on Babcock, in addition to the general sources cited, includes Nevins, *op. cit.,* 781, and articles from the *Dictionary of American Biography,* "Orville E. Babcock," by Charles Ramsdell Lingley and Paxson on Grant, *loc. cit.*

The Ring's mode of operation is surveyed in James Ford Rhodes, *History of the United States from the Compromise of 1850 to the Final Restoration of Home Rule at the South in 1877.* 8v. New York: 1920, VII, 183–186; and in Louis A. Coolidge, *Ulysses S. Grant.* Boston: 1917; 473ff. A detailed and official source is *House Miscellaneous Documents. 44 Cong. 1 Sess. No. 186 (1876). Serial 1706.* For the political situation in Missouri I have condensed material from the article, "Missouri," *Cyc. of Political Sci.,* II, 864; and the *Dictionary of American Biography* sketches "Benjamin Gratz Brown" by P. Orman Ray and Oswald Garrison Villard, "Carl Schurz." Rhodes warned that McDonald's book was untrustworthy, but accepted the story of the gift of the horses and carriage to President Grant. Modern scholarship has rejected it.

Chapter 12

General sources: *Industrial Commission. Preliminary Report on Trusts and Industrial Combinations, together with Testimony, review of Evidence, Charts Showing Effects on Prices, and Topical Digest. 56 Congress 1 Session. House of Representatives, Doc. No. 476. Part I.* Washington: 1900; Jeremiah Whipple Jenks and Walter E. Clark, *The Trust Problem.* Garden City, New York: 1929; Ernest E. East, "The Distillers' and Cattle Feeders' Trust, 1887–1895," *Journal of the Illinois State Historical Society.* 1952 45(2); Jeremiah W. Jenks, "The Development of the Whiskey Trust," *Political Science Quarterly.* 1889 4(2):296–319; *The Reports of the Committees of the House of Representatives for the Second Session of the Fifty-Second Congress, 1892–93.* 3v. Washington: 1893, v3, Nos. 2447–2621.

I have also made use of the solid chapters on "Oil" and "Trusts" in Mark Sullivan, *Our Times. The United States 1900–1925.* 6v. New York: 1926–35; II, 270–337. Material on the Whiskey Trust is included in the above. The "pools" are described in conversations some of the insiders had with the financial journalist, Clarence W. Barron. See *More They*

Told Barron. New York: 1931; 11; also William Z. Ripley, *Trusts, Pools and Corporations.* New York: 1905; 29–30, quoted in Wattel, *op. cit.,* 112.

Biographical information on Greenhut was brought together from East, *Journal of the Illinois State Hist. Soc., loc. cit.;* (H. W. Lewis), *Glimpses of Peoria.* (Peoria, Ill.) : 1898; also James Montgomery Rice, *Peoria, City and County, Illinois.* 2v. Chicago: 1912. Wattel, *op. cit.,* 114, points out the Trust's fundamental problem—the ease of manufacturing neutral spirits. The point is re-enforced by clippings and trade reports of *circa* 1903 which I studied at the National Distillers Library. For information about the Trust and successor companies, I examined "National Distillers Products Corporation," *Fortune, loc. cit.* For similar combinations in Kentucky: I found useful *Bonfort's.* 1898 28(1):63; Donald McWain, "Sales Problems Are Forcing Small Distilleries into Arms of Big Ones," *Courier-Journal,* October 26, 1941; and the *Scrapbook, op. cit.* There is some Whiskey Trust background in "Name, Schenley; Age, Three," *Fortune.* 1936 13(5).

Chapter 13

George Berkeley (1685–1753), Bishop of Cloyne, wrote the often quoted and misquoted line, "Westward the course of empire takes its way." Mark Twain's humorous improvement may be found in chapter 60, *Life on the Mississippi.* Mike Fink is quoted in Walter Blair and Franklin J. Meine, *Mike Fink. King of the Keelboatmen.* New York: (1933), 227. The source of the old Texan's observation is Sweet and Knox, *op. cit.,* 461. For the De Voto quotation: "Whiskey is for Patriots," *Harper's Magazine,* April, 1951; 69–70.

On food and drink in the old West: I used Percy Stanley Fits, *Colorado, the Centennial State.* New York: 1941. The man who ran five Indians did it by running *ahead* of them: Sweet and Knox, *op. cit.,* 462. The marksman who operated Old Ginger appears in Henry Augustus Wise, *Los Gringos* (short title). New York: 1849, quoted in Tryon, *op. cit.,* III, 662. Lay beliefs about emergency conditions for which whiskey was indicated are recited in Smith and Helwig, *op. cit.,* 74–75. That whiskey is a better cure for hydrophobia than a mad stone is the point of J. Frank Dobie's delightful folk tale, "Whiskey, Skunks and Rattle Snakes," *True West.* 1957; 22:14–15. "Whiskey fever" as an endemic disease around Topeka; *Daily Journal* (Kansas City, Mo.), November 25, 1885.

For patent medicines as a whiskey substitute, I consulted Thomas D. Clark, *Pills, Petticoats and Plows.* Indianapolis: (c. 1944), 242–243; Marshall, *op. cit.,* 205; and James Harvey Young, *The Toadstool Millionaires.* Princeton, New Jersey: 1961, 129–133. Carl Sandburg's recollection about Hostetter's Bitters: in *Always the Young Strangers*. (New York: 1952), 228, cited in Young, *op. cit.,* 130. Howell, *op. cit.,* wrote that he had tasted tequila masquerading as bourbon. I am indebed to Ramon F. Adams, *Cowboy Lingo*. Boston: 1936, 228, for the colloquial names for cheap whiskey. Bill Koch, the well-known folklorist, gave me the newspaper paragraph about Cincinnati whiskey. Marshall, *op. cit.,* describes the prefab saloons, 74. The San Francisco homicide record is taken from H. H. Bancroft, *History of California.* 7v. San Francisco: 1890; v7., 215. It is contrasted with that of the East in Lardner, *op. cit.,* 216.

For the Mastersons and the gay life in Dodge City, I have followed Nyle H. Miller and Joseph W. Snell, "Some Notes on Kansas Cowtown Police Officers and Gun Fighters," *The Kansas Historical Quarterly.* 1961 27(3):421, *passim.* The account book of G. M. Hoover, wholesale liquor merchant, Dodge City, in the Kansas State Historical Society, shows that Westerners, as Joe Snell points out, drank alcohol in whatever form it presented itself. But Kentucky Club, a well-known bourbon, shows up as a big seller. Later, during the early 1900's, John (Bathhouse) Coughlin, former Turkish bath rubber and Chicago statesman, backed an amusement park in Colorado Springs, where an elephant, Princess Alice, a Chicago *emigrée,* happily received a pint of Jim Beam bourbon every day, according to Marshall Sprague, *Newport in the Rockies. The Life and Good Times of Colorado Springs.* Denver: (c. 1961): 207. Zebulon Pike's requisition for whiskey was printed by Dr. Liebmann in *Autograph Collectors' Jour., loc. cit.*

The whiskey ration in the Army: see Cist, *Miscellany, op. cit.,* II, 252, *passim.* The issue of whiskey was abolished in 1830, not in 1832, as Cist gives it. All drinkers, in his writing, are lumped together as "inebriates." The statement that where there is money there is whiskey may be documented, if that is necessary, from George Croghan, *Army Life on the Western Frontier,* Francis Paul Prucha, ed., Norman, Oklahoma: 1958; 131; and Francis Paul Prucha, *Broadax and Bayonet. The Role of the United States Army in the Development of the West. 1815–1860.* (Madison: 1953), a work of original research. McKenzie's remark is quoted from "History Makers," *The Billings* (Montana) *Gazette,* May 26, 1962. A valuable article on the traders and the "whiskey forts" of the Northwest is Hugh A. Dempsey, "Howell Harris and the Whiskey Trade," *Montana Magazine of History.* 1953 3(2):1–8. I am indebted for information on Luke Short to William R. Cox, *Luke Short and His Era.* Garden City: 1961, 29–31, 139. The interesting question, What is an Indian? is asked and answered in *Bonfort's,* September 10, 1899, 323–324. Hiram Price's Indian story: from the *Congressional Record,* May 1, 1880, 2933. For Fred Locke: see Marshall, *op. cit.,* 212.

Frisbie's saloon and its habitués: Marshall, *op. cit.*, 153–154; and Wells Drury, *op. cit.*, 80–100. The advertisement of the Junction City (Kansas) saloon was published in the *Leavenworth Times,* May 1, 1867, quoted in *The Kansas Hist. Quar.* 1948; 16: 327. My authority for the low quality of Bob Ford's whiskey is Marshall, *op. cit.*, 147. "Sink taller" whiskey: See *American Speech.* 1936; 11:317. On the bar as the place where a man would naturally receive mail and parcels: Miller and Snell, *The Kansas Hist. Quar., loc. cit.*, 434, 442–443. Cultural and educational activities: Marshall tells of Ward's lecture, 154. Greeley's speech is reported in A. D. Richardson, *Our New States and Territories.* New York: 1866, quoted in footnote, Tryon, *op. cit.*, III, 727–728. And it should be noted that in the early days of Colorado College, when student manpower was limited, not only the faculty but also the local bartenders played on the football team. Source: Sprague, *op. cit.*, 279.

Bean's judicial procedures are described in Everett Lloyd, *Law West of the Pecos. The Story of Judge Roy Bean.* San Antonio, Texas: (1959); 53. The drunk man: *The Westerners Brand Book.* 5(3):20, quoted in Ben Botkin, ed., *Treasury of Western Folklore.* New York: (c. 1951); 15–16. Material relating to preachers in barrooms either as missionaries or ganymedes appears in Frank M. Wyncoop, "Gay Days on the Frontier," *New Mexico Magazine.* 1951 29(6):22, 40–43; and is scattered through Marshall, *op. cit.*, and Henry Chafetz. *Play the Devil. A History of Gambling in the United States from 1492 to 1955.* New York: (c. 1960). The religious services held in the Missouri saloon were reported in the *North Missourian* (Gallatin, Mo.), February 12, 1909, quoted in Lewis Atherton, *Main Street on the Middle Border.* Bloomington: 1954; 277. The eulogy of Grannan appears in Clark, *Cavalcade, op. cit.*, 113.

Women in the whiskey mills: I have synthesized data from Ramon F. Adams, *op. cit.*, 179; Lucius Beebe and Charles Clegg, *The American West, The Pictorial Epic of a Continent.* New York: 1955 (no pagination except for formal text); Dulles, *op. cit.*, 170–171; Chafetz, *op. cit.*, 123, 166ff.; Marshall, *op. cit.*, 86–89; Nollie Mumey, *Poker Alice . . . History of a Woman Gambler in the West.* Denver: 1951; Sweet and Knox, *op. cit.*, 255. An instance of the fine precision of western justice as it applied to women is recorded in Sprague, *op. cit.*, 114. When the notorious madam, Blanche Barton, was hauled into court, the judge released her on the grounds that she couldn't be running a "house" because she lived in a tent.

Chapter 14

Bill Nye's remarks: from the *Greeley County Tribune* (Tribune, Kansas), January 13, 1887. Material on the St. Louis fancy grocer may be studied in *Catalogue of Fine Wines and Liquors, Cigars and Tobacco, Fall, 1914.* J. F. Conrad Grocer Co. (St. Louis. Repro. *ca.* 1949 of 1914 catalogue). Consumption figures by whiskey types were reported in *Congressional Record,* June 8–June 23, 1896; 8065–9072. A regular advertiser in *Bonfort's* was Thompson's Prune Wine, for giving character to new liquors. Brannt, *op. cit.,* 1885, 283, gives a recipe for making twenty-three gallons of "old Bourbon" using three gallons of straight whiskey. Colonel Taylor's lament appeared in *Bonfort's,* n.d., quoted in Johnston, *op. cit.,* 267.

Mr. Gordon Bass called my attention to the fact that the modern bottle had to be perfected before whiskey could be mass-distributed in the consumer package. For the importance of this standardization see Alexander Silverman, "Michael Joseph Owens," *Dictionary of American Biog.,* XIV, 122; and Warren C. Scoville, *Revolution in Glassmaking. Entrepreneurship and Technological Change in the American Industry 1880–1920.* Cambridge: 1948; vii, 27–28, 46, 256–257. The figures on the increase in bottled whiskeys are taken from the *Courier-Journal,* March 25, 1913. George Ade, *op. cit.,* 85, describes the department store windows.

On trademark law: I consulted Frank I. Schechter, *The Historical Foundations of the Law Relating to Trade-Marks.* New York: 1925; 130–134, 143–144. Re: Hiram Walker, I am indebted to Howard R. Walton's pamphlet, *Hiram Walker (1816–1889) and Walkerville from 1858.* New York: 1958. The provision barring false information on a trademark is discussed in Walter J. Derenberg, *Trade-Mark Protection and Unfair Trading.* Albany, N.Y.: 1936; 428–429; and *Mida's Compendium, op. cit.,* 180.

Greenhut's testimony may be located in *The Reports of the Committees of the House of Representatives, loc. cit.,* III, 60. The difficulties of prosecuting imitators are outlined in *Bonfort's,* May 10, 1898; 24; and in *ibid.,* May 10, 1899; 63. The U.S. government's position on the qualities of bonded whiskeys is summarized in *Fact Book, op. cit.,* 81. The Joliet incident is reported in *Bonfort's,* May 25, 1899; 63. The confession of the Chicago counterfeiter may be found in *ibid.,* July 25, 1898; 192, with editorial comment about it, 197. The Walker advertisements naming fakers are printed in Walton, *op. cit.,* 14–15. The position of the consumer is recalled in Colonel Taylor's pamphlet, *op. cit.* I quote from a Hayner Whiskey advertisement published in the *Missouri Valley Farmer,* April, 1903. The circular exploiting Uncle Sam came to light during the Senate debate on the Kenyon-Sheppard interstate liquor bill, *Congressional Record,* December 17, 1912; 757–761.

The yarn about how to catch bass is Vance Randolph's, in *We Always Lie to Strangers. Tall Tales from the Ozarks.* New York: 1951; 225.

I summarize the points from the Falmouth Whiskey advertisement, *Missouri Valley Farmer,* April, 1903. An interesting picture-feature on old liquor advertising appeared in *The Seagram Spotlight,* November–December, 1952; 12–17. The story of the unfortunate make-up in *Puck* magazine comes from Croy, *op. cit.,* 12. I found the Old Greenbrier poem in *Bonfort's,* August 10, 1898; 240.

Duffy's Pure Malt Whiskey is treated at length in Arthur J. Cramp, *Nostrums and Quackery,* 3v. Chicago: 1912, 1921, 1936; II, 499–504. The effort to cut off liquor advertising is chronicled in Sullivan, *op. cit.,* V, 636; and Deets Pickett, ed., *The Cyclopedia of Temperance, Prohibition and Public Morals.* New York: 1917; 13–21. The Shawhan Whiskey advertisement: *The Household,* October, 1904. The sofa offer was flourished by Senator Porter James McCumber of North Dakota before the Senate Committee on Manufactures, as reported in *United States. Senate Reports,* previously cited, *Serial 4573;* 66. Information about peddlers and premiums is scattered through the folios of the Bella C. Landauer Collection, The New-York Historical Society. My Bernheim information is drawn from Isaac Wolfe Bernheim, *The Story of the Bernheim Family.* Louisville, Kentucky: 1910; 47, 54, 57–58.

Charles P. Farnsley told me of the catch in the old-time salesman's comparative test. For the Kansas whiskey salesman I used William Ansel Mitchell, *Linn County, Kansas: a History* (short title). Kansas City: c. 1928; 331–333. The ingenious Vermont drummer comes to life in "Our Story of the Month—A Tablet, a Flag, an Idea," *News and Notes.* 1952 3(6). Vermont Historical Society.

Chapter 15

Consulted generally throughout this chapter: my article, "Who Put the Borax in Dr. Wiley's Butter?", *American Heritage.* 1956 7(5):58–63, 95; Oscar E. Anderson, Jr., *The Health of a Nation. Harvey W. Wiley and the Fight for Pure Food.* Chicago: 1958; Hough, *Fable, op. cit.; Scrapbooks,* National Distillers Library; Sullivan, *op. cit.,* II, chapter on "The Crusade for Pure Food"; *United States. Senate Reports, loc. cit.; Hearings Before the Committee on Interstate and Foreign Commerce of the House of Representatives on the Pure-Food Bills* (short title). Washington: 1906; Willkie, *op. cit.;* and Henry Beach Needham, "The Senate . . . of Special Interests," *World's Work.* 1906 11(4):7208–7210. The argument between proponents of blends and straights is also rehearsed in Howell, *op. cit.,* 139–145.

The humorous dialogue referring to the battered bill appeared in *Life,* February 15, 1906, quoted in Sullivan, *op. cit.,* II, 526. For whiskey as then defined: *The Pharmacopoeia of the United States. Eighth Revision.*

Philadelphia: (1905); 418. There is also material about the struggle over blends in *Fortune* on "Schenley." 1936; 13(5); 159, footnote. What fusel oil would do to a rabbit is presented in (William Schmidt), *The Flowing Bowl. When and What to Drink.* New York: 1892; 63–64. Sherley's speech is in the *Cong. Rec.,* June 23, 1906; 9965.

Dr. Wiley's "tipple talk" is officially recorded in *Hearings,* 1906, *op. cit.;* and reported in *The World* (New York), February 28, 1906, 4. On Stanley: see *Congressional Rec.,* June 23, 1906, 9066; Stanley Papers in the Margaret I. King Library, University of Kentucky; and Sullivan, *op. cit.,* II, 510. Hough's complaint is printed in the *Hearings,* 1906, *op. cit.;* and in his own *Fable, op. cit.* What I say about the provisions of the Food and Drug Act is taken from the text of the statute, available in Chester Gwinn, *Food and Drugs Act, June 30, 1906, and Amendments.* Washington: 1914; 9–14. Gwinn also gives the incident of the seizure of the molasses-base "bourbon," 174–180. Wiley tells about making whiskey in the White House in his *Harvey W. Wiley. An Autobiography.* Indianapolis: 1930; 257–258. Izsak, *op. cit.,* gives the sequence of events leading up to President Taft's ruling, 2–6. Gwinn has the text of the decision, 831–835.

Chapter 16

Fowler's epigram is from his *Skyline, op. cit.,* 6. John W. Ripley told me about the Wyoming shepherds. James Reston wrote of "bourbon in your grits" in his column, "New Orleans," *The New York Times,* April 22, 1962. Green whiskey in Colonel Crockett's stomach: Randolph, *We Always Lie, op. cit.,* 160, a volume consulted frequently for this chapter, as was the same author's, with George P. Wilson, *Down in the Holler.* Norman: (1953); 175. I extend, too, general acknowledgment to Robert E. Gard and L. G. Sorden, *Wisconsin Lore. Antics and Anecdotes of Wisconsin People and Places.* New York: (1962); Stewart, *op. cit.;* and Sweet and Knox, *op. cit.*

Crockett's favorable impression of Philadelphia hospitality is recorded in *An Account of Col. Crockett's Tour to the North and Down East.* Philadelphia: 1835, excerpted in *Tryon, op. cit.,* I, 132. I found the riposte of Raccoon John Smith in Harlow, *op. cit.,* 364. The same story was current in the late eighteenth century in Pennsylvania, says Baldwin., *op. cit.,* 49. For luxuriant language about drinking: see Ramon F. Adams, *op. cit.,* 229, *passim;* and that engaging book of bucolic wisecracks, Randolph and Wilson, 175. The spinsters and the temperance lecture: the story is told in Dudley J. Bidstrup, "The Background of Public Speaking in Missouri, 1840–1860," *Mo. Hist. Review.* 1941 36(1), who credits the original telling to the *Springfield* (Mo.) *Advertiser,* April 6, 1847.

For the fish and Daniel Webster: see Hewson L. Peeke, cited in my text, 54. Townsend, *op. cit.*, gives the other Webster story. My sources on Mike Fink have been Blair and Meine, *op. cit.;* and B. A. Botkin, "Mike Fink," Maria Leach, ed., *Dictionary of American Folklore, Mythology and Legend,* 2v. New York: (1950), II, 724; Meine, ed., *Crockett Almanacs, op. cit.;* 149–150; and Thompson, *op. cit.,* 135–138. Major Hemphill's version of the story of the governors: *The Nashville* (Tennessee) *American,* November 15, 1906. Other embroideries upon the same yarn appear in William M. James, "Diary Reveals Familiar Saying of N. C. Governor," *Charlotte* (N.C.) *News,* March 31, 1935; H. L. Mencken, ed., *A New Dictionary of Quotations.* New York: 1942, 313; and William S. Walsh, *Handy-Book of Literary Curiosities.* New York: 1925.

The dialogue about saloon credit: Cincinnati's claim is advanced in William C. Smith, "The Cincinnati Saloon, 1800–1890," *Bulletin of the Historical and Philosophical Society of Ohio.* 1961 19(4). The Chicago version appears in Elmer Ellis, *Mr. Dooley's America.* New York: 1941; 6–7. The horse in the barroom theme recurs in Beebe and Clegg., *op. cit.;* Ramon F. Adams, *Western Words: a Dictionary of the Range, Cow Camp and Trail,* Norman: c. 1944; 46–47, quoted in Botkin, *Western Folklore, op. cit.,* 8; and Sweet and Knox, *op. cit.,* 354, 369–371.

American place names: I drew upon Herb Caen, *Baghdad-by-the-Bay.* Garden City: 1949, 117; Allen M. Trout, "Greetings," *Courier-Journal,* October 16, 1961; C. G. Coutant, *The History of Wyoming.* Laramie: 1899, I (all), 386–387; Emmett Dedmon, *Fabulous Chicago.* Chicago: (1953), 137; M. Schele De Vere, *Americanisms.* New York: 1872, 399; Aubrey Drury, *California, an Intimate Guide.* New York: 1947, 401, 439; Bil Gilbert, "Bloomers That Toppled a Throne," *Inside Michigan.* 1952, 2(1):34; File, *Distilleries,* Louisville Free Public Library; McKearin, *Two Hundred Years,* 93; Mencken, *American Language. Supplement II, op. cit.,* 171, 567, 764, 774; "Hell is Only a Small Town That Wants Own Postoffice," *New York Herald Tribune,* August 23, 1960.

Also useful was Frederic G. Cassidy, "Place-Names of Dane County, Wisconsin," *Publications of the American Dialect Society.* No. 7, April, 1947. My wife called my attention to Whiskey Island, Charles P. Farnsley to Whiskey Gut, Nyle H. Miller to Whiskey Lake. Harry Rigby, Jr., verified for me the old name, Whiskey Point, near Kingston, New York. Mr. Julian P. Van Winkle, Sr., identified the road named after the distiller, Fitzgerald. The horse, "Whiskey-peet" belonged to Charles A. Siringo, *A Texas Cowboy, or Fifteen Years on the Hurricane Deck of a Spanish Pony, Taken from Real Life.* New York: (c. 1950), 98–102. And read page 30. Read the whole book. I am indebted for the last line in the chapter to Cist, *Miscellany, op. cit.,* II, 319.

Chapter 17

For this chapter I found the following generally useful: Ade, *op. cit.;* *Bull. of the Historical . . . Society of Ohio, loc. cit.;* Raymond Calkins, *Substitutes for the Saloon.* Boston: 1901; A. S. Crockett, *Old Waldorf Bar Days* (short title). New York: 1931; *History of Chicago and Souvenir of the Liquor Interest* (short title). (Chicago: c. 1891); Frederick Lionel Holmes, *Side Roads: Excursions into Wisconsin's Past.* Madison: 1949; Don Marquis, *Her Foot is on the Brass Rail.* New York: c. 1935; Marshall, *op. cit.;* "Saloon" folders, Picture Collection, New York Public Library.

The problem of nicer ways to say "saloon" is treated in Mencken, *Language, op. cit., Supplement I,* 268, and lists various euphemisms in *Supplement II.* Saloonkeepers and Democrats: the reference is *Vogue,* October 1, 1944, 157; cited in *Dict. of Americanisms, op. cit.,* II, 1448. Slot machines: see "One-Arm Bandits," *Chicago History.* 1957 5(1):21–29. Stewart Holbrook happily describes the bartenders in *Far Corner. A Personal View of the Pacific Northwest.* New York: (c. 1952), 80–85. Fowler, *op. cit.,* 141–142, remembered the item about the Black and Tan. The bartender's duties are recited in Paul E. Lowe, *Bartender's Quick Reference Manual* (short title). Baltimore: 1908, 96–100. About writing to mother: credit for this tear-jerker goes to Chafetz, *op. cit.,* 125.

I am indebted to Miss Margaret Scriven, Librarian, Chicago Historical Society, for pulling the subject of the "Lincoln license" together. There is a full discussion in Townsend, *op. cit.,* 31–38. "Custer's Last Fight": Anheuser-Busch, Inc., have brought together extensive information in a kit they have prepared about their famous barroom lithograph, *Memorandum Respecting the Painting of "Custer's Last Fight."* The ground is traversed popularly by Paul W. Tredway, "Custer's Last Fight," *St. Louis Globe-Democrat,* July 17, 1949; and with meticulous scholarship by Robert Taft, "The Pictorial Record of the Old West—Custer's Last Stand—John Mulvey, Cassily Adams and Otto Becker," *The Kansas Hist. Quar.* 1946 14(4):361–390.

Facts regarding the Rolshoven "Venus," also known as "Repose," were checked out for me by Robert B. Johnstone, Editor, *D.A.C. News,* and James M. Babcock, Chief, Burton Historical Collection, Detroit Public Library. Carry Nation: I consulted, in addition to Marshall, *op. cit.,* Stewart Holbrook, "Bonnet, Book, and Hatchet," *American Heritage,* 1957 11(1):53–55, 120–121; "Carry Nation Journeys to Butte's Underworld and Pleads for Reform," *Butte Miner,* January 27, 1910; W. G. Clugston, *Rascals in Democracy.* New York: 1941, 185–187; Sinclair, *op. cit.,* 54–57.

Regarding the Hoffman House Bouguereau, I am indebted for useful information to Miss Sara T. Tenney, Sterling and Francine Clark Art

Institute, Williamstown, Massachusetts; and consulted also *King's Handbook, op. cit.,* 204–206; Thomas W. Ennis, "Memory of City's Great Hotels Recalls Age of Elegance," *The New York Times,* February 18, 1962; "Tales of the Hoffman House," *Time,* January 25, 1943; Frank Crowninshield, "Bouguereau's Historic Nymphs and Satyr," *Vogue,* 101 (Pt. 1), January 15, 1943.

The macabre decorative scheme of the Chicago saloon in described in Ellis, *op. cit.,* 50. The incident about Iorio's is from Fowler, *op. cit.,* 232–233. The Buckhorn's parrot: Marshall, *op. cit.;* and Sweet and Knox, *op. cit.,* 374–376. Carrie Watson's equally precocious bird figures in Dedmon, *op. cit.,* 145. On toasts: Lowe, *op. cit.,* 103–112. Tacoma case: will be found in "Tacoma Anti-Treating Law," *American Law Rev.,* v. 47, July, 1913; 576–577. Lucille Kohler's memoir: see Samuel Rapport and Patricia Schartle, *America Remembers.* Garden City: (1956).

The man who chose jail: *Chicago History, loc. cit.,* 15. The heroic Montanan: "Patient Leaps from Hospital Window, Walks to Saloon," *Montana Standard* (Butte, Mont.) *ca.* June, 1961, quoting an unnamed newspaper of 1902. Miss Geraldine Beard, Chief, The New-York Historical Society Reading Room, provided me with the pros and cons of the Brodie leap. The memory of the odd-ball saloon is preserved in Robert Joseph Casey, *Chicago Medium Rare.* Indianapolis: (1952); 294–298. Grant Talbot Dean wrote me a scholarly letter on the spelling of "Heinegebubler." For my characterization of the typical successful saloonist I studied *Chicago . . . Liquor Interest, op. cit.,* and "Other Events," *The Chicago Tribune,* December 11, 1882, 2, a society page story where the Hogans and Ritzhaupts rubbed shoulders with Farwells, Carter Harrisons and McCormicks.

"Tied house" is explained in Wattel, *op. cit.,* 156. The evils of the old saloon system are angrily reviewed by Will Irwin, *Collier's, loc. cit.* On liquor and graft in San Francisco: I drew upon Lately Thomas, *A Debonair Scoundrel.* New York: (c. 1962). I collected information on New York's Raines Law in Ade., *op. cit.;* "Regulation of the Liquor Traffic," *The Annals of the American Academy of Political Science.* 1908 32(3):556–558; Donald Barr Chidsey, *John the Great. The Times and Life of a Remarkable American, John L. Sullivan.* Garden City, New York: 1942, 221–223; and Mayer, *op. cit.;* 400.

Chapter 18

Colorful news items and flavorful episodes frequently appear in the public prints about Mr. Van Winkle, as, "Art Williams Says," *Spirits.* 1960 27(4):6; Joseph E. Kuebler, "They're Still Feuding in Kentucky Hills," *Akron* (Ohio), *Beacon-Journal,* April 8, 1962; and *Courier-Jour.,* as cited,

July 30, 1961. The blizzard man emerged in "Old-Timers Relive '88 Blizzard Here," *The New York Times,* March 12, 1961. For the nonogenarian of Buffalo see Caroline Thomas Harnsberger, ed., *Mark Twain at Your Fingertips.* New York: [c. 1948], 205. Captain Jack Haines' advice appeared in *The Sun* (New York), *ca.* 1899, quoted in "A Recipe for Longevity," *Bonfort's,* November 10, 1899. Letcher's letters, of July 16 and July 22, 1849, are in the Orlando Brown papers, Manuscript Collection, The Filson Club. American drinks for the Prussian prince: enumerated in Lucius Beebe, *Mansions on Rails* (short title). Berkeley, California: 1959, opp. 118. The salute to San Franciscans occurred in 1853, is reprinted in Caen, *op. cit.,* 229. The flourishing musical organization which took its name from a whiskey label is the subject of "Gump's Thriving on Soft Selling," *The New York Times,* July 2, 1961.

I assembled information about Jim Gore, his café and clientele from a pamphlet, *Old Jim Gore* (Chicago: 1908) and from personal communications of Grant Talbot Dean and Mrs. Bessie B. Martin Fightmaster. References to Mark Twain to which I am under obligation occur in this order: George Tressler Scott, "Illinois Testimonial to Mrs. Rutherford B. Hayes," *Jour. of the Ill. State Hist. Soc.,* XLVI, Spring, 1953; 71–78; Mayer, *op. cit.,* 221; Harry Hansen's column in *Chicago Tribune,* August 19, 1962; Malcolm Bingay, *Of Me I Sing.* Indianapolis: 1949; John A. Winkler, letter, October 28, 1958, to Lee Adler. The information regarding Ball and Black: from "Builder of Florida's Huge Du Pont Estate," *Business Week,* August 27, 1960; and James Reston, "Washington," *The New York Times,* February 18, 1962. Falk's chambermaid: steps out of Caen, *op. cit.,* 193–194.

I learned about the intimate connection between bourbon and the art of governing from: Alben W. Barkley, the late Vice President, who sometimes on non-political occasions raised a nice baritone voice in "Wagon Wheels" and left some recollections relevant to my topic in *That Reminds Me.* Garden City, New York: 1954, 158–159, 165; *Harper's Mag., loc cit.;* Luther Huston, "Bourbon on the Potomac," *The New York Times,* December 15, 1946; *ibid.,* Thomas N. Schroth, "A New Speaker Faces a Changing House," January 7, 1962; and *ibid.,* "McCormack Keeps Rayburn's Board," January 29, 1962. Murat on the same subject: Albert, *op. cit.,* 172.

Wattel, *op. cit.,* 316–317, gives consumption figures as of 1953. For information on the Supreme Court, I used Marshall, *op. cit.,* 229–237. There is a good deal in print about George Washington as Father of American Distilling. I consulted Liebmann, *Autograph Collectors' Jour., loc. cit.,* 14; Howell, *op. cit.,* 13; Townsend, *op. cit.,* 114; Weiss, *op. cit.,* 12; and Willkie, *op. cit.,* 15. When Sweet and Knox took their mustang ride through Texas and arrived at Austin, they saw a large oil painting of Washington in the Old State House. One hand rested on his sword in classic pose. The other was lifted up in an emphatic waving motion of unknown significance. The travelers advanced three conjectures about it: (1) The General was rejecting a petition; (2) He was indicating that he didn't need a shine; or (3) he was saying, "No, gentlemen, I make it a point never to enter a saloon by daylight"; 643. Material on the drinking preferences of other U.S. Presidents was located in *Bonfort's,* June 10, 1887, and September 10, 1907; and in *Kentucky Distilling Interests, op. cit.* Mrs. Longworth's observation may be located in her *Crowded Hours.* New York: 1933, 324. Mr. Truman's vote goes for bourbon, Worth Bingham, "Twosome: J.F.K. and the Press," *Courier-Jour.,* October 5, 1961.

More on the current whiskey scene in Washington: "Serving Liquor in White House Hit by Baptists," *New York Herald Tribune,* February 2, 1961. President Kennedy's personal preference is chronicled in Edward T. Ewen, "More People Drink, but Less," *The New York Times,* May 14, 1961. Mrs. Tooze on the cocktail hour: "W.C.T.U. Sees Task Bigger Than Ever," *ibid.,* August 7, 1961. The *Cong. Rec.* frequently bears witness to the beverage consumption induced by the fatigues of political life. For example, May 1, 1880, 2933; and *ibid.,* December 22, 1914, 572.

General Morgan's julep: see Coulter, *Confederate States, op. cit.,* 413–414. The Waldorf's julep is discussed reverently in Crockett, *op. cit.,* 79–81. *Fact Book, op. cit.,* 58–63, surveys some of the peaks and intervals of mint julep lore, as does "Kentucky was First in Mint Juleps, Historical Society President Asserts," *Lexington Leader,* April 29, 1960; and *Liquor Store and Dispenser, loc. cit.,* 20–23. For Cobb on Mencken's juleps, see Marion Porter, *op. cit.,* 20, *passim.* The Smith recipe has been printed many times, may be found in Thompson, *op. cit.,* and Clark, *Cavalcade, op. cit.* For what Henry Watterson said, I am indebted to McMeekin, *op. cit.,* 155. Clark, *Cavalcade, op. cit.,* 273, spoke felicitously of "no balm in Gilead, no sugar in the bottom of the glass."

Chapter 19

My treatment of the last days before Prohibition is based upon a study of New York City newspapers, various issues, 1919 and 1920; the *Herald, News, Sun, Tribune.* Also a sampling of the climate of opinion reflected in *The Literary Digest* for the same period. My information on distillery ruins was gleaned from the file, *Distilleries,* Louisville Free Public Library. For the effect of the taxing power upon small companies I am indebted to the *Courier-Jour., loc. cit.,* October 26, 1941; and ideas suggested by Wattel, *op. cit.,* 139–165. Efforts of the federal government to prevent the recurrence of old abuses are traced in Bretzfield, *op. cit.,* 215ff.; *Fact Book, op. cit.,* 111–112; Hu, *op. cit.,* 3–5, 100, 102, 156; McCarthy and Douglass, *op. cit.,* 77–78; and in a letter to the author from Dwight E. Avis, Director, Alcohol and Tobacco Tax Division, Internal Revenue Service.

An account of Georgia Moon occupied Robert Alden's advertising column, *The New York Times,* January 30, 1961: it is my source. The sign about chemists is reproduced and interpreted in Hackett, *Courier-Jour., loc. cit.* Jack Daniel's Whiskey, a kissing cousin of Kentucky bourbon, is the subject of the feature article, "Rare Jack Daniel's," *Fortune,* July, 1951. Information on manufacturing costs and the scope of the tax bite has been extracted from Spencer Klaw, "Brown-Forman's Big Time Bourbons," *Fortune,* 1955, 52(5); and *Facts about . . . the Industry, op. cit.* The effects of price on drinking habits are stated in *Schenley Twenty-Seventh Annual Report for the Year Ending August 31, 1960,* 7. Material on pricing and consumer loyalty to favored labels may be found in John McDonald, "The Perplexed Liquor Industry," *Fortune,* August, 1961. And see, *ibid.,* Richard Austin Smith, "National Pulls the Cork," October, 1953; and Wattel, *op. cit.,* 82, 574–577, 587–592, 654–657.

The complexities of law controlling alcoholic beverage advertising: I used the summary in Robert Alden, "Advertising: Laws Vary Widely," *The New York Times,* May 26, 1961. More detailed information is available in *Red Book, 1961–1962. Encyclopaedic Directory of the Wine and Liquor Industries.* New York: 1961. Covers all state as well as federal regulations. My paragraph on changing attitudes toward drinking is under obligation to *The New York Times, loc. cit.,* May 14, 1961; John Wicklein, "Methodists Ease Rigidity of Code," *ibid.,* June 3, 1961; "Farm Youth Adopt City Drinking Habits," *ibid.,* April 7, 1960; E. W. Kenworthy, "Kennedys Caper on Cape," *ibid.,* July 30, 1962—a paragraph about Hyannis, Mass., girls and their sweaters. Patrick, *op. cit.,* develops illuminatingly the role of alcohol in our cultural milieu, 57–59, 71–77, 89, 92–93, 143–144. See also Smith and Helwig, *op. cit.,* 223–224, who say of those who abuse spirits, it is not the stars, dear Brutus . . .

Consumption figures are from *Fortune, loc. cit.,* March, 1953. My data on tastes, types and trends was pulled together from "Ready-Mix Woos the Drinker," *Business Week,* September 17, 1960; "Liquor Sales Break a 15-Year Record," *ibid.,* February 4, 1961; *Gentlemen's Quar., loc. cit.;* and Benjamin W. Corrado, "Bourbon Trend Remains Unchecked," *The Journal of Commerce,* November 19, 1959.

INDEX

Abbott, E. C. ("Teddy Blue"), 143
Adams, Cassily, 192
Adams, John Quincy, 213
Adams, Samuel, 7
Adams, William Taylor, 71
Ade, George, 191, 204
Advertising, 149-162, 225
Alabama, 77
Alaska, 106
Albany, New York, 67
Albert, Carl, 212
Albertus Magnus, 2
Ale, 3, 4, 7
Allen, James Lane, 38
Allen, John Mills, 194-195
American Medical Association, 170
American Spirits Manufacturing Company, 134
American Temperance Magazine, 65
Amherst, General Jeffrey, 9
Anderson, Oscar E., Jr., 170
Anti-Saloon League, 159, 204, 221, 233
Applegate, Hamilton Clark, 84
Applejack, 5, 231
Applejohn, 4
Arabella (ship), 3

Arkansas, 106, 107
Astaire, Fred, 59
Audubon, John James, 28
Avery, William, 117

Babcock, Orville E., 115-126
Bailey, John, 27
Ball, Edward, 210
Barkley, Alben W., 211
Barnard, W. D. W., 123
Barnes, William S. ("Bill"), 87
Barnum, P. T., 194
"Barrel dogging," 109
Barrel houses, 189
Barron, Clarence W., 132
Bartenders, 189-191
Bass, Gordon, 36
Beam, Jacob, 34
Bean, Roy, 145, 161
Beck, James B., 48, 152
Beebe, Lucius, 46
Beecher, Henry Ward, 97, 123
Beer, 3, 4, 6, 12, 67, 88
Bennett, James Gordon, 194
Benz, George G., 87
Bernheim Brothers, 160
Bevis, Frazier & Co., 121

271

Bibb, Judge George M., 53
Bingay, Malcolm, 210
Bitters, 65
Black, Eugene R., 210-211
"Black Betsy," 28
Blackburn, Joseph C. S., 47, 153
Blaine, James G., 82
Blair, Walter, 51
Blended whiskey, 166-173
Blow, Henry T., 75
Boggs, Hale, 212
Bolling, Richard, 212
Bollman & O'Hara, 121
Bond, W. F., 48, 88
Boone, Daniel, 90, 178, 231
Booz, E. C., 69
Botkin, Amelia, 162
Bottled-in-Bond Act, 88, 100, 151, 166, 233
Bottles, whiskey, 68-70, 151
Bouguereau (artist), 194
Bourbon County, Kentucky, 34-36, 39, 231
Bourbon whiskey
    origin of, 33-49
    since 1920, 218-229
Bowers, Lloyd W., 172
Brackenridge, Hugh Henry, 17, 18, 19, 20, 22
Braddock, Edward, 18, 20
Braddock's Field, 18
Bradford, David, 17, 18, 20
Bragg, Braxton, 69
Bramble, E. W., 84, 85
Brandy, 2, 4, 5, 183
Breckinridge, John C., 55
Brice, Calvin S., 158
Brisbane, Arthur, 205
Bristow, Benjamin, 121-125
Brodie, Steve, 200
Brooklyn, New York, 106
Brown, B. Gratz, 118
Brown, George Garvin, 92-93, 151, 163
Brown, Joseph E., 76
Brown, Orlando, 208

Bryan, William Jennings, 2, 92, 219
Buchanan, James, 213
Buckman, John, 7
Bunyan, Paul, 178
Burns, Robert, 198
Burts, W. P., 141
Busse, George F., 201-202
Butler, Pierce Mason, 181
Butte, Montana, 144, 193, 200

Cabell, Royal E., 105
Calhoun, John, 47
California, 67
Cameron, Don, 99
Camp Follower, The, 78
Canadian Club, 153, 154-155, 172
Cannon, Bishop James, Jr., 221
Carlisle, John G., 88, 99, 100, 152
Carlisle, Pennsylvania, 20, 21
"Carlisle allowance," 99
Carroll, Charles, 68
Carson Appeal, 143
Chandler, Albert B. (Happy), 59
Chapin & Gore, 100
Charring, 36
Cheyenne, Wyoming, 196
Chicago, Illinois, 114, 122, 181, 182, 188, 193, 195, 197, 201, 204, 209
Chicago Tribune, 130, 132, 158
Churchill Downs, Inc., 153
Cider, 4, 6, 12
Cincinnati, Ohio, 66, 95, 114, 165, 181-182, 196
Cist, Charles, 66
Civil War, whiskey and the, 71-80
Clark, George Rogers, 27
Clark, Thomas D., 32
Clarke, Charles C., 128, 134
Clay, Henry, 47
Cleveland, Eli, 27
Cleveland, Grover, 88, 99, 100, 186, 194, 203
Cobb, Irvin S., 46, 105, 163, 215
Cocktails, 197

Cody, William F. ("Buffalo Bill"), 194, 209
Coffey, Aeneas, 89
Cogill, George, 143
Cole, Jack, 53
Collins, Lewis, 39
Collins, Richard H., 37, 38-39
Combs, Bert, 59
Congeners, 41
Conger, Omar Dwight, 100
Congressional Globe, 95
Congressional Record, 95, 100
Connecticut, 62
Corbett, "Gentleman Jim," 200
Corn whiskey, 27-32
Covington, Kentucky, 57
Cowper, William, 99
Craig, Reverend Elijah, 36-39, 40, 231
Craig, Reverend Lewis, 37
Crane, William H., 209
Creede, Colorado, 144
Cresswell, Nicholas, 27
Crockett, Davy, 51-52, 175, 178
Croghan, George, 141
Cronkite, Walter, 59
Crosby, Bing, 59
Crow, Dr. James C., 46-48, 88
Currie, Brainerd, 152
Custer, George A., 192
Cynthiana, Kentucky, 77, 84, 85

Daughters of the American Revolution, 162
Davis, Clyde Brion, 192
Davis, Garrett, 35
Davis, Richard Harding, 194
Dempsey, Jack, 59
Demurska, Molly, 144
Depew, Chauncey W., 194
Detroit, Michigan, 192
De Voto, Bernard, 138, 212
Dexter, Samuel, 67
Distillers' and Cattle Feeders' Trust, 130-134
"Distiller's beer," 42

Distillers' Securities Corporation, 134
District of Columbia Ring, 125
Dodge City, Kansas, 140, 142, 144, 225
Dorchester, Reverend Dr. Daniel, 9, 188
Dow, Neal, 97
Drury, Wells, 145
Dudley, Edward B., 181
Duffy Malt Whiskey Co., 158
Duke, Basil Wislon, 52
Dunne, Finley Peter, 197
Dunvaren, Lord, 52
Durritt, Reuben T., 34

Eads, James B., 117
East, Ernest E., 131
Eastport, Maine, 199
Eighteenth Amendment, 218-219, 221, 233
  repeal of, 221
"Eleveners," 63
Elizabeth II, Queen, 206
Embargo Act (1807), 10
Esch, John Jacob, 169
Estill County, Kentucky, 104
Evans, "Fighting Bob," 194
Excise tax, on whiskey, 12-22, 25-26, 37, 70, 81, 94-103, 108-109, 114, 128, 232, 234

Falk, Dave, 211
Farnsley, Charles, 54
Faulkner, William, 46
Fayette County, Kentucky, 40
Federal Alcohol Administration Act (1936), 222, 233
Ferguson, Champ, 49
Fields, W. C., 60
Filson Club (Louisville), 34, 104
Findley, William, 14, 15, 19
Fink, Mike, 137, 178-179
Fisk, Jim, 118, 126, 194
Fitzgerald, John E., 183
Flasks, 68-69
Flexner Brothers, 91

Flip, 6
Foerster, William, & Company, 98-99
Folklore, whiskey, 174-186
Foraker, Joseph, 165
Ford, C. W., 117
Ford, James, 48
Ford, Robert, 144
Forrest, Nathan Bedford, 151
Forsyth, Montana, 140
Foster, Stephen, 60
Fowler, Gene, 30, 174
Fort Fayette, 17, 18
Frank Brothers, 155
Frauds, whiskey, *see* Whiskey Ring
Freneau, Philip, 22
Fries, John, 20, 185
Frisbie, Lyman, 143
Frye, William P., 165

Gaines, B. O., 40
Gaines, Berry and Company, 47
Gaines, W. A., & Co., 47
Gallatin, Albert, 19
Garfield, James, 126
Garner, John Nance, 46, 211
Garrard, James, 39
Gates, John W., 194
Georgetown, Kentucky, 37, 38
Georgia, 31, 77, 78, 159
Gibson, George J., 132, 133
Gibson family, 110-111
Glennon, James A., 205
Goebel, William, 57
Gold Hill (Nevada) *News*, 144
Goldman, Mrs. Anna Friedman, 59
Gore, Jim, 209
Gough, John B., 3, 67, 97
Gould, Farwell, 71
Gould, Jay, 118
Grannan, Charles ("Riley"), 146
Grant, Sam, 177-178
Grant, Ulysses S., 47, 74-75, 114, 115-127, 232
Greeley, Horace, 65, 97, 145
Greenbriar Distilling Company, 157
Greenhut, Joseph B., 132-133, 154

Guinan, "Texas," 201

Haines, Jack, 208
Hale, Eugene, 165
Hall, Harrison, 28
Hallam, Theodore, 57
Hamar, General, 16
Hamilton, Alexander, 11-12, 19, 20
Hamilton, John, 34
Hammond, J. H., 181
Hanks, Dennis, 32
Harding, Warren G., 213
Harlow, Alvin W., 27, 58
Harris, George W., 63
Harrison, Benjamin, 213
Harrison, Carter, 209
Harrison, William Henry, 47
Harrod, James, 90
Hawkins, Louise, 120
Hayes, Rutherford B., 126
Hayes, Mrs. Rutherford B., 209
Hayner Whiskey, 159
Headley, John A., 221
Hearst, William Randolph, 194
Heinegebubler, Martin, 201
Heiser, "Mother," 201
Helena, Montana, 191
Hell, Michigan, 184
Hemphill, James Calvin, 179, 181
Henderson, Kentucky, 28
Henry, Patrick, 7
Henry, Prince, of Prussia, 208
Highwine Trust, 128-136
Hill, Harry, 191
Hiram Walker, Inc., 227
Hoar, George F., 165
Hobson, Richmond Pearson, 197
Hodgson, Samuel, 22
Hoffman, Charles Fenno, 50
Hoffman House (New York City), 194-195
Holcroft, John, 15, 16
Hollander, Thomas E., 172
Honorable Order of Kentucky Colonels, 59
Hooper, John J., 66

Hoover, G. M., 140
Hope Distilling Company, 86
Hopper, DeWolf, 209
Hostetter's Bitters, 139
Houston, Sam, 178
Howell, Richard, 21
Hulteen, Alvin, 200
Hyannis, Massachusetts, 226

Illinois, 28, 32, 226
Indiana, 32
Indianapolis, Indiana, 114
Indians, American, 1-2, 15-16, 22, 24,
    26, 30, 95, 139, 141-143, 178,
    185
Ingersoll, Robert G., 130, 214
Innes, Harry, 25
Interstate Commerce Act, 133-134
Iowa, 226
Ivers, "Poker Alice," 147-148

Jackson, Andrew, 47, 141
Jackson, James, 12
Jackson, Mississippi, 186
James, Jesse, 144
Jefferson, Joseph, 209
Jefferson, Thomas, 22, 94, 213
Jeffries, Jim, 33, 205
Jersey Lightning, 5
Jillson, Willard Rouse, 39
Johnson, Andrew, 114
Johnson, Jack, 33
Johnson, Robert, 13, 15
Johnson, Samuel, 14
Johnston, J. Stoddard, 56
Jolly, Jack, 144
Jones, Mrs. Ann ("Nancy"), 181
Jones, Reverend Sam P., 106
Jordan, P. H., 90
Josephson, Matthew, 116
Josselyn, John, 3
Joyce, John A., 117, 119, 120, 123
Julep, 214-215
Julian, Judge Ira, 52-53
Junction City, Kansas, 144

Kansas, 29, 149-150, 161, 183
Karpel, Leon, 198
Kazee, Clabe, 112-113
Keen, John, 165
Keene, James R., 131
Keith v. The United States and An-
    other, 142
Kenna, Hinky Dink, 204
Kennedy, John F., 213
Kenton, Simon, 90
Kentucky, 10, 20, 24-30, 31, 32, 33-
    61, 76, 106
Kentucky Derby, 53, 59, 60, 84
Kentucky Distilleries and Warehouse
    Company, 136
Kentucky Gazette, 25
Kieft, William, 231
Kilrain, Jack, 200
Kittredge, Reverend Jonathan, 65
Kline, Tom, 146
Klyman, Charles, 155
Knickerbocker, Reverend W. H., 146
Knott, J. Proctor, 152
Knott County, Kentucky, 107
Knox, J. Armony, 140
Kohler, Lucille, 199
Kramer, John F., 218
Krock, Arthur, 53

Labeling, 149-154
Lalemant, Hierosme, 26
Langdale, Lord, 152
Langtry, Texas, 145, 161
Lanphear, "Pat," 87
Las Vegas, Nevada, 143, 146
Lawrence, Hank, 184
Lee, Henry (Light Horse Harry), 20
Legends, whiskey, 174-186
Lemon, Owley, 5
Letcher, Robert, 208
Lever Food and Fuel Control Act, 219,
    233
Levy, James, & Bro., 150
Lewis, Meriwether, 20, 21
Lexington, Kentucky, 12, 33
Lexington Herald, 216

Liebenthal Brothers & Co., 159
Life (magazine), 164
Limestone, 43, 58
Lincoln, Abraham, 74, 75, 97, 191
Linn's Fort, 34
Liquor Concentration Act, 233
Littell, William, 56
Littleton, Lije, 113
Locke, Fred, 143
Lodge, Henry Cabot, 165
Long Island, 106
Longworth, Mrs. Alice, 213
Longworth, Nicholas, 211
Louisiana Distillery Company, 172
Louisville, Kentucky, 34, 79-80, 84, 86, 160, 183
Louisville Herald, 49
Lovingood, Sut, 63
Luling, Texas, 140

Macon, Missouri, 146
Madden, William, 110
Madison, James, 213
Madison, Wisconsin, 196
"Maine Law," 97
Mallon, Pat, 98
Malloy, May, 193
Mansfield, Josie, 194
Marquis, Don, 205
Marshall, Ed, 47
Marshall, James Leslie, 197
Marshall, John, 97, 212
Marshall, Thomas, 12
Maryland, 6, 9, 12, 27, 62
Massachusetts, 3, 8, 226
Masterson, Jim, 140
Masterson, William B. ("Bat"), 140, 144
Mather, Increase, 198
Mauldin, Bill, 59
May, George, 171
Mayflower, 3
McBrayer, John H., 82, 88
McBrayer, William, 82-83, 88, 92, 150
McCartney & Company, 121
McCormack, John W., 212

McCoy, Kid, 200
McCulloch v. Maryland, 97
McCumber, Senator, 170
McDonald, John A., 116-126
McFarlane, Major James, 17
McGarry, James, 182
McGehee, Micajah, 4-5
McIntyre, John, 112
McKearins, George S., 68-69
McKearins, Helen, 68-69
McKenzie, Kenneth, 142
McKinley, William, 209
McMillan, John, 175-176
McMillin, Benton, 100
McNulta, John, 134
McPherson, James Birdseye, 75
Meeting, Chester, 4
Megibben, Mattie, 84
Megibben, Thomas Jefferson, 84-85, 96
Megrue, "Con," 119
Mencken, H. L., 215
Mescal, 148
Mexico, 205
Miles, E. L., Company, 136
Miles, Nelson A., 194
Miller, H. B. ("Buffalo"), 129
Miller, William, 16
Mills, Dexter T., 132
Milton, John, 214
Milwaukee, Wisconsin, 114, 122, 188, 201
Minnesota, 226
Minutemen, 7
Missouri, 105
Molasses Act (1733), 8, 72, 231
Monarch, M. V., 82
Monarch, Richard, 28, 82
Monarch, Thomas J., 82, 83
Monongahela, Pennsylvania, 18
Monroe, James, 213
Moonshine whiskey, 102-113
Morehead, John Motley, 181
Morgan, John H., 52, 214
Morgan, Old Dan, 20, 21
Morris, Nelson, 131

Motlow, Reagor, 224
Mound City, Kansas, 161
Murat, Napoleon Achille, 212

Nation, Carry, 3, 161, 193
Nation, The, 118, 125
National Biscuit Company, 135
National Distillers Products Corporation, 135, 136, 233
National Wholesale Liquor Dealers' Association, 166
Nebraska Needle-gun, 141
Neville, General John, 15, 16-17
New England, 3-4, 6, 7, 8
New Hope Distillery Company, 136
New Jersey, 5, 165
New Mexico, 145
New Orleans, Louisiana, 114, 196
New Salem, Illinois, 191
New York, New York, 193-195, 196, 203, 205-206, 219-220
New York Commerical Bulletin, 133
New York Herald, 158, 194
New York Tribune, 125, 126
New York *World*, 89
Noble, John, 193
North Carolina, 159, 179-181
Nott, Dr. Eliphalet, 92
Nye, Bill, 149

Ohio, 62
Old Hermitage Bourbon, 100
Old Jordan Bourbon, 90
"Old metheglin," 3
"Old peach," 3
Olmstead, Frederick Law, 77
O'Rear, Jim, 43
O'Rourke, Diamond Dan, 205
Oscar of the Waldorf, 220
Osler, Sir William, 207
Owens, Michael Joseph, 151, 233

Paine's Celery Compound, 139
Paris, Kentucky, 39
Parkinson's Ferry, 18
Parrish, Maxfield, 193

Pasteur, Louis, 40
Patterson, Joseph, 176
Pearce, John Ed, 30
Peck, C. Y., 221
Peeke, Hewson, 177
Pekin, Illinois, 95, 133
Pennsylvania, 9-10, 11, 12-22, 25, 27, 36
Peoria, Illinois, 95, 114, 129-134
"Peoria pool," 129
Pepper, Elijah, 33
Pepper, James E., 33, 197
Pepper, James E., & Co., 154
Pepper, Oscar, 33, 88
Pepys, Samuel, 214
"Perry," 3
Perry, James M., 73
Pharmacopoeia of the United States, 165-166, 171
Philadelphia, Pennsylvania, 19, 22
Philadelphia Society for Promoting Agriculture, 13
Philipps, Wendell, 97
Pierce, William, 57-58
Pike, Zebulon, 141
Pilgrims, 3
Pittsburgh, Pennsylvania, 17, 18, 19
Pittsburgh Gazette, 15
Place names, associated with whiskey, 182-185
Plants, names of, associated with whiskey, 185
Platt, Tom, 194
Porter, Dan C., 220
Porter, Seton, 135
Portland, Oregon, 189
Price, Hiram, 142
Prohibition, 29, 70, 108, 135, 149, 158, 173, 187, 204-205, 218-220, 233
Prohibition Party, 232
Promotion, whiskey, 149-162
Puck, 157
Pullman, George, 209
Pure Food and Drug Act (1907), 165-172

"Raines Law sandwich," 203
Randolph, Vance, 80, 108
Rawhide, Nevada, 146
Rayburn, Sam, 211-212
Reedy, William Marion, 209
Remi, St., 2
Remington, Joseph P., 171
Reston, James, 211
Revere, Paul, 7
Rhode Island, 7, 8
Richland City, Wisconsin, 178
Richmond *Times-Dispatch*, 38
Ripley, John W., 29
Ritchie, John, 34
Roach, John G., 84
Roach, John J., 84
Robinson, Wilbert, 31
Rockefeller, John D., Sr., 131
Rolshoven, Julius, 192
Roosevelt, Theodore, 168, 170, 171
Rosensteil, Lewis S., 135
Ross, Charley, 123
Rothschild, A. M., & Co., 155
Royall, Anne, 62
Ruef, Abraham, 203
Rum, 6, 7-10, 25, 231
Ryan, John E., 207
Ryan, Thomas Fortune, 131
Rye whiskey, 10, 13, 24, 27, 28, 46, 63

St. Clair, Arthur, 16
St. Louis, Missouri, 114, 116-124, 150
St. Louis *Globe*, 121
St. Louis *Globe-Democrat*, 130
Saloons, 187-206
San Antonio, Texas, 195
Sandburg, Carl, 139
San Francisco, California, 67, 140, 144, 148, 188, 196, 199, 203, 208
Santa Fe, New Mexico, 146
Savage Club (London), 210
Schenley Distillers Co., 227, 234
Schenley Products Co., 135
Schools, John A., 38
Schurz, Carl, 117, 118, 199

Scotch whisky, 40, 48, 49
Scott County, Kentucky, 37, 39, 40
Seagrams-Distillers Co., 227
Sears, Roebuck & Co., 159
Shakespeare, William, 190, 205
Sharkey, Tom, 200
Shelby, Isaac, 25, 58
Sherley, J. Swagar, 167
Sherley, Thomas H., 136
Sherman, William T., 78, 117
Sherman Anti-Trust Act, 133, 233
Shively, Kentucky, 183
Short, Luke, 142, 225
Short, Peyton, 25
Shufeldt, H. H., & Co., 132
Simmons' Liver Regulator, 139
Siringo, Charles A., 185
Sitting Bull, Chief, 192
Slaughter, George, 27
"Slingers," 63
Smith, Raccoon John, 175
Smith, William C., 196
Smuggling, 9, 10
Solon, Johnnie, 214-215
Sons of Liberty, 7
South Carolina, 77, 159, 179-181
Spears, Jacob, 34, 231
Spelman, Edward, 129
Stalwartism, 118, 126
Stamp Act, 9
Stamper, Joe, 110
Standard Distilling and Distributing Company, 134
Standard Oil Company, 128, 129
Stanley, Augustus Owsley, 27, 169
Starrett, Vincent, 158
Statesville, North Carolina, 77
Stedman, Ebenezer Hiram, 31, 48
Stewart, Daniel, 34
Stewart, George R., 182
Stewart, Isaac, 75
Stinson, Joe, 146
Stokes, Edward S., 194
Sugar Act, 8, 231
Sullivan, John L., 189, 195, 200-201, 205

Sutherland, William, 84
Sweet, Alex E., 140
Sweet's Infallible Liniment, 139

Tacoma, Washington, 198
Tafia, 28
Taft, William H., 159, 172-173, 222,
    233
Taos lightning, 139, 148
Taste-testers, 86-87
Taylor, Edmund Haynes, Jr., 87-89,
    151, 156, 157, 169
Taylor, "Hog-Jaw," 57
Taylor, Jonathan, 42
Taylor, Zachary, 68, 69, 87
Temperance, 92, 164, 188
Temple, Shirley, 60
Tennessee, 5, 62
Tequila, 139
Thatcher, George, 25
Thomas, Jean, 112
Thomas, W. H., 170
Thomas, W. H., & Son, 150
Thompson, Frank B., 223
Thompson, J. B., 90
Thompson, Lawrence S., 39, 53, 58,
    110, 215
Thornberry, Homer, 212
Thorpe, George, 30
Ticklers, 63
"Tiger Spit," 2
Tipton, Buck, 112
Todd, Charles S., 58
Tomlinson, Jim, 161
Tooze, Mrs. Fred J., 213
Topeka, Kansas, 138
Torio, Mike, 195
Trademark Act, 151
Trademarking, 151-153
Trollope, Mrs. Frances, 64
Truman, Harry, 213
Trust, Highwine, 128-136
Tunstall, Thomas, 26
Twain, Mark, 137, 148, 208, 209-210
Tweed, Boss, 115

Twenty-first Amendment, 135, 221,
    233
Tyler, Bob, 52-53
Tyler, John, 213

U.S. Food Products Corporation, 135
Utah, 226

Vanmeter, Susan, 112
Van Winkle, Julian P., Sr., 1, 153, 207,
    223
Vermont, 3, 162
Versailles, Kentucky, 220
Virginia, 4, 12, 30, 34-35, 38, 62, 78
"Virginia drams," 4
Volstead, Andrew J., 218
Volstead Act, 218
Veronese, Paolo, 195

Wagner, John, 208
Waite, Morrison Remick, 124
Walcott, Joe, 200
Walker, Edward Chandler, 152
Walker, Hiram, 152, 154-155
Walker's Club Whisky, 152
Wantroba, Virginia, 226
War of 1812, 141
Ward, Artemus, 145
Warehouse receipts, 90-91
Warwick, Massey Hough, 166, 169,
    170
Washington (state), 226
Washington, D.C., 62
Washington, George, 7, 11, 20, 22, 68,
    213
Washington, Pennsylvania, 21
Wathen, Henry Hudson, 34
Watson, Carrie, 195-196
Watterson, Henry ("Marse Henry"),
    48, 53, 57, 99, 101, 194, 217
Watterson, Mrs. Henry, 53
Wattles, Sarah, 161-162
Wayne, Anthony, 22
Webb-Kenyon Interstate Liquor Act
    (1913), 159, 233
Webster, Daniel, 177

Weems, Reverend Mason Locke, 9
Weller, J. T., 151
West Indies, 7-8
West Virginia, 106
Western whiskey, 28
Westward expansion, whiskey and, 137-148
Wheeler, Wayne, 49
Whiskey
  apple, 5
  homemade, 4
  See also Blended whiskey; Bourbon whiskey; Rye whiskey; Scotch whisky
Whiskey Jack, 178
Whiskey Rebellion, 11-23, 25, 94, 232
Whiskey Ring, 114-127, 232
Whiskey Trust, 128-136, 164, 233
"Whiskey War," 164
Whitney, William C., 131
Wichita, Kansas, 193

Wiley, Bell Irvin, 74n.
Wiley, Harvey W., 165, 168, 170, 171-173
Williams, Evan, 34, 231
Williams, John S., 152
Willkie, H. F., 35
Wine, 3, 4, 13
Winters, Jonathan, 59
Winthrop, John, 3, 198
Wisconsin, 196
Wise, James E., 60
Women's Christian Temperance Union, 92, 213, 232
Women's Missionary Union, 92
Woodcock, Gregory, 56
Wust, Theodore, 209

"Yard of Flannel," 6
Yaryan (revenue agent), 122
Young, Hiram Casey, 99

ABOUT THE AUTHOR

GERALD CARSON was born in Carrollton, Illinois, and graduated from the University of Illinois, where he also did graduate work. In New York City he was a newspaper reporter and active later in the advertising field.

Turning from a business career to full-time research and writing in 1951, Mr. Carson has recorded aspects of the American experience in *The Old Country Store, Cornflake Crusade,* a biography, *The Roguish World of Doctor Brinkley* and *One For a Man, Two For a Horse,* a history in words and pictures of patent medicines.

Mr. Carson's reviews of current writing on the phenomena of American society, past and present, appear in *The New York Times Book Review,* the *New York Herald Tribune Book Review* and the *Chicago Tribune Magazine of Books.* He is a frequent contributor to *American Heritage* and other magazines. A member of various historical societies and associations, including the Society of American Historians, Mr. Carson now lives and writes in a country setting near Millerton, New York.